S0-BAP-532

Small Town and Rural Economic Development

Small Town and Rural Economic Development

A Case Studies Approach

Edited by
Peter V. Schaeffer and Scott Loveridge

Westport, Connecticut
London

In order to keep this title in print and available to the academic community, this edition was produced using digital reprint technology in a relatively short print run. This would not have been attainable using traditional methods. Although the cover has been changed from its original appearance, the text remains the same and all materials and methods used still conform to the highest book-making standards.

Library of Congress Cataloging-in-Publication Data

Small town and rural economic development : a case studies approach /
    edited by Peter V. Schaeffer and Scott Loveridge.
        p.   cm.
    Includes bibliographical references and index.
    ISBN 0-275-96576-7 (alk. paper)
    1. Rural development—United States Case studies.   2. Cities and
towns—United States—Growth Case studies.   3. United States—Rural
conditions Case studies.   I. Schaeffer, Peter V.   II. Loveridge,
Scott.
HN90.C6S63   2000
307.1′412′0973—dc21   99–43115

British Library Cataloguing in Publication Data is available.

Copyright © 2000 by Peter V. Schaeffer and Scott Loveridge

All rights reserved. No portion of this book may be
reproduced, by any process or technique, without the
express written consent of the publisher.

Library of Congress Catalog Card Number: 99–43115
ISBN: 0-275-96576-7

First published in 2000

Praeger Publishers, 88 Post Road West, Westport, CT 06881
An imprint of Greenwood Publishing Group, Inc.
www.praeger.com

Printed in the United States of America

The paper used in this book complies with the
Permanent Paper Standard issued by the National
Information Standards Organization (Z39.48–1984).

P

Copyright Acknowledgments

The editors and publisher gratefully acknowledge permission for use of the following material:

Excerpts from chapter 12, "Community Leadership and Vision Pay Off for Blue Mound, Illinois" by Steven Klein, developed by Illinois Institute for Rural Affairs. Courtesy of Illinois Institute for Rural Affairs.

Excerpts from interview with Sandy Maine by Ram L. Chugh. Courtesy of Sandy Maine.

Contents

PUBLIC- vs. PRIVATE-SECTOR ROLES

SUCCESSFUL RURAL BUSINESSES

Illustrations

MAPS

FIGURES

TABLES

Acknowledgments

The idea for this book is the result of our participation in sessions on nonmetropolitan and rural development at the North American meetings of the Regional Science Association International. There we met several of the contributors to this book and benefited from many formal and informal discussions. Several colleagues provided encouragement and suggested contributors. We particularly thank Emery Castle for sharing information about his own work in rural development, and Jim Hite and Niles Hansen for suggesting additional contributors. We greatly benefited from access to the Community Economics Network (CEN) listserve to communicate our idea for a collection of case studies and interest colleagues to join us. We thank David Kraybill of the Ohio State University who serves as keeper of the CEN listserve.

The Division of Resource Management, at the College of Agriculture, Forestry, and Consumer Sciences, and the Regional Research Institute supported this project. We thank them for their help.

Last but not least, we appreciate the excellent work of our staff. Eva M. Thomas and Debra Burnside typed and formatted the manuscript, and Gloria Nestor and Debbie Benson produced the figures and maps. We thank them for their patience with us when we made changes that sometimes undid their earlier work.

Introduction

Scott Loveridge and Peter V. Schaeffer

The case study approach of this book provides examples of what others have done in small town and rural development, and the opportunity to reflect on how strategies they have pursued might be adapted for use elsewhere.

Terms such as "rural areas" can easily mislead us into thinking of rural regions as homogeneous places. They differ from one another, however, in their ethnic makeup, industrial structure, topography, natural and human resources, climate, etc. (Castle 1995). This collection reflects the diversity of rural areas and presents case studies from different industries, regions, and cultures.

Many people are aware of the great transition experienced by large cities since the middle of the twentieth century. The urban majority in industrialized countries is regularly confronted with suburban growth and aging neighborhoods in the central city and older suburbs. There is far less public awareness that rural towns have also undergone dramatic change. Retailing has not only declined in the downtown areas of larger cities, but also in the centers of many small cities and rural towns. Changes in manufacturing, such as just-in-time production and the loss of jobs to foreign countries, have had a large impact on rural areas. Since rural counties were relatively more dependent on manufacturing jobs than their metropolitan counterparts, the loss of manufacturing jobs has hit them particularly hard. As in urban job markets, many of the new rural jobs are also in the service sector, therefore sharing similar concerns about wage levels and job advancement opportunities. While the rural areas have some of the same concerns about how to adjust to the changing economy, it would be inappropriate to blindly transplant successful urban strategies to rural areas. Just as the human body may reject tissue transplanted from someone else unless great care is taken to ensure a good match, rural areas may borrow some strategies from their urban counterparts, but these strategies must be well matched with the local capacity and need, or the area risks ending up worse than before.

Dramatic change is as stressful for communities and regions as it is for individuals, and not all of them cope equally well. Some communities have made it through periods of change and emerged strong and viable, while others seem to have lost hope and appear weak and dispirited. The purpose of this collection of case studies is to provide examples of communities that have tried to affect their future. The stories of small towns do not attract the attention of the national media and are, therefore, not well known outside the community. The lack of role models may contribute to a sense of helplessness that sometimes affects communities. Thus, one of the goals of this collection is to celebrate success and demonstrate that the creativity and vision of rural residents make a difference.

This volume also includes some examples of small town and rural development initiatives that did not turn out well. There are lessons to be learned from others' mistakes that can illuminate some of the pitfalls of development.

Every rural economy will face continued challenges in the future. The old ways of interacting with the rest of the world will continue to be replaced by new activities or new ways of performing familiar functions. Change is inevitable. Rural areas that embrace change which shapes the future in ways that bring new ideas to work the sparsely settled landscape will fare better than areas that passively allow change to sweep them haphazardly from one form of marginal existence to another. A proactive stance toward change requires community engagement. A single individual or a small group with creative vision can make a difference in the future development of a rural area, but ultimately success depends on how the total community interacts with and builds upon new ideas or new situations. Community engagement (or community capacity) is so important to an area's overall success that we begin this volume with a section of several case studies that illustrate, in various ways, the contribution of this building block of community development to overall outcomes. While community engagement is the subject of the first section, it remains a strong theme running through most of the cases presented in subsequent sections of this book. You will note that community capacity was usually missing when the reported outcomes fell short of what residents might have preferred.

After the section on community capacity, we turn to cases illustrating attempts to maintain and enhance existing local enterprises. An oft-quoted feature of a typical local economy is that most new jobs are created by existing businesses, not by firms attracted to the area or by small business start-ups. While the net number of jobs directly created is certainly sufficient justification for considerable attention to developing local enterprises, the true arguments for supporting existing industry go beyond mere direct job creation. First, a job that is not lost (to competition from other regions or through changing market structure) is just as valuable as one gained through an expansion, a start-up, or by attracting a new firm to the area. Second, the condition of existing industries in an area becomes a signaling mechanism for people making investment decisions. If young people get the sense that local industries are in decline, they may opt to move to another area rather than face those risks—even when they prefer to stay close to their friends and family. Similarly, declining local industry may discourage corporate investment. Corporations view declining areas as risky—the salvage value of investments is likely to be lower. Also, as the local tax base declines with local industry, either services will decline, or remaining industries may be asked to pay higher taxes to maintain services at their existing levels. Finally, existing industries become a kind of training ground for spin-off businesses or entrepreneurial spirit.

The third section deals with an aspect of small town and rural development that draws the most attention, both in the rural development literature and in the press—attracting large-scale industry. Many people regard industrial attraction and rural development as identical—a view we hope no one will hold after reading this book! Industrial attraction is so dominant in today's economic development game that no book would be complete without some attention to this subject. Industrial attraction is also very controversial.

To present a balanced viewpoint, some of our selections celebrate successful attractions, while others tell a different story—a firm was attracted to the area, but with less than satisfactory results. As with enhancing existing industry, assessing the benefits of industrial attraction is not simply a matter of counting jobs. More subtle benefits can accrue to the community. The new industry may bring to the area new skills sets that were previously unavailable locally. Even a low-wage industry may help some people in transition from poverty to a better life as they develop a positive record of work that makes them attractive to higher-wage industries.

Business leaders often rail at government as an impediment to growth and profitability. Other groups complain about Western society's "corporate welfare" systems that channel government funds into the hands of wealthy executives and shareholders. Western society is experiencing some major shifts from centralized government decision making to more localized forms of governmental intervention. Economic development is one of the few policy areas where many decisions have always been local. The section on "Public vs. Private Sector Roles" explores the relationship that the public sector can have with business in ways that go beyond traditional incentives offered to businesses to lure them to move to an area.

The final section deals with successful rural businesses. Clearly, the ultimate fate of any rural area rests on its ability to foster the growth of businesses. In this section, we feature some businesses that have managed to be internationally competitive in spite of the challenges presented by working in a rural environment. In each case, businesses were able to capitalize on the rural nature of their area. The changes experienced by these businesses were not painless. Their experience provides valuable insights for supporting entrepreneurial growth and development in rural areas.

Discussion questions have been added to many of the case studies presented in this volume. In some instances, we wished to present an alternative viewpoint—it is often the case that economic development initiatives are controversial. While we may agree with the perspective of the author of a particular chapter, it is important to know that certain types of questions will always be raised as a project moves forward. Some of our discussion questions reflect a desire to help the reader compare points made in two or more chapters. Our main intent in developing the discussion questions was to create opportunities for reflection and deeper understanding. There may be no "right" answer to our question. We encourage readers to determine on their own what might be "right" in their area. Ultimately, what is "correct" in small town and rural development results from a process of community engagement. Thinking about these case studies should help people begin—or strengthen—that process of engagement.

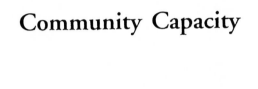

Community Capacity

CHAPTER 1

An Introduction to Building Community Capacity

Cornelia Butler Flora and Vicki Luther

Capacity building is the process whereby a community increases its well-being based on the assets—human, social, physical, and environmental—that are there. It enhances the ability of a community to access and creatively combine outside resources with existing resources and build toward a shared group vision.

In capacity building, which can be contrasted with technical assistance traditionally used for community development, the change agent is a facilitator and educator. In technical assistance, the change agent is an advisor or consultant, who maintains professional distance, protecting the territory, providing answers and the agenda for the right answers.

Capacity building focuses on process, while the technical assistance model focuses on the task. However, it is wrong to think that capacity building is only process oriented; its point is to facilitate tasks within the community, and to help the community develop the ability to decide which tasks are most important in achieving the shared vision, as well as how to discern the different ways these tasks can be addressed. Technical assistance gives the answer. Capacity building gives the ability to identify alternative solutions, to select from them, and learn from their implementation.

The basis of change for capacity building is that people can identify and solve problems collectively. For technical assistance, the model is that science provides a means to solve problems. Capacity building does not deny science, but sees it as a tool that can be used for a variety of needs.

The core problem addressed in capacity building is the ability of people to take collective action, which involves a focus on the community as a whole. The technical assistance model means the core problem addressed is harnessing science to solve human problems. The emphasis there is on the individual and the material (J. Flora et al. 1992; Christenson 1989).

Practitioners have addressed capacity building, although some research has looked at self-development, which is the use of capacity on particular economic goals (C. Flora et al. 1991; J. Flora et al. 1992; J. Flora et al. 1997; Green et al. 1990). Practitioners who worked with communities on capacity building came together in 1994 under the auspices of the Aspen Institute's Rural Economic Policy Program to discuss their approaches. In the course of that discussion, the need to measure capacity building became clear. As a result, the cluster of practitioners collectively produced "Measuring Community Capacity: A Workbook in Progress for Rural Communities" (1996).

Working on the notion of stewardship, economic capacity, and economic development, cluster members, based on their practice and conversation from communities, identified eight outcomes which indicated that community capacity was occurring. The belief that "what you measure is what you do" suggests the *activities* that occur while community capacity is increased. These include:

1. *Expanding diverse inclusive citizen participation.* In a community where capacity is being built, an ever-increasing number of people participate in all types of activities and decisions. These folks include all the different parts of the community and also represent its diversity.

2. *Expanding leadership base.* Community leaders who bring new people into decision-making are building community capacity, but the opportunity to get skills and to practice and learn leadership is also an important part of a leadership base.

3. *Strengthened individual skills.* A community that uses all kinds of resources to create opportunities for individual skills development is building community capacity in an important way. As individuals develop new skills and expertise, the level of volunteer service is raised.

4. *Widely shared understanding and vision.* Creating a vision of the best community future is an important part of planning, but in community capacity building the emphasis is on how widely that vision is shared. Getting to agreement on that vision is a process that builds community capacity.

5. *Strategic community agenda.* When clubs and organizations consider changes that might come in the future and plan together, the result is a strategic community agenda. Having a response to the future already thought through community-wide is one way to understand and manage change.

6. *Consistent, tangible progress towards goals.* A community with capacity turns plans into results. Whether it is using benchmarks to gauge progress or setting milestones to mark accomplishments, the momentum and bias for action comes through as a community gets things done.

7. *More effective community organizations and institutions.* All types of civic clubs and traditional institutions such as churches, schools, and newspapers are the mainstay of community capacity building. If clubs and institutions are run well and efficiently, the community will be stronger.

8. *Better resource utilization by the community.* Ideally, the community should select and use resources in the same way a smart consumer will make a purchase. Communities that balance local self-reliance with the use of outside resources can face the future with confidence (Aspen Institute's Rural Economic Policy Program, page 11).

These aspects of capacity building involve strengthening human capital, enhancing environmental capital, and affecting economic and built capital within the community. But most of all, building community capacity builds social capital by increasing diversity and by increasing interaction and communication. This brings more varied points of view to the table, which allows for alternative ways of addressing issues to be identified and selected.

The eight outcomes outlined by the cluster reflect the importance of individual gifts, organizations and institutions (Kretzman and McKnight 1993), as well as more effective action. Each of these eight components has been addressed in a variety of community development approaches. Good practitioners tend to combine most of them as they work with communities to build their capacity (Luther and Flora 1998).

Map 1
Location of Case Study Sites: Building Community Capacity

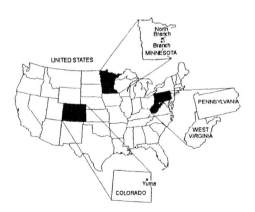

CHAPTER 2

Capacity Building and Leadership in Yuma, Colorado

Vicki Luther and Cornelia Butler Flora

June 15, 1992

    The parking lot at the community center is full. Inside, 122 residents of the town and countryside are seated at tables filling the auditorium. A community meeting is in progress. The meeting has been planned and promoted by community members and is convened and directed entirely by local residents. Staff from the Heartland Center for Leadership Development met with the organizers earlier to devise an action plan for promotions and the agenda for tonight. No outsiders are present for the meeting.

    The crowd in the auditorium is quite diverse: men and women, all ages, newcomers and long-time residents, Anglo and Hispanic. The auditorium is filled with noise, laughing and joking, as well as earnest dialogue. At each table, a group is engaged in energetic discussion. One fills a sheet of newsprint. At several tables, the recorders are high school students.

    Each small group is busy describing what they see as the desired future of the community—not what is possible or probable, but the future that is preferred. Their next step will be to consider what actions will be necessary to make that preferred future a reality. By the end of the evening, 67 individuals will have signed up for five action task forces with projects ranging from recycling to in-town school busing.

Yuma, Colorado didn't begin efforts at community capacity building in the 1990s. Certainly, many outreach programs had an impact on the town before a group of 12 citizens were engaged in a year-long training program in 1992/93 sponsored by Pioneer Hi-Bred, Inc. The group, led by a Pioneer sales representative, applied for the program and described their town as progressive, but in need of coordination among civic groups. Few efforts at citizen involvement were at play, but several civic groups were active in special projects. The group felt that training in strategic planning would be helpful to the town.

The group included a rancher, a state employee from a job training program, a school board member who was a stay-at-home mom with small children, a hospital employee, several business owners (car dealership, grocery store), and staff from the Chamber of Commerce, the recreation center, and the local economic development corporation. They represented individuals who were concerned about the future and wanted to be both realistic and proactive.

Yuma, with a population of 3,000, is the largest town in the county, which has a population of only 9,000. With cattle and irrigated corn as major economic elements, the area is typical of the high plains areas with fierce winter weather, few services and towns, and a typically hardy group of local residents. With its wide streets, ranching economy, increasing Hispanic demographics, Yuma is a classic western town, and like many small towns, is facing an uncertain future.

The Yuma group attended 15 days of training in community development and strategic planning during the year they participated in the program. They interacted with a faculty drawn from across the United States and with teams from eight other towns in as many different states. After each training, the team returned home and put into practice the theory and techniques from the session. In effect, they were already putting into practice the concept of self-reliance and immediate application that results in increased local capacity. Their successful town hall meeting was an example of this.

As the group progressed, they also put into place a systematic approach to keeping the momentum for improving and sustaining their town. A new event, a monthly breakfast of all civic club presidents and elected officials, was put into place and proved to be an invaluable setting for making and strengthening networks in the town. While the initial strategic planning program was completed in about 12 months, these breakfast meetings have continued for six years. The regular contact of volunteers and governmental leadership has offered opportunities to identify new issues and needs, and to be visible in developing new projects to respond to needs.

After two years of success, the group also began to serve as a resource in other ways. A formal leadership training program targeting the community was begun with both local government and private support. Each year, a "class" of 12 to 20 citizens attended a series of training programs that were skill-based, and were required to identify a need, develop a project, and carry out some actions. After another two years, the group was asked to assist other small communities in setting up similar leadership programs and serve as a resource for trainers, materials, and ideas. They even served the county fair board as facilitators for the board's own strategic plan.

By 1998, the group had successfully recruited others into the roles of managing regular town hall meetings and keeping the monthly breakfast get-togethers going. More community celebrations have been added to the one longtime event, the leadership program continues, and several of the original group have served as consultants to quite a few other communities in the state.

Yuma is a sterling example of community capacity building. The original investment of time and effort on the part of the local residents, and the monetary investment of the training program by a corporation have had important results. Over the past six years, the community has had ample evidence that the capacity to improve the community does exist within the residents. The successes of citizen involvement in regular town hall meetings and the highly visible and effective task force projects offer this proof, so that this type of success has become part of the community identity. In addition, the systematic maintenance of information networks and opportunities to connect have established a history of openness and involvement in local decision-making. With these simple but powerful mechanisms in place and moderated by increased skills on the part of citizens, Yuma seems to have learned that community capacity to improve and sustain a community is the most important part of making a preferred future a reality.

LESSONS LEARNED

Community capacity building is not a one-time thing. It requires multiple sources and time to develop. It is complex, iterative, and at times very frustrating. It is so much easier to bring in an expert to "fix it". But the problem is exactly that—once "it" is fixed, something else will be triggered that will once again need fixing. This is not to say that experts and technical knowledge are not important, but when technical fixes are accompanied by training, community capacity building continues to increase. When fixing is done "behind the curtain," which enhances the reputation of the fixer or person providing the technical assistance, the community learns less and its capacity is not increased.

Capacity building does not provide structure. There are early frustrations for communities that have been trained through past interactions with experts to be dependent, but the frustration itself is one of the critical factors for a community taking charge of its own destiny.

A shared vision is critical as a reference point. A vision is not gathered easily and it, too, is iterative. Management scholars profess the dangers of strategic planning because the future is increasingly unknowable, so whatever path we choose must be radically altered over time. But, a strategic vision reminds us of where we are going and allows flexibility as we choose those paths.

Capacity building by its nature tends to be shared. Those who have undergone the training share it with others in the community and with other communities. This is in contrast to training programs where the individual accumulates knowledge that becomes an exclusive asset. Exclusive access to that knowledge can then be bartered and sold. Part of community capacity is learning the mix between individual and community capacity building that yields a vital economy, a healthy ecosystem, and an equitable social setting.

Our work in community capacity building, illustrated by the case study, suggests a number of critical factors, first of which is time. Capacity building takes time because it is done by multiple sources. It is not controlled by one outside group that can claim the community, yet there is the ability to go back to the various institutions for support and council.

A critical mass is achieved through multiple interventions. Community capacity building is community-based instead of externally based. Core volunteers who went through the original program in skill building immediately began to apply those skills inside the community, which became a resource for other citizens for other communities in the region.

Capacity building is community-based rather than individual. When the community creates a leadership program, rather than sending off one of its members to leadership training, it builds on the strengths rather than the weaknesses of the community. This is where the momentum comes from and why it is sustainable. If you are working on deficiencies and needs, the momentum is gone once the need is met or the problem is solved.

Many communities engage in "crisis response." They can provide wonderful things when a house burns down, but that effort is completely exhausting. Getting everyone up and in place so quickly can often lead to the networks and plans disappearing between that and the next emergency response. As community capacity is built, communities still respond to emergencies, but more effectively and with more continuous follow-up.

Communities learn "consumer skills." They learn to access resources on their own terms. You don't immediately hire a grant writer until you first begin to look for the variety of resources you need to meet your goals. Thus, you know what grants to go for rather than being driven by random funding opportunities.

Communities with a high level of capacity can demand services that provide them help in addressing local issues rather then just taking their packaged programs. For example, many economic development experts are really good at surveys. They will go in and do a survey for a community at the drop of a hat. The community with a high degree of capacity says, "Wait, we have already gathered some data. We would like you to help us analyze it." They recognize the importance of expertise, but they understand it well enough to know what pieces they need to make things move forward in this community.

IMPLICATIONS FOR SERVICE PROVIDERS

Building community capacity does not just change communities, it changes the market for community-building services. As community capacity grows, the roles and relationships of a variety of technical experts and service providers must change. Communities no longer seek problem solutions, which we can then generously give them. Instead, they see a variety of issues as a part of a whole. Different responses will be required by service providers. As we train communities, we must also build new capacities for service providers.

The ability to deal with a capable community rather than a needy one will require an enormous change in the mind-set of community development professionals. The Heartland Center for Rural Development's project, Getting the Help Your Town Needs (developed with support from the Ford Foundation), is an example where training to adjust this mind-set on the part of community service providers has been developed.

DISCUSSION QUESTIONS FROM THE EDITORS

1. Most local organizations need to show short-term results to maintain their funding, yet capacity building and leadership development for communities are long-term objectives. How can agencies balance the need for short-term results with the long-term nature of the development process?

2. Is a community that has a lot of open disagreement about its path for the future a community with high capacity or low capacity?

3. How would you go about deciding whether a particular community has high capacity or low capacity?

CHAPTER 3

Catalyzing Local Leadership and Infrastructure Development

Scott Loveridge and L. Christopher Plein

INTRODUCTION

This case study examines communities that applied to receive assistance from a program called the Community Design Team (CDT). It follows the communities from their application to outcomes.[1] The purpose of this presentation is to provide a learning module that introduces the CDT concept and invites readers to think through the planning and implementation stages associated with a CDT visit to a community. After providing a brief overview, we discuss four stages of the CDT process: (1) the applications, (2) the selection and team development process, (3) the site reconnaissance visit, (4) the team visit, and (5) project outcomes.

THE COMMUNITY DESIGN TEAM APPROACH

The Community Design Team is a multidisciplinary group of volunteer professionals who donate their time to communities wishing to improve their future. The West Virginia CDT model is based, in part, on a design charette model, which is distinguished by an intense, short-term visit ·by a team of professionals to a community or locale. The West Virginia model has benefited from initiatives pioneered by the Minnesota Design Team (Mehrhoff 1995).

In general, design charettes for communities have focused on tangible and well-defined matters of space and location in a community. Thus, for example, in the Minnesota experience, landscape architects have been primary players in helping to visualize and plan for public space development in a community. The West Virginia CDT emphasizes this component, but in the larger context of community and economic development. A distinguishing feature of the West Virginia experience is a focus not only on physical improvements in a community, but a building of local social capacity through economic planning, community development, and civic engagement.

In pulling together a CDT team, professionals are drawn from a number of disciplines, but typically include landscape architects, architects, planners, civil engineers, and historians, as well as community economic development and local government experts. The process begins with an application from the community, in which the physical scope of the community and the issues to be addressed are defined. A screening committee reviews the applications and selects communities for reconnaissance visits. The reconnaissance visit involves a face-to-face meeting with community leaders, discussions of the issues, collection of topographic maps, and a tour of the area during which sites are photographed. Once the community is accepted into the program, 10 to 20 professionals are recruited to become team members. The exact composition of the team varies according to volunteer availability and the issues to be addressed. The CDT visit begins on a Thursday with an informal reception during which the team meets members of the community. Team members stay with community host families to increase the level of interaction between the community and the team. Most of Friday is devoted to a listening project. Community members make formal presentations about the history, natural resources, economy, and government of the area. The full team is given a tour of sites of concern to the community. The team has a special meeting with representatives of the area's youth to discuss their concerns for the future. On Friday night, the team facilitates an open community meeting, in which anyone with an opinion about the future development of the community is invited to express their views. Most of Saturday is devoted to a team work session. On Saturday night, the team's suggestions on how the community might achieve its goals are shared in a presentation to the community. After the visit, the team's presentation is produced into a report, which is delivered to the community within a month of the visit.

The West Virginia CDT received start-up funding from a grant. The grant provided money for some travel, development of materials, and publicity. The grant proposal promised that at least one community would receive a visit during the first 12 months. Promotional materials describing the program stated that its cost was $3,000, but that some grant money was available to communities with strong applications.

THE APPLICATION PROCESS

Three communities responded to the initial call for applications. This section summarizes the applications, and asks the reader to assess them from the perspective of the Community Design Team steering committee.

1. The mayor of the town of Bigwater chaired the local application committee. The committee also included a well-respected local businessperson, a retired teacher, and a town council member. The town is small (less than 700 people), and located near an interstate highway. The population is relatively stable. It has a large number of commuters, and its incomes are slightly lower than the county averages. Recent demographic changes mean that its elementary school is threatened due to a declining enrollment base. The application requested a $1,000 grant, with the remaining $2,000 coming from the county commission, town funds, and a local business. Major issues expressed in the application were cleanup of the interstate exit, murals for downtown buildings, and traffic patterns in the core downtown area. The application included letters of support from a number of local people and institutions. A notable aspect of the application was that it had broad support from the business community and local government.

2. A recent retiree who was new to the area chaired the application committee for Forest Grove, a relatively isolated area with a declining population of about 1,000 people close to a major national forest. While not a member of any official organization, the committee chair had the endorsement of the town council to investigate and develop the application, which included written comments and endorsements from roughly 100 persons. The area described in the application included an incorporated town, as well as several nearby unincorporated areas. Issues described in the application touched on historic preservation, but emphasized economic development. The area's largest private employer had recently shut down. The application indicated that the city council would pay the full $3,000 and provide host families for team member accommodations during the visit.

3. A city staff member chaired the application committee for Adamsville. Adamsville is a city of about 15,000. The application focused on historic preservation of the downtown area, with additional concern about better markings to the entrances to town, and developing walking and biking areas. Located on an interstate, and the largest city in the county, Adamsville is growing and feeling some of the urban sprawl commonly found in much larger cities. The application included letters of support from several civic organizations and businesses. One business was donating the use of its fully furnished condos for team member accommodations during the visit. The application indicated city council would pay the full $3,000.

Discussion I

Put yourself in the role of the CDT steering committee. As a member of the leadership group for this new program, you must decide which of these applications (if any) to pursue. List strengths of the three applications and any concerns you might have. Make a recommendation about next steps for each application. Recall that the grant funded is expecting at least one program to be completed within the first calendar year of the program.

STEERING COMMITTEE DELIBERATION AND ACTIONS

1. *Bigwater.* The steering committee recommended that this community move to the next stage of the program, i.e., the site visit. Although this was the only applicant unable to produce the entire $3,000, the committee felt that the community's small size and variety of sources of support mitigated this shortfall. The steering committee was also impressed with the support from local government and the letters of support from other organizations. The application was also seen as strong because it focused on a small geographic area and dealt with issues the CDT felt were well within its scope of action.

2. *Forest Grove.* The steering committee also recommended this community for the next stage of the program. However, there were some reservations. Foremost was the geographic area of the community. As part of a county but more than a city, the lines of governance seemed awkward. The size of the area was also more than that envisioned for a typical CDT visit. It was proposed to go forward with the reconnaissance visit, and use that venue to convince the community to narrow its geographic focus to the incorporated city that was financing the effort.

3. *Adamsville.* The steering committee recommended that this city amend its application, so a reconnaissance visit was deferred. Two major concerns were raised. First, the city's application asked the CDT to address items that were already available to the city through another program, so the scope had to be narrowed to avoid duplication of effort. Second, the city's offer of accommodations in a condo instead of with families was seen as detracting from the team's ability to obtain information about the community, and possibly a sign of lack of community buy-in.

RECONNAISSANCE VISITS

As part of the CDT planning process, representatives from the CDT steering committee conduct a reconnaissance visit in preparation for the full-team visit. The purpose of the reconnaissance visit is to gain a clearer sense of needs and issues facing the community, to establish closer contacts with local leaders, gain a sense of place and community, gather information (maps, photos, details on issues) for the team visit, and work out agendas and logistics for the team visit.

Bigwater's reconnaissance visit went very smoothly. Representatives of the team held good discussions with community leaders about the issues that concerned the community. Appropriate maps and other background information were collected. The part-time mayor, who revealed that the job of mayor paid $500 per month, personally arranged all the steps that were needed up to that point.

Forest Grove's reconnaissance visit went quite well at first. The team representatives met the application committee chair and were introduced to the mayor, the recorder, the district ranger for the U.S. Forest Service, and other interested citizens. All were supportive and enthusiastic about the process, and promised to support it in any way possible. In the course of discussions with these local leaders, it became clear to team members that their original plan to reduce the geographic scope of the project was probably not a good idea. While the area did not have a formal government holding it together, there were a number of joint activities that made the area a functioning community. Among these were a local park located outside the city limits and maintained by area people, a public radio station, and an area-wide fire and emergency medical service system. Towards the end of the site visit, local organizers held an open community meeting. During this meeting, it became clear that local support for the project was far from unanimous. The mayor of the town had been involved in a fracas with a landowner who was a prominent member of the volunteer fire department. The argument had to do with cleaning up a certain piece of property. The CDT visit became associated with local cleanup efforts, and was viewed by some as a means of forcing the issue between the mayor and this property owner. Members of the fire department were therefore not supportive of the team's visit. Citizens from the unincorporated areas saw the team's visit as a first step towards an unwanted annexation. Longtime citizens mentioned that the effort seemed to be getting most of its support from people not born in the area, and indicated they resented efforts by these "outsiders" to upset the status quo. The team representatives explained that the team had no legal rights to impose any of their recommendations, which could be used or not used as the community saw fit.

Discussion II

Based on the information obtained during the site visits, should the CDT go forward with either or both of these visits? Why or why not? Recall that the grant required at least one visit in the first calendar year.

THE TEAM VISITS

The steering committee recommended going forward with both visits. It was recommended to visit Bigwater first, to allow Forest Grove more time to work out its internal differences.

The visit to Bigwater went very well. The team included 11 volunteer professionals from disciplines such as planning, architecture, landscape architecture, economics, civil engineering, sociology, and public administration. The mayor personally recruited host families and arranged for wonderful home-cooked meals for the team. The team's recommendations included ideas on land use and historic preservation, but focused on how the community could best make use of a county rail trail project that will convert a rail bed running through town into a pedestrian and bicycle path. The team designed a way to make part of the trail into a new road, reducing congestion for the EMS, while still maintaining adequate space for walkers and bikers. The plans also included ideas for better connections between the local elementary school, the downtown, and a local park.

The run up to Forest Grove's visit took some interesting twists and turns. Because of various needs and questions arising from the application committee in Forest Grove, a few members of the CDT applications committee were in regular contact with the local organizers through the planning process. In addition to a reconnaissance visit, CDT team members made two other trips to the community. The reason for this intensive interaction prior to the visit was two-fold. First, the long six-month lead time between the acceptance of the Forest Grove application and the CDT visit contributed to more interactions than might otherwise be expected with a shorter time horizon. Second, because the effort was generated by those outside of existing community power structures and because of a lack of institutional participation, there was more of a need to rely on the CDT for assistance and direction in the planning of the process.

The mayor of the area's only incorporated town withdrew his support for the project. As a result, the local application committee lost its source of funding. They first obtained replacement funds from a local business, but that business withdrew its support when it learned of the controversy surrounding the visit. Meanwhile, it emerged that the town council had not been consulted about withdrawing funding for the visit. A regularly scheduled election resulted in a new mayor-elect, who was supportive of the visit, but could not promise funds until after taking office and examining the town's finances. Ultimately, the funds were raised through contributions from a variety of individuals, businesses, the Forest Service, a bake sale, and a small grant from the CDT. At the same time, members of the application committee became embroiled in a dispute with county officials over an environmental cleanup in Forest Grove. This meant that the local economic development authority and the county commission became lukewarm to the CDT project because of the local personalities involved.

Eleven volunteer professionals participated in Forest Grove's visit, representing architecture, landscape architecture, economics, organizational development, public administration, history, and civil engineering. Despite earlier reservations, members of the volunteer fire department made their hall available for some of the meetings, and the county economic development authority was well represented in presentations and discussions. The team's report included aspects of historic preservation, but focused mostly on economic development and community organization. It emphasized amenities as an important aspect of many modern industrial location decisions, and that development of local amenities could benefit local residents, the local tourism industry, and possibly make some of the old industrial sites more attractive to potential investors.   The report also concluded that lacking a unifying government, the interwoven communities could greatly benefit from forming a local nonprofit to serve as a mechanism through which many things (bigger than the town but smaller than the county) could be accomplished.

Discussion III

Which community (Bigwater or Forest Grove) seems likely to have the greatest impact from a Community Design Team visit? Why?

OUTCOMES

In Bigwater, the mayor immediately began working to implement the CDT recommendations. A plaque celebrating the history of the local library was installed, and a project was begun with a local nonprofit to develop grants and other funding mechanisms to implement the plan for the new road suggested by the CDT. However, shortly after the grant application was in place, the mayor placed a letter of resignation on the front door of city hall. Citizens of Bigwater were surprised that their hard-working and popular mayor had resigned. In retrospect, it seems clear that this was almost inevitable. The mayor had done wonders for the town, but had done all the work personally, putting in hundreds of hours a month for a low-paying, part-time job. When leaders try to do it all themselves, they often don't last very long.

In Forest Grove, the open process and the controversial positions taken by some of the parties involved with the application committee led to greater public awareness of the suggested projects. It also resulted in the realization that various factions could work together on some issues even though they differed on others. Like the mayor of Bigwater, the chair of the application committee also stepped back from the implementation process, but not before finding and mentoring others who could fill the void. A new nonprofit was formed, with lifelong residents and "newcomers" on its board, which has successfully obtained funds to renovate the local park, is working on a local crisis center, purchased land to convert an abandoned rail line into a tract for the area, and is preserving local history. It also created a high school equivalency program to help unemployed people become more able to compete for jobs. The non-profit has developed a strong collaborative working relationship with the county economic development authority on issues of mutual interest.

CONCLUSION

The CDT is truly outcome-oriented, and it is difficult to track success. We found that there are stages of success which are both tangible and more process-oriented. There are tangible successes in the form of the various planning meetings organized by the local application committee leading up to the team visit. By the same measure, there is the success of the team visit itself. What determines the success is if an interactive experience has been facilitated that would not otherwise have been provided, and which allows for ideas to be shared, issues raised, and relationships to be formed and strengthened among community members. It is difficult to account for successes at this stage, but we can argue that there is a certain "enlightenment effect" involved in this process. Subsequent stages of success can be identified in the downstream effects of a community design team visit. For example, in the Bigwater visit, the Community Design Team recommendations regarding downtown revitalization helped to energize efforts to apply for and secure grant funds. In the Forest Grove visit, the Community Design Team suggested that a community development corporation or some other community organization be created to take up the perceived slack the region was receiving from government authorities in the county. In the six months following the visit, a community development corporation was formed and a number of small-scale and visible projects were undertaken aimed at addressing the community's infrastructure and recreational needs.

The importance of institutional commitment became clear in both the planning and outcome stages of the CDT initiatives in Bigwater and Forest Grove. Institutional commitment can be defined as the interested participation of established governmental and nongovernmental organizations in the community design process. These institutions have the resources, mission, and legitimacy to champion a project and can help in efforts to follow through on project objectives.

One of the purposes of the application process is to establish the level of institutional commitment to the project. One of the goals of the design process is to enhance institutional arrangements through their greater involvement in communities and with citizens.

In the Bigwater initiative, it appeared that institutional commitment to CDT process was substantial. The application received the endorsement of many actors in the community. During the team visit, numerous business and local government leaders made presentations. It was not anticipated, however, that institutional support was somewhat superficial. After the visit, most of the responsibility for project follow-through seemed to fall into the hands of one person—the mayor. Thus, institutional commitment became personified and when the mayor resigned, the outcomes became uncertain.

In the case of Forest Grove, the CDT screening committee quickly determined that there was a lack of institutional commitment to the initiative from local government and the business community. Indeed, the site visit revealed that there was divisiveness in the community between local government leaders. It was also discovered that there was very little in the way of established nongovernmental institutions, such as chambers of commerce and citizen groups. While much of the energy for initiating the process came from dedicated individuals, the success of the initiative was in large part due to efforts by the local district of the U. S. Forest Service to serve as one of the sponsors of the visit. Their commitment added a level of credibility and legitimacy to the effort that was necessary for a successful visit. The issue of institutional commitment became critical during the team visit, as it became apparent that there was a need for more local leadership and organization to address community and economic development issues. One of the most significant outcomes of the visit was the development of a citizen group organized around planning and development activities. In essence, this group recognized that there was a vacuum in local governmental and nongovernmental arrangements and sought to fill this void.

The Community Design Team experience shows that outside experts can help catalyze the development of new leaders and stronger leadership within communities. More successful efforts will backstop attention to the community's immediate goals (such as economic development or historic preservation) with attention to how existing social structures might be adapted to carry the community forward in the long term. The open process adopted by Forest Grove led to more controversy and difficulties as the project was getting under way, but it also established a precedent for communication and trust within the community. As communities seek to develop leaders, a tangible set of goals and a workable structure are vital ingredients to positive outcomes.

NOTE

1. This case is based on real communities, but the names have been changed.

CHAPTER 4

The Case of the Community Collaborative, Inc.

Rachel B. Tompkins

The Community Collaborative, Inc., grew out of the work of many individuals and organizations in West Virginia that were frustrated by four common occurrences:

- short-term community projects that were not part of an overall community development plan;
- strategic planning processes that left community groups with a vision, a plan, but no additional help to implement the ideas;
- lack of coordination among community and economic development groups which reduced the cumulative impact of everyone's work; and
- the emphasis of state and local development groups on industrial recruitment and infrastructure building to the exclusion of other development work.

CONTEXT

In West Virginia in the early 1990s, several groups began to encourage local community planning and improvement activities. The Claude Worthington Benedum Foundation launched a new program to build grass-roots leadership. This program offered community-based organizations small grants to complete projects that grew out of planning done by teams during a structured training. After the grant-making and the completion of the projects, local leaders were on their own.

The Brushy Fork Institute of Berea College in Kentucky began a community leadership program in 1988 serving the mountain counties of

Kentucky, Tennessee, Virginia, and West Virginia. This program combined training for diverse community teams with small grants for team projects. Participants were asked to commit six months to the process. The projects served as a laboratory to apply new skills and perspectives. At the end of the program, participants are expected to continue to use their new skills in other organizations and projects.

The Community Development Division of the West Virginia Development Office began to offer strategic planning services to local economic development authorities. The training focused on vision-to-action planning and created plans, task groups, and to-do lists.

The Center for Economic Options, a West Virginia nonprofit working on community-based economic development especially for women, received funding from the Benedum Foundation to train facilitators for local grass-roots planning efforts like the mini-grant program.

The West Virginia University Extension Service created its Division of Community Economic Development, and assembled a small campus-based staff focused on entrepreneurship training and business retention and expansion. A few county extension faculty members were involved in community development activities, but most had neither the skills nor interest to provide leadership for local planning efforts.

Each of these organizations had one or two people working part of the time on these community capacity-building efforts. While they knew each other and went to national training meetings together occasionally, they did not share work plans or work jointly in target counties. In 1992, a facilitator from the West Virginia Development Office went to a community meeting in a county and discovered the community group had received similar training the week before from Brushy Fork. Following this event, the program officer at the Benedum Foundation convened a meeting of all organizations working on community capacity building to discuss how to coordinate and communicate.

Discussion I

Multiple groups doing the same or similar good work are typical. What would you suggest for these groups? What forces are at work to cause collaboration? What forces are at work to push the groups apart?

BEGINNING STEPS

From 1992 until 1995, members of the group of organizations met regularly to share work plans and ideas. This helped avoid duplication and allowed some value-added activities to occur in communities.

The world kept changing and it was hard to have all the players in the community planning arena in the room at the same time. Some participants changed jobs or dropped out, and new organizations with community planning missions were created. One of the new organizations was the West Virginia Rural Development Council, a state agency whose director had been involved in community planning for years. Two new state rural health organizations were created—the Office of Rural Health in the Department of Health and Human Resources, and a nonprofit affiliated with higher education called the Center for Rural Health Development. A new structure for planning and delivering comprehensive coordinated services for children and families called the Governor's Cabinet for Children and Families began to create family resource networks in each county in the state. On the nonprofit side, refugees and spin-offs from the Center for Economic Options created three nonprofits—one focused on dispute resolution (West Virginia Center for Dispute Resolution), another operating a home-based microenterprise network of knitters (Appalachian By Design), and the third offering training and technical assistance in community planning (Rural Strategies). The new groups joined the conversation. The Benedum program officer left the region for another job, but the group continued to meet, with different members taking responsibility for arranging times and places.

By late 1994, when the federal government announced the Empowerment Zone Enterprise Community (EZ/EC) program to assist persistently poor communities who had a strategic plan developed with broad community input, there were many West Virginia community groups with skills and capacity to respond. West Virginia generated 15 proposals, three of which were funded as enterprise communities. The two funded rural communities could trace their success directly to one or another of the training and support programs offered by members of the collection of community development organizations.

All of the communities in the EZ/EC process were, however, struggling with a new set of relationships with county political leaders and local economic elites, most of whom had not participated in the training and planning work prior to EZ/EC. Conflicts, lack of knowledge about possible development strategies and tools, not knowing how to negotiate governmental mazes, fragile board and staff relations, and more plagued all of the groups. They needed continuing coaching, training, and technical assistance. The thrill of having hundreds of people create a vision and plan was followed by the hard reality of implementing the ideas.

In 1994, the governor of West Virginia participated in the Commission on the Future of the South and visited Tupelo, Mississippi, the poster child for long-term community development leading to economic success. He decided to create some Tupelos in West Virginia, and recruited to his office as adviser on the effort a loaned executive from West Virginia University who had been Associate Provost for Extension and Economic Development. He committed several million dollars from various sources to support the highest priority items in the strategic plans developed in the EZ/EC process. The governor's adviser became a regular member of the group of organizations now calling itself the Community Collaborative, Inc.

The group had long discussions about whether to become a formal organization and offer training and technical assistance to local groups. What should be the structure of the organization? Should it become a membership organization for local groups? How should the work be funded? How can members avoid competing against each other? What was the work, anyway? What was needed that was not being offered by someone somewhere?

After an all-day retreat around the dining room table of one of the members facilitated by a colleague not previously involved, the group decided to form a new nonprofit corporation, the Community Collaborative, Inc., which would focus on providing continuing long-term support to communities focused on community transformation. The definition for that was a little vague, but everyone understood that it meant long-term systemic change for communities and not just individual and organizational skill development. Increasing group process, decision making, and leadership skills of individuals, and shoring up fragile grass-roots groups whose voices often were not heard in development conversations were important. The focus, however, was to be on building good communities. Integration of planning among "developers" of health, human services, education, transportation, and job creation was to be a priority.

The first organizational decision of the newly created group was to ask each member who wanted to participate to contribute equally to the filing fee for state and federal nonprofit status. Thus was established a guiding principle: the Community Collaborative, Inc., is a group to which you give, rather than a group from which you take.

Discussion II

How would you answer the structural and programmatic questions raised by the members of the Community Collaborative, Inc.? Keeping organizations flexible enough to respond to dynamic changes and yet coherent is troublesome. What strategies work?

CURRENT GOVERNANCE AND PROGRAM

After much debate, the group decided on the basic structure of a collective in which each organization is equal and has one vote regardless of size, budget, or number of people involved in Community Collaborative, Inc., work. The members meet regularly by conference call or in person and usually make decisions by consensus. After a few years, two categories of members were defined—those who wanted to participate all the time, and those who could only participate on a limited basis. Some new groups joined; some original groups dropped back to part-time involvement.

Each representative of an organization is expected to contribute time; those on the public payroll write Community Collaborative, Inc., time into work plans; nonprofits contribute several days a year and charge additional time off to grants. Three of the organizations have staff located in the same office complex so fiscal and grants management and events coordination are handled by them for a fee written into grants. Together, the organizations have skills that cover a wide range of the assistance a community would need to nurture and support a long- range development process.

The Community Collaborative, Inc., offers three major programs:

1. Community Team Building
2. Community Fellows
3. Topical Workshops

Community Team Building is funded by the Appalachian Regional Commission and includes six to eight workshops offered over a period of several months for diverse teams of eight people from a county. These workshops are then followed by small grants to each team for projects they have devised during the training. The same training is offered to three different teams from the same county, with some activities knitting the three teams together. At the end of a three-year cycle, each county will have a diverse group of 25 people who have learned and planned and worked together on community improvement over three years.

The curriculum includes three categories—knowledge, skills, and networks. Knowledge includes understanding the local economy, its history, and trends and its place in the international economy; local and state government structure, history, and political attitudes; the network of family and social relations, and various institutions and their roles in the community. This might be called "know thyself" work. Some of this is taught by lecture, some by getting team members to share their knowledge with each other, some by teaching teams to do surveys, focus groups, listening projects, and other types of information collection and analysis to learn for themselves. Successful models from other places are highlighted in presentations and visits—"know others like yourselves." Skills include facilitation and group process, decision making, planning and assessment, asset mapping, interviewing, survey design, public presentation, and forum design.

Network building focuses on creating more dense community networks crossing traditional boundaries that fragment. This is the reason behind diverse teams and multiple years. People are encouraged to first use all their own assets before looking elsewhere. Participants link with state government units and higher education institutions. They are introduced to others like themselves inside the state and out. They are linked to national and international sources of assistance through face-to-face meetings, as well as the Internet.

The second major program of the Community Collaborative, Inc., Community Fellows, is operated by the West Virginia University Extension Service under subcontract to the Community Collaborative, Inc. It brings seven to ten community leaders to campus two days a month to learn about and get linked to campus resources, to participate in a lecture series, and to develop support for a specific project or work activity back home. The Fellows are economic development directors, family resource network directors, community health planners, extension agents, local elected officials, business organization activists, and community action staff. Several of them come from communities involved in the team training.

Each campus visit follows the same pattern. Fellows come to campus on Thursday afternoon and spend that evening becoming a peer support and consulting group for each other. Guided dinner conversation focuses on reflection and problem solving. The environment and the distance from home and the telephone allows them space and time to think.

A typical Friday morning agenda might focus on student resources for community work and include visits by faculty who lead internships and senior projects in social work, public administration, landscape architecture, and parks and recreation. The head of West Virginia University's Office of Service Learning might discuss opportunities for student placement and give the Fellows a briefing on a new grant to create community partnerships for faculty and students. Another Friday, the College of Business and Economics would give a preview of the economic outlook for the state and link the Fellows into their data bases and analytical assistance.

At noon on the Friday of several visits a noted national scholar or development official is invited to speak to social science faculty and graduate students, as well as the Fellows. This provides more opportunity for interaction between community and campus. The Fellows have some time of their own with the presenters. Prior to the visit, they get readings by and about the visitors so that they can be prepared.

The third major program of the Community Collaborative, Inc., is topical training designed to meet needs identified by the teams and the Fellows. These have included sessions on group facilitation, workshop design, and conflict resolution. While recruiting for this training is done in the communities with teams and Fellows, the sessions are open to anyone in the state. A series of forums on community development corporations and finance institutions is planned.

The work of the Community Collaborative, Inc., provides each organization with sites for work that creates cumulative impact. USDA Rural Development will use counties in the Community Collaborative, Inc., for its new targeted community program. Communities have used the Community Collaborative, Inc., Small Grants Program to fund WVU Extension's Community Design Team and First Impressions program. WVU Extension has also done a business retention and expansion program in one of the counties. The Center for Dispute Resolution (conflict resolution for a school board), Brushy Fork Institute (leadership development in a Fellows community), and the Center for Economic Options (consulting on micro-enterprise development) have been invited to work in counties in which the Community Collaborative, Inc., has been active. In turn, communities in which WVU Extension has done a business retention and expansion program have signed up for the team training. The Community Collaborative, Inc., has struggled with the question of outcomes and measuring outcomes. What should happen and how will we know when it has? After much

---

Discussion III

How does one evaluate the work? When will we know that a community is transformed? What is a good community?

---

discussion, a simple definition and set of criteria have been devised to guide our work.

A good community is a place where residents can earn a living, and those who visit want to stay. Specifically, it has an *economy* in which locally controlled assets and wealth are expanding; *equity,* which means that those expanding assets are shared fairly and public decisions are inclusive and democratic; and a concern for *ecology,* stewardship of natural and human resources.

Communities are asked to test their projects, their capacity building, and their development against the three "E's." Is the idea, process, or project moving the community in the proper direction? If not, what changes could be made to build local assets, include people left out, distribute resources more fairly, be better stewards? Groups struggle to be more inclusive of old and young, newcomers and fifth generations, working class and poor folks, as well as managers and shop owners, diverse religions, ethnicity, and races. They make certain women lead, as well as make coffee. The definition and the criteria serve as core values.

CONCLUSION

The Community Collaborative, Inc., is a creative way to coordinate resources for community development. The structure is flexible enough to accommodate members moving in and out, changes in community needs, and shifting public priorities. Its structure and specific programs may be unique to West Virginia and to the organizations and people involved, but the problems of long-term support and cumulative impact in community change are universal. As a case study, the Community Collaborative, Inc., raises the issues, gives one set of answers as an example, and invites others to create their own best practice.

CHAPTER 5

Identifying Community Needs and Preferences: Community Forums as an Emerging Option

Drew Hyman

INTRODUCTION

Local issues forums are a new way for communities to identify their needs and preferences in relation to growth and the quality of life. Traditional methods used by decision makers include personal relationships and political networks, constituent mail and phone calls, sample surveys, media coverage, reactions of people at public speeches and appearances, and public hearings. These approaches tend to focus on the opposing positions of different interests and interest groups. Such methods tend to be adversarial, pitting individuals and groups against each other. Theorists call this a zero sum game, in which the winnings of one group are offset by the losses of another.

Deliberative democracy is an emerging movement that advocates a new way of acting which emphasizes areas of agreement among different parties. It is based on the democratic ideal of a "common good," which balances the different interests for the good of the community. Instead of debate, a deliberative process is used to allow the parties to identify policy choices based on their mutual interests. The different sides are asked to focus on areas of agreement, not areas of disagreement. Deliberation is a way to engage participants in a process through which they discover their "common ground" and work toward a consensus for action among what are otherwise conflicting interests. Theorists call this a variable sum game, in which all can benefit.

DELIBERATING CHOICES FOR THE FUTURE IN NITTANY VALLEY

A community we will call Nittany Valley has been using deliberation in a series of local issues forums (LIF) for considering choices for the future. Nittany Valley is a complex community with 36 municipalities divided into seven planning regions. This mostly rural locality includes a small metropolitan area (center region) and several moderate-sized towns surrounded by rural agricultural and mining communities. In the 1990 U.S. Census, Nittany Valley had a population of 123,786. Of these, 70,607 lived in its six-municipality center region. The median Nittany Valley income was $26,060, and incomes in its center region municipalities ranged from a low of $18,000 to a high of $42,000. Unemployment is typically several points higher in rural communities than in the center region. Median housing costs in Nittany Valley are $74,700, compared to about $115,000 in its center region. The center region municipalities have higher average levels of education as well. Two forums, in March and November 1996, explored alternative paradigms for change, and a range of strategies, techniques, and mechanisms for action.

The first forum examined alternative visions of the future. Using materials and a booklet created by a local task force, participants concluded that efforts were needed to constrain and redirect economic growth and address quality-of-life issues including health, social, educational, cultural, recreation, infrastructure, housing, and environmental systems. The second forum explored three strategies for action: Individual Choice and Expanding Economic Opportunity; A Sustainable Mosaic of Diverse Communities; and Ecological Sustainability. Postforum surveys show a shift in perspectives and the emergence of agreement among most participants. Contrary to expectations, 84 percent asked for increased government regulation and involvement. In both forums, there was a notable difference between what participants prefer, what they believe decision-makers are doing, and what they believe should be done. This experience suggests that local issues forums can provide a nonconfrontational process for citizens and leaders to become informed about public issues, seek common ground, and measure support for public actions.

NATIONAL AND LOCAL ISSUES FORUMS

The Nittany Valley forums followed the format of the National Issues Forums Institute (NIFI 1996). The full range of local issues was "framed" in advance, and a booklet was prepared to guide participants' deliberations. Small group discussions focused on identifying areas of agreement, not on debating areas of disagreement. It was thus a *deliberation,* not a *debate.*[1]

The NIF model was used to develop a process for engaging local citizens and leaders in a deliberative process for understanding different perspectives on development, appreciating their implications for public policy and governance, and considering types of strategies that might be required to move in a given direction. As noted by Hyman, Steff, and MacIsaac (1996), a local issues forum (LIF) *is not* a place where advocates argue the merits of their positions seeking to "defeat" others, but *is* a place where all perspectives are welcome, providing an opportunity for participants to share how they see the future emerging with friends and neighbors, leaders, and government officials. Forums seek to hear all local voices, to consider the major policy choices for an issue, and to work toward a shared direction for public policy.

THE LIF PROCESS IN NITTANY VALLEY

In Nittany Valley, the process begins in the local Public Issues Forum (PIF) Steering Committee. This local group of volunteers handles policy issues and plans for the national issues forums held locally. (Any local group of citizens and/or leaders could perform this function.) The process is as follows.

Initiation

Co-conveners are appointed by the local NIF Steering Committee and charged with creating a task force.

Creation of an LIF Task Force

Following the decision to create an LIF, the co-conveners and interested members of the NIF Steering Committee brainstorm a list of local people whom they consider to represent the full range of different interests related to the topic. This list is refined and prioritized, and personal contacts are made to invite participation. People who decline are asked to suggest others who might become involved. In Nittany Valley this "snowball technique" leads to a task force of 15 to 25 people.

Task Force Responsibilities

Task force members are asked to make a commitment to meet monthly for six to nine months to plan, frame the issues, and implement the forum. They take responsibility for, and/or recruit others to assist in, the following tasks:

Preparation of Materials: Nittany Valley local issues forums include materials similar to the booklets provided by Kettering and NIFI for the national issues forums. In Nittany Valley, this includes identifying and framing the policy choices to be deliberated, preparation of a booklet explaining the choices and the rationale, pros and cons for each, and background information related to the topic. A key operating principle is that *all* voices (perspectives) in the community need to be reflected in one or more of the choices to be deliberated.

Guest Columns in the Local Newspaper: In Nittany Valley, the local newspaper is a cosponsor of both the local and national issues forums. It contributes by printing guest columns by local citizens (usually task force members) about each of the policy choices to be deliberated to put a local flavor on the deliberation, to interest people in attending, and to highlight the fact that this is a locally created and organized event.

Preforum Outreach and the Media: People attend forums if they know about and are interested in the forum topics. Forums are announced in the local media months in advance, guest columns and follow-up letters are printed in the local newspapers, and shows on the local cable TV channel and radio stations prepare people for the forum. Videotaped copies of the forums are placed in community libraries to be used by citizens and teachers.

Preforum and Postforum Questionnaires: The Nittany Valley local issues forums follow the practice of the national issues forums (NIFI 1996) by administering preforum and postforum questionnaires to participants. The questionnaires ask for participants' perspectives on the major public policy choices to be deliberated, opinions about how local officials are approaching these issues, and how participants think officials should be proceeding.

Logistics: Arrangements for forum day are sometimes complex. In Nittany Valley, the school district's Community Education Program cosponsors the forums and takes responsibility for facilitating the logistics, space, and location of the forums. Forums pay for direct costs for postage, printing, refreshments, and other specific items through voluntary contributions from several organizations, businesses, and individuals in the community.

Moderators: Most deliberation takes place in small groups. In Nittany Valley, the steering committee recruits and trains moderators to guide the groups through the process.

Post-Forum Activities

Following the forum, a committee compiles results and prepares a brief report. This report is sent to participants and officials of all local municipalities, state representatives, the media, and local groups. The task force meets once again to review and authorize the report and consider further action. When a subsequent forum is proposed, a recommendation is made to the steering committee, which then forms a new task force (for which many members of the previous task force volunteer). This latter process allows people to be invited to be task force members with only a one-forum commitment.

WHO ATTENDED THE NITTANY VALLEY FORUMS?

In Nittany Valley, the number of participants exceeded 200, a response that impressed local officials, who tend to get perhaps 25 to 30 people for input on local planning efforts. The forums were open to citizens of all 36 municipalities in the county, leading to a diverse group of participants who identified with different localities. While about four out of ten identified with the more densely populated core, another three out of ten considered themselves to be residents of broader Nittany Valley rather than a specific region, township, or borough. This was true for both forums.

Forum Day

The typical agenda for the Nittany Valley forums is as follows:

Registration and Continental Breakfast. Local organizations and planning agencies are encouraged to provide displays. 8:30–9:00 a.m.
Welcome to the Forum and overview of the policy choices. 9:00–9:30 a.m.
Small Group Deliberation of the Choices. The process asks participants to first indicate their stake in the issue and then to discuss their understanding of the policy choices one at a time. 9:30–Noon.
Lunch and informal discussion. Noon–1:00 p.m.
Small Group Deliberation for Seeking Common Ground. Areas of agreement and disagreement from the morning are summarized and moderators guide participants toward identifying areas where they could achieve agreement. 1:00–2:30 p.m.
Group Reports and Identifying Overall Common Ground. All participants gather together in one large group. The small group reports are heard and commonalties are identified. 2:30–3:00 p.m.

The forums were successful in attracting both citizens and leaders. Sixty-three percent said they were citizens and not leaders, developers, officials, or government employees; 14 percent said they were community leaders; 7 percent were developers; 7 percent were elected officials; and 9 percent were government employees. Thus, as the organizers (steering committee and task force members) desired, the attendees were a mix of citizens and leaders.

The gender, age, and education distributions also suggest that this was a diverse group of participants. We compared forum participants to census data on the overall population. Forum 1 had identical percentages of females and males when compared to the census. Forum 2 had a smaller percentage of females. In general, however, both genders were well represented in both forums.

All ages were represented, although the age distribution of participants was skewed considerably toward older citizens. Compared to census data, the younger age groups were highly underrepresented in the forums. The young adult group—ages 30 to 49—was fairly well represented. Over half of the participants were 50 years of age and above. Thus, the majority of voices heard in the forums were those of the more mature citizens in the community.

All levels of education were represented, but participants tended to have higher levels of education than the general population. College graduates significantly outnumbered the other categories of participants in terms of education. Both forums had similar percentages of participants with high school degrees or less and those with some college or with technical degrees.

The majority of forum attendees had lived in the Nittany Valley for 15 years or more. However, many attendees at both forums were people who had lived in the Nittany Valley for less than a year to four years, five to nine years, and ten to fourteen years. The proportions of different age groups are similar for both forums.

Finally, about half of the people at each forum said they had not attended either a local or national issues forum before. This means that the forum process was reaching new people—a plus from the perspective of the task force and local leaders.

THE RESULTS OF DELIBERATION

The first Nittany Valley local issues forum on *Growth and the Quality of Life in Nittany Valley* considered four choices for the future, which were identified through an "issue framing" process by the task force over a three- to four-month period. They represent the major choices voiced by citizens of Nittany Valley as desirable directions for community change. During the forum, more than 250 people explored strategies, techniques, specific programs, and mechanisms that could be used to work toward common perspectives. This was a deliberative dialogue about several different perspectives on community change and development.

Choice 1: The Status Quo was favored by those who believed that Nittany Valley has the benefits of a small town atmosphere and the advantages of a mini-metropolitan area, but, they said, the benefits are disappearing fast. Growth is bringing traffic jams, pollution, and unanticipated demands on infrastructure, community systems and environmental resources. Supporters of this perspective wanted to find ways to stop development and keep the rural communities intact.

Choice 2: Economic Growth or the Free Market Model was advocated by those who seek to sustain and enhance growth. From this perspective, Nittany Valley had the opportunity to create a dynamic major metropolitan center. Supporters of this perspective wanted the community to build the infrastructure to attract investors, create jobs, and encourage more intense development of the land and natural resources.

Choice 3: Sustainable Communities or Emphasizing the Quality of Life for Nittany Valley Residents was favored by those who believed that growth provides opportunities on the one hand, and threatens to destroy the small town character of local communities on the other. Supporters of this perspective believed in restraining growth efforts that place additional costs on the broader community, and requiring development activities to meet the criteria for improving the quality of life for all major groups and residents of Nittany Valley.

Choice 4: Dealing with Embattled Downtowns was shared by those who believed that the problem is not growth, but unbalanced growth. From this perspective, core business districts are declining relative to the peripheries—which are growing. Supporters of this perspective wanted to find ways to protect and enhance downtowns as centers for shopping and community interactions (Hyman, Steff, and MacIsaac 1996).

Citizens' preferences on the desirability of these four choices for Nittany Valley were provided in pre- and postforum ballots. By the end of the forum, most participants thought that Choice 3—Sustainable Communities—was the most desirable. Almost 80 percent gave this a "very desirable" rating. The task force agreed that the first forum provided the impetus and direction for a second forum focusing on the sustainable community-of-communities perspective. The first task force disbanded and a new one was created with about one-third of the membership agreeing to serve on the new task force and to recruit others for the second forum.

Eight months later, the second Nittany Valley local issues forum focused on the main issue that emerged from the first forum—creating a sustainable community of communities in Nittany Valley. More than 200 participants from many Nittany Valley communities considered ways for all communities to create a valley-wide mosaic based on the many visions of its individual communities. The issue framing by the task force for Forum II identified three possible strategies for creating the future that was envisioned in the first forum.

Choice 1: Individual Choice and Expanding Economic Opportunity (the Market Model) would trust individual decisions in the marketplace to achieve sustainability and a high quality of life. Supporters of this choice would encourage continued economic growth in the Nittany Valley with a concern for increasing jobs, investment, and some attention to the environment.

Choice 2: Strengthening Local Communities (Social Capital) suggested that only concerted community action based on the visions of many communities would achieve sustainability and a high quality of life. Supporters of this choice would seek to change the direction of development toward a county-wide mosaic and would "spread the wealth" throughout Nittany Valley communities. It would include creating quality of life criteria for the human and natural environments to guide and manage proposed changes.

Choice 3: Ecological Sustainability (Ecological Footprint) envisioned significant changes in lifestyle directed toward long-term ecological sustainability and quality of life. This would require action toward decreasing reliance on nonrenewable resources and to increase local self-reliance. Supporters of this choice would apply the "clean, healthy, friendly" principle to set performance milestones for land use policies, zoning ordinances, building codes, and other aspects of development to reduce the "ecological footprint."

In the pre- and postforum questionnaires, the majority of Forum II participants emphasized the importance of the second and third choices, which address concerted community action and a commitment to ecological sustainability as the most desired strategies. Small group reports suggested that economic growth should be directed to those areas that want it and away from others.

OUTCOMES

The Nittany Valley experience suggests that public deliberation based on the NIF model can provide a format for moving a community toward a consensus on issues of development, growth, and the quality of life. About 80 percent of the participants in the forums changed their opinions. Clearly the deliberative process had an impact on the majority of the participants.

The first Nittany Valley forum led toward the community-of-communities idea. These results surprised most planners and officials since for three decades the area has been growing rapidly. As a result, plans are under way to create a growth boundary around the metropolitan area, protect open space and promote agricultural preservation, and direct growth toward economically decimated communities.

Participants were also asked to what extent local government should be involved in the management of community growth, protection of the environment, and the quality of life in Nittany Valley communities. The overwhelming majority—more than 60 percent—favored increased levels of regulation and government involvement to promote quality of life. Contrary to common belief that we are in a time of reducing government involvement, very few advocated reducing regulations and government involvement in these areas. Forum II shows a similar pattern. As occurred in Forum I, there was a significant difference between what participants preferred, what they believed decision makers to be doing, and what they believed should be done. The need to act "before more excessive development occurs" was a common theme.

Participants were also clear in their belief that local issues forums are a good place to discuss and become informed about public issues. The percentage of participants who said they now understand the issues and have a position increased from 52 to 79 percent during Forum I and from 59 to 78 percent during Forum II. In their open-ended comments, participants said they enjoyed the participation, deliberation, and presentations, learning about new ideas and information, meeting other people, and gaining a general understanding of these issues.

CONCLUSION

Deliberative democracy as implemented through the local issues forums shows a potential for providing a path through the adversarial debates that occur in so many of our local governments, hearings, and commissions. The outcomes of these forums are not binding decisions—that is the role of local government and community organizations. By not taking sides, the forums provide an arena where all interests can feel comfortable deliberating important issues. In the Nittany Valley scenario, issues include the implications of more shopping centers and "big box" retailers; new mines and quarries; additional housing developments; upgrading a major highway to interstate status; expanding the airport to allow for big jets that will approach over populated areas; preservation of forests, farms, and streams; and the future of downtowns and neighborhoods. The forums explored strategies for guiding and controlling the future. They addressed the need to find ways for guiding and directing development that improve the quality of life while protecting the environment and restraining efforts that place unwanted costs on the broader community. Deliberative demo-

Table 5.1
Comparison of Adversarial and Deliberative Approaches

Assumptions	Approach	
	Adversarial	*Deliberative*
Communication Style	Debate	Deliberation
Interests and Values	Conflicting Interests	Shared Values
Decision-Making	Top Down	Bottom-Up
Structure of Decision-Making	Elitist	Pluralist
Interaction	Conflict	Consensus
Search for Solutions	Positional Debate	Seeking Common Ground
Point of Reference	Power Network	Community
Power Structure	Cumulative Inequalities	Dispersed Inequalities
Nature of Conflict	Win-Lose, Zero Sum	Variable Sum
Participant Attitudes	Fixed Preferences	Open Discovery Process
Citizen Involvement	Passive Citizens	Active Citizens

cracy offers leaders and citizens a choice about the democratic process. Table 5.1 compares the main characteristics of these two approaches.

The postforum surveys revealed strong support for additional forums in different regions, as well as Valley-wide. About eight out of ten said there should be more forums and they would plan to attend, and most of the remainder said there should be more and they might attend. As a result, a third forum on *Transportation Choices for Nittany Valley Communities* was held the fall following the second forum, and a fourth forum is being planned on *Open Space, Watersheds, and Agricultural Preservation* at this writing.

In a separate action, the intermunicipal council of governments began small group deliberative processes about a metropolitan growth boundary and preserving open space. The county commissioners established a commission to address watershed issues. A coalition of government and community leaders was formed to address development around a planned new interstate on a multimunicipal basis. An LIF steering committee was established to create a process for encouraging Nittany Valley residents to create visions of the future for their communities. The idea is that the many community visions would be woven into a "Nittany Valley Mosaic" during a general forum in spring of 2000.

In summary, the LIF methodology is a way for leaders, citizens, and officials to deliberate sensitive public issues without the acrimony and conflict that so frequently attend public debate. It may provide a bridge to the future for this community of many communities, old and new, small and large, some gathered in towns and neighborhoods, some spread across regional landscapes. It brings home the fact that if we want to have some control over what happens to our own communities, if we want to change the direction of development—toward or away from growth—we must begin thinking, speaking, and acting differently in our communities and governments. The methodology of deliberative democracy pushes us to clarify our values and confront essential truths while seeking common ground among diverse interests. Deliberation is not a panacea. The process takes work and commitment. At the same time, the right kind of deliberative collaboration and constructive local activism can create paths to a sustainable future where all sectors of the community benefit.

DISCUSSION QUESTIONS FROM THE EDITORS

1. Why might deliberation rather than debate be a useful approach to citizen participation in your community?

2. Why do you think turnout for the forum was so much greater than a typical town meeting?

3. Nittany Valley has plans to create a growth boundary around the metropolitan area. What will likely happen when the area reaches its full potential growth within the boundary? Will growth stop or will it leapfrog the boundary?

4. To what extent do small towns or groups of small towns have control over the nature of future development?

5. When a town decides to limit growth, it takes future income away from certain property owners and creates wealth for other property owners. Should those who benefit pay those who lose? If yes, how would you accomplish this?

NOTE

1. The National Issues Forums Institute (NIFI) indicates that there are more than 5,000 communities and organizations using the national issues forums process (NIFI 1996). Each local group is organized and operated independently. How many of these create local issues forums is not known.

CHAPTER 6

Community Well-Being and Local Activeness

Lumane P. Claude, Jeffrey C. Bridger, and A. E. Luloff

INTRODUCTION

Over the last two decades, many rural communities have experienced major structural shifts away from agriculture, manufacturing, and goods-producing industries toward technological and service industries (Johansen and Fuguitt 1984; Congress of the United States 1991). The losses in traditional industries are seldom offset by gains in new jobs or income (Nord et al. 1994; Pulver 1995). This shift has been accompanied by out-migration and concomitant alterations in rural social organizations that weaken the ability of many rural communities to overcome economic distress (Summers and Branch 1984; Luloff and Swanson 1995). Taken together, these trends have left many communities vulnerable to extra-local influences as they try to find a niche in the global market and compete in an information-based economy (Lovejoy and Krannich 1982; Blakely and Bradshaw 1985; Dillman 1985; Krannich and Luloff 1991; Pulver 1995).

Despite this bleak picture, some rural communities have successfully retained their population and compensated for job losses in traditional industries (Nord et al. 1994). Many communities adopt new and/or altered strategies to deal with emerging concerns and adapt to changes by coordinating their actions toward shared goals (Kaufman and Wilkinson 1967; Wilkinson 1991). New patterns of cooperation often surface as residents mobilize resources to solve problems threatening common interests and establish strategies to prevent similar situations in the future (Luloff and Wilkinson 1979; Wilkinson 1991).

This chapter investigates the relationship between residents' perceptions of community well-being, levels of community activeness, and success in four rural Pennsylvania communities. An interactional field theory of community

(Wilkinson 1970, 1991) provides the framework for linking the concepts of community action and success to social and economic well-being. Our aim is to provide a better understanding of residents' perceptions of community well-being through a central claim of field theory: community well-being depends on the purposive involvement and participation of both government and citizens in actions that sustain and improve the local quality of life (Bridger and Luloff 1999).

We assume that the community is composed of several more or less distinct interactional fields through which actors pursue or express particular interests. For instance, there are interactional fields concerned with the provision of public services, education, economic development, and so forth. Community development occurs as *members of these fields interact with one another on projects and around issues that transect interest lines*. The linkages that are established during this process are important in creating and/or altering the community structure so as to improve the general quality of life of local residents. This structure, the community field, is distinct from other interactional fields in that the interests pursued

are generalizable and intrinsic; they are not specialized or instrumental. The community field cuts across other interaction fields in a local population. It abstracts and combines the locality-relevant aspects of the special interest fields, and integrates the other fields into a generalized whole. It does this by creating and maintaining linkages among fields that otherwise are directed toward more limited interests. (Wilkinson 1991, 36)

The community field, arising as it does in the course of actions undertaken to deal with local problems, represents a structure capable of responding to the challenges posed by rapid change. And of equal importance, it is through this process that such other aspects of community well-being as attachment and solidarity are generated (Wilkinson 1991).

THE STUDY

Knowledgeable informants in 170 rural communities throughout Pennsylvania were surveyed about initiatives undertaken over a ten-year period (1985–1995) to improve a range of aspects of community life. After computing an activeness score for each community, those that fell into the highest and lowest tertiles were classified respectively as high and low active.[1] Successful adaptation to economic restructuring was measured using Census data. A community was classified as successful if, over the last decade, employment and income levels stabilized, community services were maintained or expanded, or out-migration slowed.

These data were used to sort each of the 170 communities into those indicating that they were high active/high success; high active/low success; low active/high success; and low active/low success. Respectively, the selected study communities were Coudersport, Emporium, Liberty, and Austin.[2] In each case study site, we conducted key informant interviews and a citizen survey that asked about local perceptions of quality of life and community well-being

Table 6.1 Case Study Communities		Success	
		High	*Low*
Active	High	Coudersport	Emporium
	Low	Liberty	Austin

measured across six broad categories.[3] We used a multidimensional measure of community well-being (combined perceived changes across all six categories) as our dependent variable. The inclusion of multiple indicators of community well-being provided a means of capturing both objective, structural changes, as well as residents' perceptions of local life.

FINDINGS

We expected to find positive associations between high success and perceptions of community well-being. Upon analysis, however, we discovered that the objective measures of success did not confirm our expectations, especially in Liberty. In contrast, we found a strong positive association for this relationship in Emporium.

To further examine these seemingly counterintuitive results, we developed a series of hierarchical regression models to assess how the independent variables simultaneously accounted for variation in perceptions of community well-being. In model 1, demographic variables were regressed on community well-being. In model 2, we incorporated a community contextual factor, namely site (measured by a set of orthogonal contrasts with Coudersport treated as the comparison category), to capture differences across the study communities. This variable highlighted the process by which individual characteristics were affected by group context. Finally, in model 3, all independent variables and interaction terms were included.

In the first model, households with people 65 and older was the only demographic variable found to have a significant and positive predictor effect on community well-being. The effects of the other demographic variables (gender, income, education, and length of residence) were negligible. When the site variables were entered (model 2), households with persons over 65 remained significant. More importantly, we found distinct differences between communities. Compared to Coudersport, residents of Austin and Emporium, the low-success communities, reported lower levels of community well-being. And, while residents of Liberty, a high-success community, also had lower perceptions of well-being than Coudersport, they nevertheless indicated higher levels of community well-being than either Austin or Emporium. Thus, when not controlling for activeness or perceived level of influence of local organizations and government, perceptions of well-being appear to be closely related to objective level of success.

Consistent with the theoretical expectations of the interactional perspective, model 3 (which included all independent variables and interaction terms) indicated that perceptions of well-being increased with increases in perceptions of levels of local activeness and influence of groups and local government. Moreover, this relationship held regardless of community of residence. In each case, increases in perceived level of local activeness were significantly related to increases in perceived community well-being.

However, this picture became more complicated when the interactions between influence and site were examined. Here we uncovered substantial differences between communities. Compared to Coudersport, perceptions of well-being among Austin residents did not change with perceptions of greater influence of local groups and government. When the same relationships were examined for Emporium respondents, we found that perceptions of well-being increased with increases in the perception of level of influence of local groups and government. Finally, when we compared Liberty to Coudersport, we found that perceptions of community well-being actually declined with increases in perceived level of influence of local groups and government. Thus, in both communities rated as low in activeness, perceptions of increases in level of influence had either no impact or a negative impact on perceptions of well-being, suggesting again that success is not necessarily key to perceptions of community well-being.

The relationship between involvement in various community activities and perceptions of well-being also differed by site. Compared to Coudersport, Austin residents reported increased perceptions of well-being with increases in involvement in community affairs. In both Emporium and Liberty, the relationship was reversed. Initially, these findings seemed counterintuitive. After all, our analyses thus far suggested that community well-being depended on high levels of activeness. A clearer understanding of this issue was gained by considering more carefully the relationship between activeness, success, and perceived well-being in each of these communities. Austin has historically been characterized by low levels of activeness and low levels of success. Here, involvement in community activities appears to be associated with perceptions of improved community well-being primarily because levels of activeness there were so low. Thus, any involvement in community activities appears to be seen as a sign that things are improving. Emporium, on the other hand, has a long tradition of activeness. Unfortunately, this activeness has not translated to many economic successes. Over time, such repeated failures have contributed to a certain level of pessimism about current and future possibilities here. Finally, despite the absence of a tradition of activeness, Liberty has experienced consistent economic growth. In this type of community, residents may not see an obvious relationship between their involvement in local affairs and the fate of their community.

CONCLUSION

As the findings presented above indicate, the relationship between community activeness, economic success, and perceptions of community well-being is more complicated than is often assumed. Economic success is only one of the criteria by which residents make judgements about the local quality of life. Equally important are such intangible and frequently ignored factors as levels of activeness and perceived level of influence of local groups and organizations. The interactional approach outlined in this chapter stresses that, in addition to meeting the sustenance needs of residents, community well-being depends on the active involvement of individuals, groups, and organizations in matters that arise in the course of living together in the same place. Not only does such involvement build capacity to meet new challenges, it also creates a more holistic local society, one characterized by the broad range of interpersonal contacts that contribute to healthy individuals (Wilkinson 1991).

With this point in mind, it is useful to recall the distinction that is typically made between development *in* the community and development *of* community (Summers 1986). Development in the community refers to such activities as job creation and income generation. Development of community, on the other hand, focuses on the social aspects of local life, including the building of relationships across interest lines and the creation of local networks that can be mobilized for collective action. In policy discussions, these two forms of development tend to be treated as separate phenomena, with development in the community taking precedence. Of course, in many rural communities there is a pressing need for jobs, income, and services. However, to focus solely on the sustenance needs of local residents is to miss the important contribution that development of community can make to well-being. Community development is a broader process in which development in the community and development of community should be mutually reinforcing activities. When specific projects are undertaken with an eye toward building the relationships and lines of communication that comprise the community field, community development has occurred—regardless of whether a project met specific outcomes or not (Wilkinson 1991). In fact, from the perspective articulated here, success, as measured by objective standards, is not the sole or most important benchmark against which to gauge community development. Communities develop, and well-being is enhanced, when residents work together to address issues and problems that affect them all.

IMPLICATIONS FOR COMMUNITY DEVELOPMENT RESEARCH AND PRACTICE

The familiar tendency for community development researchers and practitioners to rely primarily on macro, secondary indicators for background information on locality specific issues may be problematic. As we discovered in this study, traditional sources (such as the Censuses of Population and Housing,

County and City Data Books, and the Statistical Abstracts) provide important but incomplete data on most localities, particularly small and rural communities.

Developing useful community development strategies requires detailed information about such issues as local activeness, organizational capacity, and information networks. Macro indicators do not tell us about these hard-to-measure aspects of community life. In the communities we studied, our chief concern was the relationship between levels of local activeness and perceptions of community well-being. As we discovered soon after beginning our research, however, consolidated sources of information on the number or types of activities in which municipalities were engaged was not available. Using key and action informant surveys and methods associated with community ethnographic approaches (narratives, histories, searches of newspaper morgues, and the use of newspaper clipping services), we were able to gather such data. And, as we learned, knowing levels of local activity was critical to a proper understanding of community well-being.

The combination of quantitative and qualitative research techniques is essential to community development research. Macro data can provide an important starting point, but to tell the story of what is happening in particular places requires additional information derived from interviews, observations, and local histories. Without going into the field to gather real-time data from discussions with real people, our community and community development analyses are bound to be incomplete. The only way for researchers, practitioners, and students to know, is to ask. They cannot get the answers from secondary data or even survey data. What is needed is the existential experience of being in the study site, knowing something of its history and recent past, and, of course, talking to the people who live there.

DISCUSSION QUESTIONS FROM THE EDITORS

1. The authors conclude that using published or publicly available statistics to characterize communities can be problematic. When is it important to rely on statistics and when is it important to develop "on-the-ground" knowledge of a community?

2. How will the Internet increase community activeness? How will the Internet decrease community activeness?

3. The authors cite a distinction between development in the community and development of the community. While most people probably prefer development of the community, generally most development activity revolves around development in the community. Can you provide some potential explanations of why this is the case?

NOTES

Support for this work was received through Cooperative State Research Service, United States Department of Agriculture, National Research Initiative Project 92-37401-8285. The authors acknowledge the assistance of Kenneth P. Wilkinson, Steve Smith, Craig Humphrey, Mark Nord, Myron Schwartz, Kathleen Miller, and Patti Fickes.

1. See Luloff (1996) for a detailed description of the key aspects of community life, the methodological procedures used in this study, and the identification of key indicators used for determining level of success.

2. To minimize both regional differences and data collection costs, we selected case study sites in the north-central region of Pennsylvania.

3. For information on the surveys, including the seven broad themes of community well-being used in this study, contact A. E. Luloff.

CHAPTER 7

Studying a Controversial Local Issue

Beth Walter Honadle

INTRODUCTION

In 1991, citizens from Branch and North Branch, Minnesota, signed petitions in favor of consolidating these two small cities in Chisago County. (For more information about this case study, see Honadle 1998, 1996, 1995; and Busse 1994. These studies deal with different aspects of the case, including legal, process, and financial analysis issues.) The petitions cited economic development, planning, duplication of services, and environmental concerns as reasons for the proposed consolidation. The citizens presented the petitions to both city councils, who were known not to favor consolidation. In fact, the two city governments did not have a cooperative, friendly relationship. Reluctantly, the two city councils passed unanimous resolutions asking the Minnesota Municipal Board to appoint a consolidation study commission, which was to conduct a study and make a recommendation within two years. The reason the city councils approved the resolution was that it assured a citizen referendum before consolidation could occur. A group of 20 citizen-volunteers studied the proposed consolidation from 1992 to 1994 and recommended (by a vote of 14 to 6) consolidating the cities. Ultimately, the citizens in both communities approved the consolidation and the new city came into being in the fall of 1994.

This case study examines the process that the commission used to reach its conclusions. The stages in the process were designed to maximize citizen participation and openness. The steps were: (1) review of state law and initial work plan, (2) solicitation of public input to the commission's study agenda, (3) draft report and resource fair, (4) solicitation of public input on draft report, and (5) preparation and presentation of final report.

THE CONSOLIDATION STUDY COMMISSION APPROACH

The Consolidation Study Commission was a group of 20 citizen-volunteers. They were nominated by their respective cities and appointed by the Minnesota Municipal Board (MMB), a quasi-judicial state agency that dealt with boundary adjustments involving municipalities. Both cities nominated potential chairpersons and the MMB appointed the chair, who had to be a resident of Chisago County, but not a resident of either city. The nonvoting chairperson was a professor specialized in the organization and delivery of local government services. The role of the chairperson was to facilitate and provide organizational and technical assistance throughout the process. The commission also appointed a steering committee. It consisted of the chair (nonvoting), a vice chair from each city, and a secretary. The study commission's expenses, totaling less than $2,000, were borne equally by the two city governments.

Commission members included elected officials from both cities, municipal employees, a civil engineer who specialized in municipal infrastructure, an accountant, schoolteachers, a banker, a home builder, and a real estate agent. They brought with them a host of skills that proved useful in studying a proposed consolidation, as well as perspectives and biases for and against consolidation.

REVIEW OF STATE LAW AND INITIAL WORK PLAN

The commission began by reviewing its legal mandate. The law enumerated specific subjects and factors the study commission had to study. These were:

- present population, past population growth, and projected population in the two cities;
- quantity of land within the two cities; and natural terrain, including general topography, major watersheds, soil conditions, and such natural features as rivers, lakes, and major bluffs;
- degree of contiguity of the boundaries between the two cities;
- analysis of whether present planning and physical development in the included municipalities indicates that the consolidation of the two cities will benefit planning and land-use patterns in the area; the present transportation network and potential transportation issues, including proposed highway development;
- analysis of whether consolidation of the two cities is consistent with comprehensive plans for the area;
- analysis of whether governmental services now available in the two cities can be more effectively or economically provided by consolidation;
- analysis of whether there are existing or potential environmental problems and whether municipal consolidation will help improve such conditions;

- analysis of tax and governmental aid issues involved in the consolidation of the municipalities;
- analysis of the effect of consolidation on area school districts; and
- analysis of the applicability of the state building code.

In addition, the law required the commission to hold at least one public hearing regarding consolidation to discuss the contents of any city charter or the form of government for the proposed consolidated city, and whether a ward system should be included in the form of government of the proposed consolidated city.

After reviewing these mandates from the state, the commission clustered the work into four topical areas for study: (1) public services and finance; (2) planning and land use; (3) environmental issues; and (4) a structural issues category, including naming the new city, whether there would be wards in the new city, and the form of government for the new city. The commission divided itself into four "work groups" to specialize in the four areas. The term work group, as opposed to committee, was used to emphasize their role as researchers for the entire commission. Their purpose was to divide up the workload rather than give the groups autonomy in their respective areas.[1]

Discussion I

Put yourself in the role of the Study Commission Steering Committee. As a member of the leadership group for this new commission, you must decide how to organize it. List criteria you would use to decide how to divide the work of the commission among its members. Recall that you have members from two communities, people with different backgrounds and skills, and a deadline. Also recall that you have at least three audiences for your report: the MMB, the two city councils, and the voters in the two communities.

Each work group developed a preliminary work plan and presented it to the full commission for discussion and approval. These plans included the scope of their investigations, questions they wanted to have answered, and their proposed sources of relevant information (e.g., interviews, maps, government documents, etc.). For example, the public services and finance work group planned to look at municipal debt, intergovernmental grants, expenditures, and property taxes, among other considerations. In this way, the commission managed the task of developing its agenda.

SOLICITATION OF PUBLIC INPUT TO THE COMMISSION'S AGENDA

Having addressed the state's mandate and incorporated their own ideas on the scope and content of their report, the study commission involved the public in shaping its agenda. The commission opened up a post office box and maintained it throughout the process so that citizens could send the committee comments at any time. The commission held its first public hearing six months into its process. Prior to the hearing, the commission sent flyers to each household in the area with information, inviting people to the hearing, and asking what questions they wanted the commission to study in its deliberations. This gave the public an opportunity to write down any questions they had and to mail them to the commission or bring them to the public hearing and insert them in special boxes located in the auditorium where the meeting was to be held. The hearing was well attended. In addition, it was broadcast live on a local radio station and was played again a week later for people who may have missed it.

The hearing began with brief presentations by the commission chair and chairs of each of the work groups. The commission chair introduced the 20 commission members and explained how the commission came to be established, its legal framework, and the timeframe for completing its work. Then, the work group chairs made brief presentations on their group's preliminary plans and any progress to date.

A former radio announcer and city administrator from another community in Chisago County was the moderator for the evening. The majority of the hearing involved the commission listening to citizens express their views on concerns they wanted the commission to address. Some attendees needed to be reminded that this was *not* a hearing about the public's opinions for or against consolidation, but rather a forum for them to tell the commission their *questions*.

At one point, a citizen who was decidedly proconsolidation and believed the commission membership was stacked against it demanded commission members stand up and state publicly their bias either for or against consolidation. The chair explained that this would not be done, and that to do so would compromise the integrity of the investigation. Within a few days, this individual wrote a letter to the editor of the local paper reiterating his desire for the commission to state its prejudices regarding consolidation up front. The commission chair responded to this request by likening it to a jury in a criminal trial stating at the outset whether they thought the accused was guilty or innocent. The editor of the paper also wrote a column stating her objection to this request and expressing her confidence in the commission's integrity. This initial criticism by one person never progressed beyond this exchange and that person eventually saw that the commission was studying the consolidation openly and thoroughly.

Discussion II

Put yourself in the role of the study commission chair. As someone who does not live in either community, you must be a neutral facilitator and assistant to the project. How would you handle citizens who might disrupt the process while still maintaining a value of openness and responsiveness to the community?

The public input process at this initial stage produced a couple of modifications in the study plans. A group of farmers expressed their concern about the possible effects of consolidation on their property taxes. There were also citizens who wanted to know how consolidation would affect electric power. This was because North Branch had a municipal power plant and Branch did not. Branch was served by Northern States Power Company and a rural electric cooperative. The issue was whether residents of former Branch would be saddled with costs incurred by the power plant. So, the commission collected information and discussed the probable impact of consolidation on farmers and looked into any implications of consolidation on local electric power provision. This work was distributed to the work groups in an equitable manner. Since the work group dealing with public services and finance had three people associated with the North Branch power plant on it, the steering committee (the chair, two vice chairs, secretary, and treasurer) suggested assigning the power plant issue to another work group. This avoided the perception by some citizens that those people had a conflict of interest and might present a biased presentation of the financial implications of the power plant for a consolidated city.

DRAFT REPORT AND RESOURCE FAIR

A year after the commission held its first public hearing, it produced a draft report, which covered all of the areas the work groups had been studying. Each section of the report included factual findings and conclusions. The commission also made some preliminary recommendations on key issues.

The commission decided to make preliminary recommendations at this point so the public would have a clear idea of what the consolidated city would be like, if consolidation were to occur. Thus, the commission recommended the name North Branch, a mayor and council form of government, and no wards in the newly consolidated city. The commission also recommended consolidating the outstanding municipal debt of the two cities after consolidation.

The commission made a public presentation of the draft report and took questions at a well-attended meeting in January 1994. After this presentation and question-and-answer period, the commission hosted a resource fair. The resource fair was organized around the four work groups. Attendees were invited to visit tables displaying various materials the work groups had studied in their research. These included maps, reports, budgets, and other pertinent documents. Members of the work groups were stationed at these tables to answer questions and discuss people's thoughts on the issues. This was an advantage to having commission members specialize in the various areas. The public's reaction to the resource fair was very positive. They were impressed with how much material the work groups had studied to reach their conclusions. Residents also appreciated having an opportunity to converse with commission members about the report.

SOLICITATION OF PUBLIC INPUT ON THE DRAFT REPORT

The commission had only a few copies of the report at the public meeting, but had decided to make copies available at the local library, both city halls, and the county extension office. The commission did not expect a lot of demand for personal copies of the draft report and thought it would be acceptable (given the cost of producing each copy) to give copies to the press and anyone who asked for one. The copies that were placed in the public locations around the two cities were for people to check out and return. The copies had forms on them for receiving comments and input about the draft report. The only criticism the commission received about this approach was from the editor of the local newspaper who thought that the commission should have had a large supply of copies at the public meeting for everyone who came.

Discussion III

Put yourself in the role of a commission member. How would you solicit public input on preliminary findings, conclusions, and recommendations of the commission? How would you present the draft report to the public so that you could obtain this feedback?

The commission received a small amount of criticism from the public on the draft report. This included some complaints about the use of the economists' term "free-riders" to describe benefits Branch residents were receiving from North Branch public services without having to pay for them. The Branch City Council hired a consultant to criticize the report and sent this critique to the commission. This generated no small amount of consternation and discussion at the next monthly commission meeting. The Branch members on the commission were especially offended that their elected representatives (including two members of the commission) had hired a consultant to attack their work.

PREPARATION AND PRESENTATION OF FINAL REPORT

The commission considered all of the input it received about the draft report. It went through the comments point by point and discussed them. Where appropriate, they made clarifying changes and added material. The most substantive change was the decision not to recommend consolidating the outstanding debt if the two cities were consolidated. Instead, the commission recommended that the two city councils decide prior to consolidation whether to merge the debts. This removed from debate perhaps the most controversial issue about the proposed consolidation.

The commission completed its final report in the spring of 1994. It presented the report at a public meeting at about the time it was sent to the MMB. The MMB held a hearing on the consolidation in June 1994. After listening to anyone who wished to speak, the hearing was adjourned. In several weeks the MMB ordered the consolidation. Both city councils then voted on it. It passed in North Branch, but failed in Branch. At that point, citizens from Branch circulated a petition and succeeded in calling for a September referendum in both cities.

The study commission had no role in the campaigns and debates over the initiative. However, the chair of the commission accepted an invitation to present the final report and answer questions at a public meeting a week before the referendum. It was the same presentation of the commission's findings, conclusions, and recommendations given in the spring at the conclusion of the commission's work, and to the MMB at its hearing. The consolidation passed by more than 60 percent in Branch and more than 90 percent in North Branch. The newly consolidated city of North Branch officially came into being in November 1994, right after a general election to seat a new city council.

Discussion IV

Put yourself in the role of the study commission chair. How would you balance your duty to be a neutral party in the process against a responsibility to present the commission's work to the public? Remember that the process was instigated by citizens. After the commission had voted to recommend consolidation, would it have been appropriate for the commission to take a public position in favor of consolidation?

CONCLUSION

The process used in this case shows that citizens can study a complex and controversial issue with the help of outside experts. It was important to delineate the mission of the commission at the outset and to organize its work in an efficient and equitable manner. It was also necessary to assign work in a way that avoided the appearance of impropriety or conflict of interest. This case study emphasizes the importance of public input in studying a controversial community issue. It is essential that the public be involved in the setting of the study commission's agenda to ensure that salient issues are addressed. On the other hand, it is imperative that the study commission resist being drawn into political debates before they have had time to gather, analyze, and reach conclusions about relevant facts. This process can be used to reach a decision about a wide range of public policy issues in a community.

NOTE

1. The commission elected a steering committee to help guide the process. The steering committee included two vice chairs (one from each community), a treasurer, a secretary, and the chair of the commission. Unintentionally, the commission chose the

treasurer from one of the cities and the secretary from the other, so the steering committee had balanced representation from the two cities.

Maintaining and Enhancing the Community Economic Base

CHAPTER 8

Introduction: Maintaining and Enhancing the Community Economic Base

Scott Loveridge

When economists speak of an area's economic base, they generally mean those industries that sell to customers outside the region. In this section, we focus on efforts to maintain and expand the economic base. We broaden the standard definition of economic base to include those industries that sell to nonlocal customers, but inside the region (as in tourism) and industries in which businesses compete with companies outside the region for local dollars (as in retail).

With the increasing globalization of the economy, it is no longer safe to assume that an industry that is viable today will continue to be healthy next year or even tomorrow. A political decision made in a distant continent can change world commodity prices, wreaking havoc on local natural resource-based economic systems. Similarly, an investment decision made in a distant boardroom can make local manufacturing facilities obsolete. A new highway can bring new competitors into a local retail market, putting locally owned enterprises at risk. While each of the changes described above may promote better world prosperity, these kinds of developments also have negative—even potentially disastrous—effects on the local economy.

In urban areas, the negative consequences of changing economic and environmental circumstances may be more easily overcome than is the case in rural areas. Rural areas have fewer employment opportunities. A worker specialized in one type of activity may find it difficult to be reemployed in a job using that skill if his or her job comes to an end. Workers in rural areas may also have less access to retraining opportunities than do workers in urban areas. Workers need jobs, so much of economic development revolves around job creation strategies.

Economic development professionals began devoting more attention to creating jobs by working with existing industries after a study by David Birch (1979) became well publicized. While some of Birch's findings have since been debated, the main message—that most new job creation is the result of growth in small to medium-sized local firms—remains valid. While job creation is a fundamental reason to focus on existing industry, other benefits come from attention to the existing local industries. These include:

Increased Community Engagement. Local businesses have made a commitment to the region. Existing local businesses may be more willing and able to contribute to community engagement than businesses brought in from the outside. Another community engagement benefit is that enhancing the local economic base usually helps local government better understand and respond to existing industry concerns. If existing industry is well satisfied with local government services, the area becomes known as a good place to do business. This may attract additional investments to the region.

Early Warning. Even when an existing business cannot be saved, a strong program of working with local businesses can help the community better forecast and prepare for the departure of a major industry. With better prior warning, support systems for displaced workers are likely to be better managed. Early warning might also help the community begin devising industry replacement strategies to make the best use of the resources that become available as the industry declines.

More Complete Information. Decision-makers in the region typically know a lot more about industries related to the existing economic base than they do new industries. It is therefore easier to get good information about the probability of success of future investments if the investments are related to existing industry. A focus on existing industries therefore helps avoid costly mistakes.

Reduced Probability of Local Conflict. When proposed activities add value to an existing industry, there is usually minimal opposition to the concept. The new activities will likely enhance the operations of those who have made prior investments in the impacted industry. In contrast, a new industry may draw customers, workers, or government resources away from existing employers.

In this section, we explore community experiences in working with their local economic base through eight case studies. The contributions by Darling and by Kline demonstrate how community engagement can result in improved performance of the local retail sector. The contributions by Morse and Lazarus, and by Leistritz show how communities can identify potential value added opportunities within the agricultural sector, and secure investments that increase the marketability of local products. The chapters by Barkley and Henry, by Bender and Davis, and by Albrecht provide examples of communities that are transitioning away from agriculture to tourism-related economies. Finally, the chapter by Rosenfeld shows how targeted investments in education can promote local enterprise development.

Map 2
Location of Case Studies Sites: Maintaining and Enhancing The Community Economic Base

CHAPTER 9

Building a Healthy Retail Community: Lessons from Two Towns

David L. Darling

INTRODUCTION

Retail trade is a dramatically dynamic sector. One major trend is the consolidation in the sale of everything from toys to fabrics. Currently, Wal-Mart dominates the competition in the general merchandising retail sector. Due to consolidation, small towns have lost retail services to larger towns. The only retail services that are sure to stay are those that provide a product which is bought based on the customers' desire for convenience. In fact, research by the author has found that there is a high level of dissatisfaction with local stores and shopping (Coulson and Darling 1996). Thus, many rural and small-town residents are interested in the issue of retaining retail services.

This chapter examines two similar-sized towns in central Kansas that have diversified retail sectors. One retail sector is strong, while the other town's is weak. The author compares the two towns and contrasts them using a number of characteristics. From this analysis, it is possible to explain why one town outshines the other. Next, the author presents important lessons that can be learned in this case study. Finally, an economic development model is applied to the retail trade issue to provide some prescriptive advice.

BACKGROUND

The primary and traditional role of the retail sector is to provide goods and services to a local customer base for their convenience and at a reasonable price. Customers expect most of their household needs to be met locally, and the products offered to be of an acceptable quality. In addition, service at and after the sale, which is the hallmark of the traditional small-town merchant, is expected to be part of the bundle of benefits to shoppers in small towns.

In return, the business community hopes to earn a comfortable, middle-class income. Often, the social status of a merchant is defined by the business he owns and operates. Collectively, the business community makes up the majority of the middle and upper class, and often provides key leaders such as the mayor, the president of the Chamber of Commerce, or the chairperson of the United Way.

The community gains by recycling new dollars through the local banks, grocery stores, specialty shops, and doctors offices. From this turnover, new income is created. Economists measure the strength of these local linkages with income, sales, and employment multipliers.

THE CASE STUDY

To measure the performance of the retail sector, the author uses local sales tax collections to generate city trade pull factors and trade area capture numbers. Both towns have similar populations, but have very different pull factors and trade area capture numbers. A city trade pull factor measures the ratio of in-shopping to out-shopping (leakage); a pull factor of one means the city has no net in-shopping or out-shopping, while higher numbers indicate in-shopping. Trade area capture measures the size of the customer base supporting the retail sector. In these two towns, community A had a fiscal year 1998 pull factor of 1.26 and a trade area capture of 3,012 full-time equivalent customers. Community B had a fiscal year 1998 pull factor of 0.63 and a trade area capture of 1,705 full-time equivalent customers. Table 9.1 presents the comparison of numbers, and figure 9.1 presents the differences visually.

Table 9.1 Retail Sector Performance		
	Community A	Community B
1998 Sales Tax Collections at 1 percent rate	$164,287	$92,988
1998 City Trade Pull Factor	1.26	0.63
1998 Trade Area Capture	3,012	1,705
Estimated Personal Income Multiplier	1.50	1.32
1996 City Population	2,395	2,702
1997 Zip Code Area Population	3,615	4,447

Figure 9.1
Retail Area Comparison

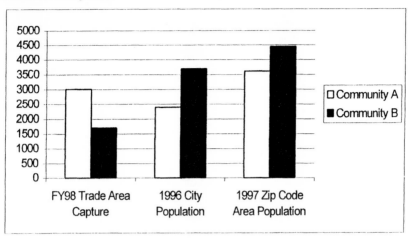

One might expect that city A and city B are very similar in almost every way. About 98 percent of the population is white. The median household incomes are $23,046 and $20,197 respectively. In Kansas, the 1997 comparable number is $28,041. The author estimates that 44.5 percent of all households in community A are in the middle class, based on 1997 incomes between $25,000 and $100,000. In community B, the percentage drops down to 40.3 percent.[1] The median age in both towns is around 40. In community A, 23 percent of the population is 65 or older and 22 percent for community B. Thus, the difference in their pull factors and their trade area capture numbers make this comparison interesting.

Communities A and B have very different histories and cultural backgrounds. Community A was settled by Mennonites who immigrated from Poland, Germany, and Russia in the 1870s. The city was established as a farm service trade center on a rail line. Community B also is a farm service trade center on a rail line, but its people have more diverse religious affiliations. Community B also became a railroad town with many railroad functions added such as switching, train servicing, and overnight lodging services. The community solidarity in city A has grown out of their strong sense of identity. City B has a weaker sense of solidarity which has been exacerbated by a population of transient families renting and buying inexpensive homes, while one or more of the adults in the family commute to work at a military fort, and, most likely, shop on post at the commissary and PX.

Community A has a history of stamina. For 30 years, the Arts and Crafts Association has put on a fall fair. The 1998 fair was attended by 45,000 people and 400 vendors sold about one million dollars worth of arts and crafts. Separately, but closely connected, The Development Corporation has a history dating back to July 1, 1968. This for-profit corporation bought land and developed a 160-acre industrial park. Stock sold in the corporation was used to buy the land. In 1972, the Ozark Regional Commission provided a $194,000 grant to further develop the industrial park. By 1998, ten industries were manufacturing products in the park.

DETAILED COMPARISON

In summary, some of the most important differences are the following:

- Community A has a very successful fall arts and crafts fair.
- Community A has been more successful creating job opportunities than Community B.
- Community A has two grocery stores, and that competition actually helps improve in-shopping and discourage out-shopping. Community B has only one.
- Community A has a large discount department store and community B does not.
- Community A has three new-vehicle dealers, and these are a magnet that draw in trade as well as hold automobile trade locally. Community B has only one auto dealer and it only sells used cars and trucks.

These five strengths of community A are enough to explain the higher pull factor and higher trade area capture. The strengths of community B over community A are the existence of two drugstores and one local radio station. However, these strengths are not of the same magnitude as the ones already highlighted for community A. (See table 9.2.)

Table 9.2
State of Kansas Per Capita Sales Tax Collections by Business Class

Business Class	Taxable Trade Per Capita ($)
Grocery and Meat Stores	1,245
Department and Discount Stores	1,103
Auto and Truck Dealers	1,051
Restaurants and Other Eating Establishments	661
Variety, Hobby, Gift, and Antique Stores	329
Drugstores	320
Building Material Dealers	317
Engine Repair Shops	295
Rental and Leasing Businesses	280
Plumbing, Heating, and Air Conditioning Contractors and Service Businesses	258
Office Equipment and Stationary Stores	204

Source: Darling, Ariyaratne. 1997. "Spending Patterns across Business Groups by Kansas Consumers: An Analysis of Data from Fiscal Year 1996." C. D. Study Report #167, KSU Department of Agricultural Economics, Manhattan, KS.

OTHER DIFFERENCES

Community A has a long history of successfully planning and implementing community and economic development projects and programs. They tapped into state programs to help get them started and keep the momentum going. For example, they joined the *PRIDE* Program when it was just getting started. This Kansas-wide small town betterment program was initially designed to help communities prepare to attract new industry. Community A won annual competitive awards and successfully completed all their *Blue Ribbon* categories to become a *Pace Maker* community. This designation allowed them to state that they had been judged competent in 22 major categories, including commercial and industrial development.

Community B also joined the PRIDE Program, but unlike community A, had less success in the program and dropped out after struggling for six years to achieve the *Pace Maker* status. They never won an annual competition, however, they did get certified in 20 out of 22 categories by outside judges, including the commercial and industrial *Blue Ribbon*.

The lesson learned here is that sustained efforts can make a difference. Community A is well organized and uses a large pool of people to act as volunteer leaders. Some of these people have been trained in a county-wide leadership program that has been in place for more than ten years. Community B relies on the city manager to keep programs moving forward, and he has to overcome negative attitudes and a reactive city council. Community A is a proactive place.

The collective energy and intelligence of a positive group of people is more powerful than the efforts of just one. Dr. Glen Pulver, past president of the Community Development Society, likes to say: "It takes smarts, sweat and stamina, to build a successful community."

PRESCRIPTION FOR SUCCESS

The leaders of community A understand that the ideas captured in figure 9.2 relate just as well to the retail sector of their community as well as to their economy in general. The community has to be organized to effectively address the issue of a healthy retail sector. This organization has to build trusting partnerships with city government, the local banking community, appropriate regional and state organizations, and others. The business environment will be enriched over time as cooperation builds and one successful project leads to more successes. Once the leadership is ready to plan and implement an effort to build a healthy retail community, five basic strategies should be considered. Existing retail businesses should be encouraged and assisted to survive and thrive (strategy 1). New businesses should be incubated and grown. The downtown is America's historic incubator facility (strategy 2). Local, area, and outsiders should be encouraged to shop locally. This includes local households, local businesses, local governmental units, and local nonprofit organizations (strategy 3). The leadership of the town and the Chamber of Commerce should look for ways to capture outside dollars to be channeled through the retail community and build the capital stock that is an asset to the retail community (strategy 4). This could include grants from higher governmental units and investments by business people who live elsewhere but see an opportunity worth pursuing. Finally, new firms can be targeted and attracted to be added to the mix and strengthen the retail community (strategy 5).

Figure 9.2
Economic Development Pyramid

Table 9.3
Checklist for the Success of Your City

	Communities			
	A		B	
	YES	NO	YES	NO
Strong downtown shopping district	x		x	
Two or more grocery stores	2		1	
Large department store selling general merchandise	1			x
Forty or more miles from a Wal-Mart Store		x		x
Two or more new/used vehicle dealers	3			x
Variety of restaurants and taverns	x		x	
Building materials and supplies business	x		x	
Drugstore		x	2	
Hospital	x		x	
Strong medical service community	x		x	
Strong local newspaper	x		x	
Local radio station		x	x	
County seat status		x		x
Job center status (at least one job for every two people)	x			x
Strong attractions such as college sports events, festivals, and natural wonders	x			x
Above-average family incomes and net worth		x		x
Trade area population is growing at an average or faster rate		x		x
Household incomes are growing at an average or faster rate		x	x	
Daily traffic volume ≥ 4,000 cars and trucks on a nearby major highway		3,555		1,630
Farm-related businesses, implement dealers	1		1	

DISCUSSION QUESTIONS FROM THE EDITORS

1. Community A had a natural comparative advantage in that the population consists predominately of members of a close-knit religious community. How do tight social bonds help promote economic development? What might community B do to promote better social cohesion?

2. The author mentions that many members of community B shop at the local military base where goods are sold at lower prices, so the military base

reduces opportunities for local retail sales. What other impacts, bad and good, does close proximity to a military base have on small communities?

3.   What does the author mean when he says, "The downtown is America's historic incubator facility"?

NOTE

1. All demographic and income statistics come from the twelveth edition of "The Source Book of Zip Code Demographics" published by CACI Marketing Systems, Arlington, VA.

CHAPTER 10

Local Economic and Fiscal Impacts of a Planned Retirement Community in South Carolina

David L. Barkley and Mark S. Henry

INTRODUCTION

For many years, McCormick County served as the "poster child" for rural economic development in South Carolina. McCormick's residents (7,800 in 1980) exhibited all of the characteristics associated with geographic isolation and an absence of economic opportunity. In the early 1980s, the unemployment rate hovered around 15 percent, per capita income remained below 60 percent of the U.S. average, more than one-fourth of the households lived in poverty, and approximately 60 percent of the adult population had less than a high school degree. Tax revenues for public goods and services were limited by low property values resulting from extensive forest lands (31 percent of county land area is in public lands).

In response to the economic development needs of McCormick County and surrounding areas, the state of South Carolina established the Savannah Valley Authority to plan and stimulate economic development in the upper Savannah River Valley. In 1986, the Savannah Valley Authority obtained 3,159 acres of federal land in McCormick County for development. The U.S. Army Corps of Engineers land was obtained as compensation for state land needed for construction of Clarks Hill Reservoir (later Lake Thurmond). Accordingly, there was little net impact on McCormick County fees in lieu of taxes. Proposals were requested to determine how to develop the property in a way that would enhance local economic development and expand the county tax base. In 1987, Cooper Communities, Inc., a residential development company based in Bella Vista,

Arkansas, contracted with the Savannah Valley Authority to develop a planned retirement/recreation community named Savannah Lakes Village (SLV). Construction for SLV began in 1988 and development plans included 5,100 home sites, extensive recreational facilities, and business properties to serve the needs of village residents.

The purpose of this chapter is to report the economic and fiscal contributions of SLV to McCormick County in 1995. By the end of 1995, more than 3,000 lots were sold to individuals and construction was completed on 32 townhouses and 204 single-family residences. Infrastructure investments completed at SLV include water and sewer lines, streets, a golf course and club house, hotel and sales center, restaurant, village store, bank building, emergency medical service/fire station/security facility, marina, boat docks, and recreation center. Activity at SLV resulted in 610 jobs and $18.8 million in income in 1995, numbers that are anticipated to increase significantly as the village adds approximately 80 residences each year. In addition, McCormick County and county schools received almost $1.1 million in tax revenue from SLV, residents and property owners. Approximately one-third of McCormick County's property tax revenues is attributable to SLV, with projections that SLV will contribute one-half of these revenues by 2000. The methods and data used to derive the above economic and fiscal impacts are summarized in the following sections.

RETIREMENT COMMUNITIES AND ECONOMIC GROWTH

Private Sector Impacts

Planned retirement developments serve as "basic" industries, and thus provide the stimulus for local economic growth and development. The potential impact a retirement development has on a county may be illustrated by tracing the flows of goods and payments through the local economy (Figure 10.1). The retirement development initiates the growth process by bringing new dollars to the local economy. The principal sources of these dollar flows will be retirement income (A) and spending by tourists and visitors to the community (B). Many of the dollars attracted to the planned community are then distributed throughout the local economy to: households for labor services (C), local businesses for goods and services (D), local building firms for new home construction (E), government for public services (F), and local financial institutions for financial services (G).

The income and jobs generation process generally does not stop after only one round of spending. Households and businesses spend their new incomes for locally provided goods and services, and this round of spending creates new jobs which in turn stimulates additional rounds of spending. Each round, some of the income received by households and local businesses is spent on goods and services acquired outside the local economy (e.g, purchases of goods in neighboring communities, state and federal tax payments, profits or savings invested elsewhere, nonlocal input acquisitions). These flows of funds outside the community ("leakages") result in less spending available for following

Figure 10.1
Goods and Payments Flows: Direct Economic Impacts

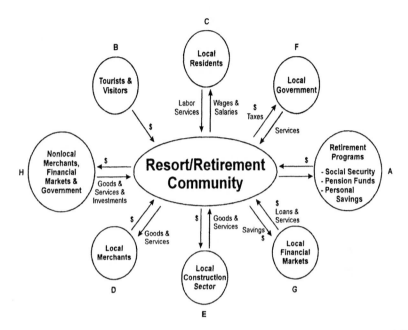

rounds and a smaller multiplier effect. Rural communities such as McCormick have relatively high leakages due to the scarcity of services and shopping opportunities.

In sum, a planned retirement community attracts people who spend money earned elsewhere, which stimulates employment growth in the local economy. The jobs provided are primarily construction, retail, and service oriented, a good fit for rural areas whose labor supply consists of many individuals with limited education and training. In addition, economic activity in retirement areas is relatively stable over business cycles since the principal income sources (pensions, annuities, social security) vary little over time.

Public Sector Benefits

Some of the money spent by new residents of and visitors to retirement/recreation communities goes to pay local taxes, including property, sales, and use taxes. The additional revenue raised from the new residents and visitors provides local governments with opportunities to invest in infrastructure and services for local citizens. Also, an influx of people who build houses but do not have school-age children, provides school districts with additional revenue without the responsibility of providing education to more students.

ECONOMIC IMPACT OF SLV ON MCCORMICK COUNTY

Savannah Lakes Village provides two principal private-sector economic benefits to McCormick County:

1. Construction, marketing, and facilities operations at Savannah Lakes Village create new jobs and income. And as SLV adds more full-time residents to the county, these residents purchase new homes, consume local goods and services, and draw visitors to the county *(direct effects)*.

2. Jobs and incomes generated at SLV lead to additional economic activity in the region as dollars are re-spent for local goods and services *(indirect and induced effects)*.

The direct effects are translated into their corresponding total impacts using the IMPLAN data and software. Since McCormick County is small and isolated, many of the purchases of goods and services by local businesses, Cooper Communities, Inc., and residents of McCormick are made outside the county. Thus, the multiplier effects attributable to SLV are relatively small. As the McCormick County economy grows in response to SLV, some of these leakages will be reduced and multiplier values are likely to become larger.

In reporting our results, we group the private-sector benefits into four categories: Cooper Communities, Inc., Savannah Lakes Village Property Owners Association, Inc., residents of Savannah Lakes Village, and marketing tour participants and tourists to Savannah Lakes Village. Our focus is the contribution of each component to the employment and income in the county in 1995.

Cooper Communities, Inc.

Cooper Communities, Inc. provides direct employment and income impacts on McCormick County through infrastructure development and administrative and marketing activities at SLV (including lodge and restaurant operations). In 1995, infrastructure construction expenditures were $1,840,000 for roads, $494,094 for utilities, and $1,600,000 for a new activities center. These construction expenditures directly generated 52 jobs and $1,756,850 in income in 1995 (table 10.1). After including all multiplier effects, we estimate that infrastructure activities resulted in $4,621,224 in total expenditures, 69 new jobs, and $2,135,673 in total income.

In 1995, Cooper Communities, Inc. spent more than $4 million for administration, marketing (including sales commissions), and operating the lodge and restaurant at Savannah Lakes Village. These activities resulted in 121 full-time equivalent jobs. The 1995 total effect of Cooper Communities, Inc. administration, marketing, and service expenditures was $5,433,319 and total employment and income associated with these expenditures was 159 jobs and $3,971,860 in wages, salaries, and commissions.

Property Owners Association

The SLV Property Owners Association, Inc. independently provides services to village residents, including administration of the association; management and maintenance of the golf course, pro shop, clubhouse, and recreation center; EMS, fire protection, and security services; and maintenance of roads within SLV. The infrastructure investments, expenditures, payroll, and employment associated with these activities are summarized in table 10.1. In 1995, the Property Owners Association's expenditures were $2,429,590, resulting in 32 jobs with a payroll of about $880,000. The cumulative impacts of expenditures by the Property Owners Association were 40 jobs and more than $1,400,000 in income.

Savannah Lakes Village Residents

The most important and enduring economic impacts from SLV on McCormick County result from the residents of the retirement community. Residents stimulate the local economy through home construction and expenditures for goods and services.

In 1995, 67 single-family residences were completed. The average value of homes under construction (excluding lot) was $157,597 and total construction expenditures were $10,559,017. The 1995 construction expenditures resulted in 107 jobs and $4,342,924 in income in the construction sector (table 10.1). The total impacts on the local economy (direct plus indirect and induced) were 154 jobs and $6,014,081 in income.

Two hundred thirty-six families resided in SLV in 1995 (177 full-year and 59 partial-year). We estimate that residents of SLV generated about $5.3 million in personal consumption expenditures in 1995 based on an average family income of $72,000 and partial-year residents staying in the community approximately three months a year. Residents' expenditures generated direct effects of 94 jobs and $3.0 million in income and total effects of approximately 120 jobs with $4.0 million in local income (table 10.1). The local business sectors most affected by residents' spending are miscellaneous retail, eating and drinking establishments, food stores, auto service, and apparel.

Tour Participants and Tourists

The final source of spending attributable to Savannah Lakes Village is by individuals participating in marketing tours of SLV (referred to as *tour participants*), and individuals either visiting SLV residents or attracted to the area by the development's recreational facilities (referred to as *tourists*). In 1995, Cooper Communities, Inc. conducted 6,235 tours of SLV properties. Each tour averaged two individuals and took an average of two days. Thus, the marketing tours resulted in 24,940 tour participant spending days (6,235 tours x 2 persons per tour x 2 days per tour). In addition, some 3,460 room-nights at the Savannah

Lakes Village Lodge were used by tourists. On average, two people were registered for each room, thus tourists to the area contributed 6,920 (3,460 room-nights x 2 persons per room) tourist spending days.

Table 10.1
Economic Impacts of Savannah Lakes Village

Cooper Communities, Inc.		Residents Construction and Consumption	
I. Infrastructure Construction		I. Residential Construction	
A. Direct Effects		A. Direct Effects	
Expenditures	$3,934,094	Expenditures	$10,559,017
Employment	52	Employment	107
Income	$1,756,850	Income	$4,342,924
B. Total Effects		B. Total Effects	
Expenditures	$4,621,224	Expenditures	$13,784,797
Employment	69	Employment	154
Income	$2,135,673	Income	$6,014,081
II. Administration, Marketing, Lodge & Restaurant		II. Personal Consumption	
A. Direct Effects		A. Direct Effects	
Expenditures	$4,052,394	Expenditures	$5,282,713
Employment	121	Employment	94
Income	$2,940,057	Income	3,024,189
B. Total Effects		B. Total Effects	
Expenditures	$5,433,319	Expenditures	$6,880,183
Employment	159	Employment	119
Income	$3,971,860	Income	$3,901,568

The tour participants and tourists contribute to the McCormick County economy through their local spending for lodging, food and drink, recreation, and other services and retail goods. We estimate these expenditures at $52 per day per person for 1995 ($30 for meals, $10 for recreation, $10 for retail and services, $2 for gas and oil). To avoid double counting, we consider only the expected spending of tour participants and tourists that is made in McCormick County but outside of the Savannah Lakes Village facilities. The estimated expenditures from tour participants and tourists are provided in table 10.1.

Tour participants and tourists are not expected to be a major source of spending in the area. Estimated direct spending in McCormick County by tour participants and tourists was $1,656,720 for 1995, and employment generated by this spending is estimated at 57. Estimated total spending (direct plus indirect and induced) in McCormick County is $2,353,562 for 1995, and total employment generated by tour participants and tourists is estimated to be 69.

Table 10.1 continued

Property Owners Association		Tourists and Tour Participants	
I. Direct Effects		I. Visitor Days	
A. Administration			
Expenditures	$1,200,360*	Tour Participants	24,940
Employment	5	Tourists	6,920
Income	$182,700		
B. Golf Course/Clubhouse		A. Direct Effects	
Expenditures	$770,052	Expenditures	$1,656,720
Employment	20	Employment	57
Income	$517,950	Income	$970,436
C. Activity Center		B. Total Effects	
Expenditures	$12,382	Expenditures	$2,353,562
Employment	3	Employment	69
Income	$52,800	Income	$1,362,682
D. EMS/Fire/Security			
Expenditures	$191,625	Total Private Economic Impacts	
Employment	3		
Income	$52,800	I. Direct Effects	
		Expenditures	$27,914,528
E. Road Maintenance		Employment	463
Expenditures	$255,171	Income	$13,915,306
Employment	4		
Income	$127,400	II. Total Effects	
		Expenditures	$35,634,379
F. Total POA Activities		Employment	610
Expenditures	$2,429,590*	Income	$18,791,391
Employment	32		
Income	$880,850		
II. Total Effects			
Expenditures	$2,561,294		
Employment	40		
Income	$1,405,527		

Note: *Includes payment to depreciation accounts and interest and principal payments for loans. These expenses were estimated at $647,200 for 1995. These expenditures are not included in the direct effect stimulating the multiplier process and total effect.

Total Economic Impacts

The jobs and income generated by SLV provide a significant contribution to the economy of McCormick County. In 1995, 463 direct jobs and 610 total jobs were created by SLV direct expenditures of almost $28 million. Income resulting from these jobs was $13.9 million for direct effects and $18.8 for total effects. Many of the people working at SLV live in neighboring counties; however, over time more jobs are expected to go to county residents as local firms and workers adjust to opportunities available at the development.

PUBLIC BENEFITS AND COSTS

Tax Revenues for County Ordinary Operations

Savannah Lakes Village affects the fiscal structure of McCormick County by increasing both revenues for and costs of public goods and services. McCormick County tax revenues are funded primarily by taxes on real and personal property. Additional sources of county revenues are: a 1 percent local option sales tax (net of property tax rebates from this fund to SLV residents); accommodations tax (2 percent of hotel/motel receipts); and state tax distributions to the county (distributions from state liquor, bank, gasoline, and income taxes are based on population). Property development at Savannah Lakes Village, spending by SLV homeowners, and visitors/tourists expenditures in the county will generate additional dollars from all sources of tax revenues.

The principal source of new tax revenues is the increase in real property values in the county (primarily lot sales and home construction at SLV). The 1995 appraised market value of real property at Savannah Lakes Village was approximately $82.6 million. Tax collections on SLV real property for county ordinary purposes (using a millage rate of 105) were $476,532. County revenue from personal property taxes attributable to SLV was approximately $37,000 in 1995. SLV residents also contributed about $17,000 in additional state aid to McCormick County based on per capita state aid to counties of $42. Finally, accommodation taxes are paid by visitors to the Savannah Lakes Village Lodge. In 1995, the lodge revenues were about $1,136,000, resulting in about $22,700 in accommodations taxes at a 2 percent rate (10.2).

McCormick County also has a 1 percent local option sales tax. As SLV expands, new residents increase the volume of purchases of taxable goods in the county. In addition, Cooper Communities, Inc., the Property Owners Association, and tourists and visitors also spend money in local stores, adding to retail sales volume in the county and the local option tax revenues for McCormick County. Most of these revenues are used to reduce property taxes, and the remainder is shared between the county government and municipalities. In 1995, the net local option sales taxes to McCormick County attributable to SLV were estimated to be about $9,300. Note that this estimate is new revenue for the county government only. Property owners throughout the county will receive another $45,838 in property tax rebates in 1995 because of added local sales taxes from Savannah Lakes Village activities.

In sum, the total Savannah Lakes Village based revenues that accrue to McCormick County for ordinary uses were $563,000 in 1995. Thus, about 35 percent of all tax revenues in the county for ordinary purposes came from SLV sources in 1995. Savannah Lakes Village lots and residences are a relatively important source of the county's tax base because a large proportion of the county's land is not subject to property taxes (state and federal lands) or the land is in a low-valued use (forestry).

Table 10.2	
McCormick County Public Benefits and Cost, 1995	
Ordinary Operating Budget	**School District Budget**
I. Ordinary Operating Revenues	I. McCormick County School District Revenues Total
Local Options Sales Tax $9,361	Property Tax – SLV $528,636
Total Property Tax – SLV $513,952 State Aid to Political $17,136 Subdivisions	II. McCormick County School District Net Benefits from SLV $0
Accommodations Tax $22,720 Local Options Sales Tax $9,361 Total $563,169	III. McCormick County School District $528,636
II. McCormick County Ordinary Operating Expenses $65,000	
III. McCormick County Ordinary Operating Net Benefits from SLV $498,169	

Added Expenses to McCormick County

Economic growth and development generally create costs to the public sector, as well as benefits. New residents require public services (e.g., education, police and fire protection, emergency medical services, and trash collection) and increase the demand on public goods (parks, sewer and water systems, roads). Expanding public service delivery and infrastructure generate additional costs to the county.

In the case of Savannah Lakes Village, however, new costs to the county are relatively low. Police protection, fire protection, and emergency medical services are funded 80 percent by the Property Owners Association and 20 percent through a special tax district at SLV. Thus, other county residents will not bear additional costs for these services. The expansion of off-site water treatment, wastewater treatment, and distribution and collection facilities may be required to serve additional SLV residents. Cooper Communities, Inc. has established an aid-to-construction fund of $6 million to fund the county for such an expansion.

The county will have the responsibility to maintain the roads of Savannah Lakes Village. By agreement with the Savannah Lakes Village Property Owners Association, Inc., McCormick County will set aside 19 percent of the "new money" (i.e., property tax revenues attributable to SLV) for fiscal year 1995–

1996 for the maintenance and upkeep of Savannah Lakes Village roads. The Savannah Lakes Village Property Owners Association, Inc. will supplement this road fund as necessary to maintain roads. This agreement means that road maintenance is not projected to be a relatively large expense.

Benefits and Costs for Public Schools

A principal beneficiary of an expanding property tax base is the McCormick County School District. Of the county's total 223 mills, 108 were designated for county schools in 1995. The SLV contribution to current school operating funds was $490,148 from real property tax revenues and $38,000 from personal property tax revenues. These two sources accounted for approximately 35 percent of the county's public schools revenues from property tax sources. Few school-age children are expected at SLV; therefore, we assume there will be no added school costs as a result of the development of Savannah Lakes Village. Thus, almost all of the expected school revenue from SLV is a net benefit to the McCormick County School District.

In summary, Savannah Lakes Village provides a substantial net fiscal benefit to both McCormick County and the McCormick County School District. Because of the "own-provision" of many local services through the Savannah Lakes Village special purpose district and because few children are included in the new households, added costs to local governments are small compared to new tax revenues. Moreover, most new jobs are in the trade and service sectors. These jobs are likely to be filled by unemployed residents of McCormick County or commuters from nearby places since wage levels in these sectors are likely to be too low to induce in-migration. Accordingly, little added pressure on new public services is anticipated from the new jobs in the service and trade sectors. Similarly, the economic impacts associated with new consumer spending could be less than reported if there is simply a relocation of McCormick County residents to the SLV from other places in the county. However, data on lot and home sales from Cooper Communities show that almost all SLV residents have in-migrated from places outside McCormick County.

Finally, on a broader scale, the sale of land obtained by the developer from the Savannah River Authority at prices lower than market cost of purchase and Cooper Communities' investments in the project can be viewed as a public subsidy to develop this retirement village. A complete benefit-cost analysis of the development would incorporate this subsidy in finding the rate of return to the government in using these public lands as a development tool.

CONCLUSION

Although only eight years old in 1995, Savannah Lakes Village was making significant economic and fiscal contributions to McCormick County and the surrounding area. Employment (610 jobs) and income ($18.8 million) attributable to SLV represent almost 15 percent of the county's totals in 1995.

And by the year 2000, SLV is anticipated to be responsible for approximately 25 percent of the county's jobs and income. The retirement development also provided about 35 percent of the county's tax revenues for general operations and public schools. And the outlook over the next 10 to 20 years suggests that these net fiscal benefits will continue to increase significantly, as about 80 new homes are added each year to the development.

In addition to the positive net economic and fiscal benefits provided by SLV, residents of the retirement community enhance the county's stock of human capital and are active in local civic and public service organizations. For example, retirees at SLV and employees at Cooper Communities assisted with the downtown revitalization program for the city of McCormick and volunteered for programs at the local public schools. There does not appear to be any political initiative by SLV residents to restrict public spending and taxes, a concern typically associated with the attraction of retirees. The "fiscal generosity" on the part of SLV residents may be attributable to their perception that tax rates are low and local services and schools are underfunded (relative to the communities from which the retirees moved).

The success story of SLV may not be replicable for many rural communities. McCormick County offered an attractive location for retirees because of its mild climate, rolling wooded hills, and access to Lake Thurmond. The development also was "jump started" when the state made available a large tract of lakefront land for a very attractive price. And Cooper Communities, Inc. is an experienced developer of retirement communities, with other developments in Arkansas, Tennessee, and Missouri. Thus, SLV benefited from good location and planning and public support.

DISCUSSION QUESTIONS FROM THE EDITORS

1. Traditionally, industries that sell goods or services outside the region are known as "basic" industries. The authors characterize Savannah Lakes Village as a basic industry. Why?

2. Assume that overall, McCormick County obtains a net economic benefit when retirees move into the development. Are there people living in the county who experience net costs?

3. The authors list jobs created by construction and services to retirees as benefits. Over the long run, which of these two benefits is likely to be the most important?

CHAPTER 11

Failures Lead to Success in Dairy Business Retention and Enhancement Programs

George W. Morse and William Lazarus

INTRODUCTION

The goal of business retention and expansion visitation (BREV) programs is to build the capacity of a community to help its existing businesses survive and grow (Morse 1990; Loveridge and Morse 1997). This case study presents an application of a BREV program to the dairy industry in two different regions in Minnesota. When applied to agricultural industries, the name of the program was changed to retention and enhancement because expansion is an emotionally and politically charged term in the agricultural community. This was one of several changes required to adjust the BREV program from manufacturing/mainstreet businesses to an agricultural business. Not all of our efforts were successful on the first try. Fortunately, lessons learned in the first program led to changes and successes in the second and third dairy programs. After giving a brief overview of the Business Retention and Expansion Visitation Program, we describe the differences in success in two dairy programs. Then we discuss four lessons we learned in doing the first dairy BREV programs that helped make the next one successful.

OVERVIEW OF DAIRY RETENTION AND ENHANCEMENT VISITATION (BREV) PROGRAMS

The overall goal of the dairy BREV programs was to build the capacity of a community to retain and enhance its existing dairies. The two areas that used this approach defined their specific objectives as (1) demonstrating to dairy producers that area residents want them to stay in business and prosper; (2)

demonstrating to agribusiness firms throughout the state that local dairy producers plan to stay competitive; (3) assisting local dairy producers in using local, state, and federal programs; and (4) developing an action plan to help local dairies stay in business and grow.

To achieve these objectives, teams of two community leaders visited dairy farms for hour-long interviews. The community leaders included farmers, agribusiness persons, bankers, local economic developers, local government officials, and educators. During these visits, the interviewers asked questions on the future plans of the farmers, as well as concerns on which they wanted additional information and assistance. After completing the interviews, the surveys were used in two ways. The local task force reviewed each survey to see if there were immediate concerns (or "red flags") that could be addressed (for discussion of the "red flag" review process, see McLaughlin 1990). At the same time, the surveys were sent to the University of Minnesota where a research report was written to summarize the concerns of the firms. The university's report included a set of potential local projects for responding to these concerns. During a four-hour retreat, the local task force reviewed the research report and set project priorities. In some cases, the local group selected new projects developed at that meeting. After sharing the results with community leaders, the priority projects were implemented. The first dairy project didn't run smoothly, but the second one did. Here's what happened and why there were major differences.

FAILURES AND SUCCESSES IN DAIRY BREV PROGRAMS

Region A, located just outside a major metropolitan area, includes five counties. While they are all outside the state's primary dairy area, two of the counties were in the second tier of dairy production, two in the third tier, and one in the lowest group (Hunst and Howse 1998). Dairy production, though one of the most important agricultural commodities produced in region A, is not a major source of income for the region, constituting only 1 percent of the total income in these counties. A leadership team of five people (four were county extension educators and one was from a milk processing company) guided the program. Fifty-nine community leaders participated in a two-hour training session and then visited 45 dairy producers in the fall of 1994. Stratified random sampling was used for the survey, and the process proceeded as outlined above until the "red flag" meeting.[1] Then the program started to come apart. The four-hour retreat for reviewing the overall results had such poor attendance that it was rescheduled. Attendance at the second meeting was slightly better, but still too low for any decisions made at the meeting to represented the consensus of a cross section of community leaders interested in the dairy industry. In the end, no local priorities were set on the long-term projects.[2]

Region B, located over three hours from Minneapolis-St. Paul, includes only two counties. One of these two counties (Otter Tail) was the second highest milk producer in the state, and the other (Becher) was in the second tier of dairy counties. Milk production accounted for 2.3 percent of the total income earned in the county. The leadership team for this project included ten persons (three county extension educators, five dairy farmers, a farm credit services official, and an economic development consultant). Seventy-four community leaders visited 132 dairy farms. This project went through all the recommended steps, set priorities, and implemented seven major projects. Responding to the need for business and financial planning, a conference was held for building a financial network and distributing information about assistance available from the U.S. Small Business Administration. A dairy reception group toured dairy operations in Idaho and California and met with the commissioners of agriculture to lure diary operations from New Mexico and California. Two new large dairy herds were attracted, adding 3,000 new cows to the region and reversing previous trends. The group worked with the Minnesota Department of Agriculture to employ a full-time dairy specialist. The group worked with both the Department of Agriculture and the Minnesota Pollution Control Agency on county options for planning and zoning to protect the interests of the dairy and tourism industries. A series of newspaper stories was developed to educate the public on the importance of the dairy industry to region B. Based on these achievements, the program won Business Retention and Expansion International's Exemplary Program Award in 1996. The results in region B were so different from those in region A largely because of the lessons learned in region A. What were the key lessons learned?

LESSONS LEARNED

We learned four major lessons with respect to applying a BREV program to an agricultural sector. Because the educators in region A were willing to share these lessons with the educators working in region B, the latter went on to develop an outstanding program.[3]

Lesson #1: Focus on Major Production Areas

One of the motivations of doing BREV for a specific livestock species was to help nonfarm community leaders learn about the importance of that sector to the community's economy. In region A, although dairy was the most important agricultural commodity, it accounted for only 1 percent of the total value-added of the region. The counties included ranked 18th, 26th, 36th, 37th, and 56th in milk production within the state, accounting for 4.7 percent of the state's total. In contrast, region B is located in the heart of Minnesota's dairy country and includes the county with the second highest milk production in Minnesota; the second county is ranked number 19. Together, the two counties account for 7.3 percent of the state's milk production. Milk production contributes 2.3 percent of region B's income. Because of its proximity to a large metropolitan area, many farmers in region A hope to sell their farms for residential development. This option is far less available in region B. Further, more people in region A expect to commute to the metro area and work in nonfarm jobs than is the case in region B. Finally, milk processing accounted for only 91 jobs in region A, but for 286 jobs in region B. Ensuring a sufficient milk supply to keep the plant open was therefore more important in region B.

In summary, the regions differed in the following ways. First, dairy was not as important to the economy of region A as that of region B. Second, milk processing accounted for only 91 jobs in region A, compared to 286 jobs in region B. Because of the number of jobs, there was great concern in region B that there was a sufficient supply of milk to keep these processing plants open. While dairy was the most important agricultural commodity in region A, it was simply not important enough to hold the attention of community leaders over the entire BREV program. From this we learned that when your project focuses on a specific commodity, it is wise to focus only on those counties that are major producers of that commodity.

Lesson #2: Keep the Region Relatively Small

A BREV project covering five or six counties is appealing when it focuses on a single commodity or industry.[4] The larger number of counties in region A (five) than in region B (two) made collaboration more costly. Since task force members do not know each other very well, building social capital among them requires that the group meet frequently. Long distances in a large region make it difficult for volunteers to engage in the process. In region A, the overall visitation coordinator found it difficult to push those in other counties to complete the surveys. The response rate was 98 percent in region B versus only 56 percent in region A.

Lesson #3: Recruit a Diverse Leadership Team

Region A elected to have five of the six members of the Leadership Team be from one organization—the Extension Service. The sixth member was from a milk processing company that purchased milk in this region. While this team worked together extremely well, the larger task force interpreted the program as simply a process for setting priorities for extension programs rather than something much broader. This narrow interpretation of the program was never suggested by anyone, but happened nonetheless. In region B, the leadership team included three extension educators, five farmers, one farm credit service manager, and an economic development consultant. While this made the group slightly large, it provided the diversity and perspectives necessary to maintain momentum for the program. This reflects a greater interest of industry participants, and the high response rate generated more representative and reliable information. A diverse leadership team is also more likely to successfully recruit a diverse task force, as leadership team members tend to each recruit from among their peers.

Lesson #4: Red Flags (Urgent Issues) Must Be Handled Differently

Each industry has its own characteristics and needs. The experience with a BREV program in region A taught us that in agricultural programs, the red flags must be handled differently than in manufacturing/main street programs. To understand the difference, we need a definition of "red flags" and a description of the standard approach to them. Red flags include the following issues: firms that are planning to move or close; information requests on issues impacting the firm's survival or growth; problems or concerns with local governments; or other important issues that can be resolved by local action with common sense on a firm-by-firm basis. To handle the red flags in the standard program, the entire task force meets to review each survey. They look for: (1) clues that the firms will close or move, (2) information request, and (3) local government issues. If any of these exist, someone on the task force is asked to follow up with the firm and with other agencies.

This approach was first developed by a local group in Ohio. McLaughlin (1990) found that this process was the key aspect of the program in building social capital among task force members. It encouraged trust, the development of more open channels of communications among task force members, more realistic expectations regarding organizational capabilities, greater cooperative coordination, and new forms of accountability. In addition, solving some of the immediate short-run problems builds goodwill between the groups sponsoring the BREV effort and local firms. That goodwill makes it easier for the BREV group to then tackle more difficult long-term issues. This approach had been used in more than 40 communities prior to its application in region A. The program in region A was the first application of the BREV approach to an agricultural project.

When the red flag review was performed in region A, an influential community leader asked why the extension staff had not done the review of individual surveys rather than having the entire task force do it together. None of the teams in prior BREV programs had challenged this approach. In fact, just the opposite had been the case. In earlier groups, many participants saw this as the "real analysis" of the firm's concerns. Thus, the community leader's comment caught us by surprise. We asked other team members present at the meeting whether they agreed with the community leader's view that extension staff should have performed the review, and they agreed. When confronted by several outspoken local leaders, the extension educators agreed to assume responsibility for doing the review.[5]

Region B had no problem using the standard approach to dealing with red flags, but it did change the approach in one small but important way. The leadership team explained why it was essential for the group to perform the review rather than delegate the task to the extension educators. The reasons they gave were that (1) the review by the full task force gives a broader set of perspectives to evaluate the responses; (2) the full group has more contacts for making referrals; (3) the review by the task force helps those who might need to respond (local government officials and school officials) learn about concerns directly; and (4) the full review results in a more timely response. From these experiences, we learned that the method of handling red flags had to be different for agricultural groups than for nonagricultural groups.

SUMMARY AND CONCLUSIONS

In the Dairy Business Retention and Enhancement Program, we did not get it right the first time, even though we were trying very hard. However, based on the lessons from the first project, our second and third projects were recognized with exemplar awards from Business Retention and Expansion International. There were four specific lessons we learned from these experiences. They are:

Lesson #1: Focus Specific Commodity BREV Programs on Major Production Regions for That Commodity. This lesson probably applies for any type of business retention and expansion program, and not just the BR&E visitation programs.

Lesson #2: Keep the Region Relatively Small. Two or three counties might be OK if these units are used to working together. However, it is probably better to do individual county level programs, encouraging collaboration across a number of communities than to push collaboration to the point that the program is a weak one. After each county has done an individual program, the leadership teams can explore multicounty collaboration on common problems. This lesson probably carries over to many types of community economic development programs.

Lesson #3: Recruit a Diverse Leadership Team. This lesson probably seems obvious and, in fact, had been a BREV guideline for many years. However, the large size of region A led us to ignore this, forcing us to relearn it. This lesson applies to nearly all local community economic development efforts. Without a diverse leadership team, it is more difficult to build bridges to the different groups which will need to support either the BREV efforts or other types to local community and economic development efforts.

Lesson #4: Red Flags and Other Issues Must Be Handled Differently with Different Audiences. These differences in handling red flags with agricultural and nonagricultural groups and handling the name were outlined earlier. While these might seem like small points, they can have major impacts on the overall program.

Importance of State Program Assistance

An overall lesson from this experience relates to the importance of having a state or regional program that provides technical and organizational assistance to communities starting BREV programs. If there had not been a statewide organization providing technical assistance, the lessons learned in region A might never have benefited region B. Initially, many of the lessons from region A were transmitted to region B's consultant by the authors. In each instance, the authors encouraged the second region's BREV consultant to call the first region's BREV consultant. As the program proceeded, the consultant in region B called the consultant in region A directly. In region C, most of the lessons were transmitted both directly from the state office to the new team, as well as via discussion with the leaders in the other regions.

Often a community starting a new BREV program will not know which other communities have done similar programs. Even if they know this, they might not know who the key contacts are and what they might be able to learn from them. Further, sometimes those that have learned lessons the hard way are unwilling to share. If you are a community leader about to call a stranger and ask them about their failures, it is nice to know they will be willing to share what they have learned. Consequently, the state office's educational role often consists of putting new community leaders in touch with those that have learned these lessons the hard way but are willing to share them.[6]

While region A's dairy BREV program was not as successful as we had hoped, its failures led to successes in future programs because of the collaboration between the regions.

DISCUSSION QUESTIONS FROM THE EDITORS

1. Milk is a highly perishable product. How would this characteristic affect the potential for success of a program of this type? Would wheat producers have as many local processors in their county?

2. The authors report on a program focused on dairy, but note in passing that similar programs have been in place for manufacturing and retail for many years. The manufacturing and retail programs visit many types of businesses. Why do you suppose the authors decided upon such a specific sector—dairy— in the program, instead of visiting every kind of farm?

3. The authors note that the effort in one community was not as successful as they had hoped. What are the risks associated with implementing this kind of program (in terms of the local organizers)?[7]

NOTES

The authors recognize the valuable contributions of the 421 people who took active roles in the three dairy BR&E programs discussed in this chapter. In particular, they recognize those on the leadership teams in the programs: Rodney Elmstrand, Theron Salmela, Steven Drazkowski, Ralph VanDixhorn, Stephen Watrin, Ken Herbranson, Mark Helland, David Rupp, Allen Schroeder, Julian Sjostrom, Jerome Sternberg, Gene Zepper, Lisa Axton, Denizl Copper, Harold Stanislawski, Nancy Nelson, Lee Gross, Jim Salfer, Bob Swanberg, Art Kerfeld, Jerry Jennissen, Bernie Quist, Marke Wehlage, Joseph Conlin, Brian Buhr, Inhyuck Ha, and Patricia Love.

1. The extension educators held a series of seven meetings for dairy farmers on issues that were also found in the survey responses (forage issues, agricultural trends, enterprise analysis, facility tourism, heifer contract raising opportunities, rotational grazing and seasonal grazing). These were scheduled before the survey results were available and were not in response to the survey.

2. For those readers wanting to pin blame on someone, pin it on the senior author. The local leadership team worked very well together. They followed the approach suggested by the senior author at every step. However, the agricultural audience required some different approaches than manufacturing programs or other main street programs. These changes were more than just a new survey.

3. A third region, Stearns County, Minnesota, also went on to have an outstanding dairy BREV program and to win Business Retention and Expansion International's Exemplar Program Award. This region is not discussed in this case study.

4. Not only might there be economies of scale from doing several counties at a time, the Extension Service was promoting multicounty specialization and collaboration. While the specialization aspect probably made sense, in the project we found that the multicounty collaboration did not.

5. In none of the 40 prior programs to use this red flag review approach had community leaders suggested that extension educators do the review by themselves. One hypothesis on why this happened in an agricultural program is that extension has done a great deal for agricultural groups and programs over the years, but not as much for nonagricultural groups. As one person put it: "Extension has 'pampered' agricultural groups too much but the other groups just figured they would need to do it themselves."

6. The Extension Educators in Region A should be recognized with a great deal of the credit for the results in Region B. Region A's willingness to unselfishly share what they had learned was a major reason for turning later programs into successes.

7. Only three of the ninety-four local BREV programs that involved the senior author were failures, or slightly over three percent.

CHAPTER 12

Community Leadership and Vision Pay Off for Blue Mound, Illinois

Steven Kline

INTRODUCTION

Subsequent to the completion of a comprehensive community and economic development plan in the early 1980s, local leaders in Blue Mound, Illinois (pop. 1,161) faced a dilemma. The plan presented an overwhelming set of recommendations for improving the community. How could the village defy countywide population declines and economic hardships and still achieve all of the recommended objectives? The answer came in the form of unprecedented community support for a vision of the future, a shared strategy for improving the economy, and widespread acceptance that the village expected to achieve success with the help of people, not just the taxpayers' money. Blue Mound's small business development strategies illustrated how a small town, even during difficult times, could combine a powerful vision with leadership, civic participation, and partnerships with public- and private-sector agencies to expand the local economy and preserve a rural way of life.

Of all the recommendations in Blue Mound's 200-page comprehensive plan, local leaders decided to first focus on revitalizing downtown with an aggressive approach to small business development. Within eight years, community leaders successfully attracted 20 new businesses and revolutionized downtown's role as a commercial hub for the area. Some of the new businesses were created with local development corporations that sold shares to Blue Mound residents. Other businesses, such as a new dentist's office, video store, small motor repair, and a clothing alteration shop were borne out of other innovative strategies. Local enthusiasm for community entrepreneurship even impacted public services. Blue Mound's police department eventually became a state-of-the-art division of local government with sophisticated communications and data retrieval systems that began with less than $6,000 in grants and donations. Blue Mound's story demonstrates how the keys to success are often held locally and that positive results occur when people empower themselves to change their community's future. Originally documented in 1993, this case includes updated information about Blue Mound based on interviews with local leaders in August 1998.

HOW DID THEY GET STARTED?

Organizing for economic development became a central issue in many small communities in the 1990s. Establishing an economic development structure, developing a sustainable budget, identifying community goals, and even hiring a small staff to coordinate local activities was often part of a community's plan for improving economic, social, and environmental conditions. For Blue Mound, planning was important and it was the residents who actualized the community's goals.

As of 1980, the Blue Mound Village Board had accrued a long list of supporting activities for new development by establishing positive relationships with local residents, private firms, and service clubs. The local Rotary Club, in tandem with the village's Community Development Committee, actively assisted the community in bringing new businesses to Blue Mound. Central Illinois Public Service (now Ameren, Inc.) had always demonstrated a willingness to extend natural gas and electricity to new businesses that required new lines or substations. The village had also been successful in matching community dollars with state and federal funds. In 1977, a new sewer system doubled sewage handling capacity, and in 1978, low-income housing programs were financed with HUD funds.

In 1971, the Illinois Department of Conservation created the Griswald Conservation Center. The Griswald area is one of two public parks in Blue Mound where amenities such as a baseball field, shelter houses, and a walking trail had been created.

The village's other recreational area, Wise Park, was designated as the official site for hosting the Blue Mound Fall Festival (established in 1906). Still in operation today, the festival occurs during the third week of August and attracts more than 10,000 people annually. Wise Park was so heavily used that a third park was created near the Rainey Development, a recently constructed housing subdivision. The new park offered a children's playground, a ball diamond, and other recreational facilities.

With the improvements of so many quality-of-life amenities, residents continued to become involved in community development. In a recent interview, Blue Mound's mayor applauded the local citizenry for its interest in the community's future, and indicated that "when we do something in Blue Mound its not one person doing it, everybody has learned to get involved." In fact, prior to when Blue Mound formally organized for community and economic development, local residents joined forces and raised close to $100,000 to convert what was once a run-down firehouse into a new public library.

The mayor admitted that "a few people thought we were touched in the head when a group of us said we were going to raise $100,000 in Blue Mound. They said we must be crazy." Nevertheless, the entire community including schools, churches, and local service clubs supported the proposed library. Gathering funds became a community effort as progress was measured with a thermostat tally board displayed at Blue Mound's Fall Festival. Within 18 months, enough money and equipment was collected to renovate the firehouse and create a successful rural library.

The library project was not only a huge success, but was a milestone for community and economic development in Blue Mound. Local residents became convinced that they could work together to plan their community's future. However, what they would learn later is that even though residents were willing to work, skillful leadership was the essential element that stimulated their success.

WORKING FOR A VISION OF THE FUTURE

Despite the village's past success, the mayor of Blue Mound and a concerned citizen from the local zoning commission in 1982 observed a persistent deterioration of the downtown and decided to devise a plan of action. Knowing that fiscal conditions within state and federal government showed little promise for local assistance in the future, the two leaders in Blue Mound sent letters to more than 60 residents and businesses in the community. Each person was invited to attend a community wide meeting addressing critical issues affecting the future of their town. Representatives from Richland Community College were also invited to discuss various types of assistance available to small communities. Richland was, at that time, beginning to work with the Department of Urban and Regional Planning at the University of Illinois in Urbana-Champaign to develop ways to help residents of small communities improve their local economies.

The first town meeting resulted in several subsequent meetings with the University of Illinois, after which a local citizen assumed a central leadership role for Blue Mound's development efforts. Local leaders were soon convinced that "small communities simply couldn't do much without having some kind of a plan for community development." Unfortunately, as is true with many small towns, funds to create a comprehensive plan for Blue Mound were not readily available. However, given the positive attitudes and persistence demonstrated by Blue Mound residents, the University of Illinois agreed to provide a team of graduate students to help the village create a comprehensive development program through the year 2000. The village invested $1,500 in the project and the university absorbed other costs.

The plan called for the formation of the Blue Mound Business Association, which, by 1983, evolved into the Blue Mound Development Corporation (BMDC). In addition to forming the development corporation, the village identified a central theme around which the community could rally. The vision statement, which captures the best of what Blue Mound had already become and what it hoped to be in the future, was proudly posted throughout the community and in the community's brochure:

Essentially rural in character, our village lies in the southwest corner of Macon County, Illinois. Blue Mound encapsulates much of what people typically expect in a small town in central Illinois, yet the village welcomes new business and a moderately increasing population. Ours is financially a very sound community. Reasonable taxes, adequate public services, and a balanced municipal budget, together with a surprisingly diversified local economy, suggest the excellent potential for further development in the village.

The comprehensive plan described numerous ways to improve Blue Mound, including recommendations for designing appropriate land use ordinances, expanding public services, improving the local business and economic climate, upgrading the appearance of downtown, providing adequate housing and social services, and strengthening the village's financial condition. Leaders quickly learned that for a community the size of Blue Mound, this comprehensive plan would indeed require many years to complete.

Although Blue Mound was primarily regarded as a farming community located between three larger cities (Decatur, Springfield, and Taylorville), its economy was quite diversified and deemed capable of hosting many small retail, service, and manufacturing businesses. Therefore, after adopting its vision of the future, Blue Mound's first objective was to improve the downtown business climate while continuing to expand public services. This approach, while only emphasizing the achievement of one or two major goals at a time, actually increased the community's capacity for several more development projects. Community leaders continued to advocate their strategy of slow, steady progress, because they believed other towns had tried to do too much, too quickly. Most agreed, however, that "to attract new (and retain existing) residents to the community, it would be necessary to first continue developing an environment that appealed to more people and was worthy of new economic investment."

The BMDC, managed by a seven-member board, operated on an annual budget of less than $1,000 and was financed through donations and local memberships at $1 per member annually. To this day, the role that the BMDC plays is one of coordination and unity among the community's residents. The mayor points out that "the Village of Blue Mound doesn't want to do (community/economic) development with money, we want to do it with people." The methods employed in Blue Mound exemplified that philosophy because the results have been significant.

A FOCUSED APPROACH PAID OFF

Although Decatur, Springfield, and Taylorville offered a vast selection of retail goods and services, Blue Mound sought to attract businesses by appealing to a variety of niche markets. In addition to providing goods and services to residents, several Blue Mound businesses already brought dollars into the community from the outside by offering products and services that were different than what was sold at discount chains or shopping malls. The astonishing result that Blue Mound was able to realize between 1984 and 1992 was an unprecedented expansion and/or addition of more than 20 new small businesses to the downtown. Examples included a new grocery store financed by local shareholders, a hardware store, a craft store, a video rental operation, and a bicycle shop. New businesses also included services such as an attorney's office, an insurance agency, an alterations shop, a small-motor repair business, two tanning spas, a fitness center, a barber shop, a construction company, an auction/realty firm, and a restaurant that drew patrons from nearby communities and catered special events. Nearly all of these businesses were created and owned by local residents (most are still in business today, however three of the businesses had closed and some changes in ownership of others had occurred since the original interview in 1993).

Firms like Macon Metal Products Company and Beckenmar Church Furniture were two long-standing businesses that exported goods from Blue Mound. Macon Metal Products Company, a metal fabrication firm contracted with Caterpillar Tractor Corporation for small lot jobs (e.g., toolboxes for mounting on construction equipment). The BMDC and Richland Community College worked with Macon Metals to provide workforce training for an upcoming expansion. Fifty percent of the costs for the training were reimbursed to the company within six months of the expansion, which created 13 new jobs. Interestingly, since the original interview in 1993, the company expanded so much that it became Illini Metals, completely outgrew its space in Blue Mound and eventually moved to nearby Taylorville in 1994—taking 30 to 40 jobs with it. The community regretted the loss of such an important employer and learned that successful economic development could bring unexpected consequences.

Beckenmar Church Furniture has a long history of manufacturing quality church pews and other specialized furniture in Blue Mound. At the time of the last interview, the company had six full-time employees and had been in business for more than 50 years. Although Beckenmar mainly serves Illinois, its clients have come from as far away as Virginia. The majority of Beckenmar furniture is sold to churches, but some has been sold as private household furnishings.

The *Blue Mound Leader*, a locally owned newspaper serving Blue Mound and the surrounding area, was credited with providing an efficient conduit for information among the community's residents. The newspaper changed ownership in July 1986 and relocated to a larger building (a former furniture store) on Main Street. After the newspaper remodeled its own space, it created several additional locations for other businesses. Excess space on the lower and upper levels of the former furniture store were converted for use by the newspaper, a barber shop, an attorney's office, and a golf pro shop that manufactured and reconditioned clubs and other golf equipment. The mayor reported that "part of Blue Mound's strategy had been to encourage development of small businesses that may each contribute only a small amount to the village's economy. . . . it's the small parts that add up to a strong reversal of the economic decay along Blue Mound's downtown."

An alteration shop was formerly located in the owner's home, but with encouragement from Blue Mound residents and the BMDC, the business relocated to downtown where it continues to do business today. The owner admitted she was skeptical at first about making the move, but the community's support and assistance with setting up the new location persuaded her to follow through. The shop primarily serves local residents and nearby communities. Services range from simple alterations to designing and making wedding gowns. Since 1993, Fran's Alterations has become a very successful business with a customer base far beyond Blue Mound.

When a prospective entrepreneur was ready to expand her home-based craft and floral business, but was unable to secure an appropriate location in a nearby community, the mayor responded by showing her a vacant building in the downtown. The result was that a new store moved into another of the village's empty Main Street locations—it is still there today and doing well. This business, Fran's Alterations, and many of the others were made possible through volunteer labor and support for repairing and renovating empty buildings.

Blue Mound residents generally agreed that community and economic development most often occurred when *everyone* participated. However, many people in Blue Mound also agreed that daily attention to community and economic development by a key individual was also essential. The publisher of the *Blue Mound Leader* believed the mayor's daily stroll to visit with local businesses and his frequent trips out of town to investigate new opportunities were essential to Blue Mound's success between 1983 and 1993 when so much economic development occurred there. Note that between 1994 and early 1998, Mayor Bonn retired from public life. The new mayor during that period was a conscientious administrator and a responsible public servant, but he was part-time. The community had grown accustomed to seeing Mayor Bonn strolling the streets and stopping by each day—as of 1993, the mayor's communication and attention to detail had become an inspirational part of Blue Mound's daily routine. The consensus seemed to be that strong personal relationships had won half the battle for economic development when business growth was strong. With part-time leadership, there was less time for nurturing those relationships, and the creation of new ones was even more difficult.

A community volunteer and writer of the *Leader's* "News and Views" column, agreed and suggested that another quality of good leadership was the ability to get other people together for a cause. Local volunteers believed that "building the library was one of the community's greatest accomplishments, but the village's successful efforts to bring in a dentist and build a new grocery store also illustrated how the persistence of a few individuals and the BMDC could gather community support."

In the early 1980s, Blue Mound had been fortunate to have a resident physician for more than 30 years, but the community lacked a dentist. So, in 1985, the recently formed BMDC began to aggressively search for a dentist who would locate in Blue Mound. Fortunately, because the village had worked so closely with University of Illinois students in the past, a prospective dentist, who was a recent graduate of the University of Illinois, contacted BMDC about possibly locating a clinic in Blue Mound.

After several months of discussing the possibility, the BMDC invited the young doctor to meet the community. At a BMDC-sponsored potluck dinner, the school district, churches, business owners, and local residents invited the doctor to make his home in Blue Mound. After deciding to locate his practice there, the dentist purchased a vacant building downtown. Although it was the BMDC's policy to avoid providing financial assistance to new businesses, the development organization did organize volunteer assistance to help remodel the new Main Street location. A local carpenter, a plumber, an electrician, and other local residents donated their time and expertise. As soon as the new dental clinic opened, the BMDC sponsored an open house and promoted the practice to area residents, just as it had done for other new business that located in Blue Mound.

It was shortly after bringing a dentist to town (July 1986) that the BMDC faced its first real crisis. The grocery store, which had been in business for many years, burned in late 1985. A few months later, the former grocer decided not to rebuild and retired. In response, the BMDC began a painstaking search for a new grocer. It made several attempts to attract a new grocery company, but most were interested in only serving larger communities. After a rather exhaustive search, the BMDC decided that the village would have to create its own local grocery store by forming the Blue Mound Store Corporation (BMSC).

Again, the BMDC's policy was to only coordinate community and economic development and not to make financial investments. Every project that required financing and full-time management was organized as a separate corporation with a different board of directors. The new library, the Blue Mound Fall Festival, and the new grocery store were each incorporated separately. Doing it that way ensured that the BMDC, the foundation for all community and economic development efforts, would not be seriously hurt if a development project turned out less than favorable. Separate boards also provided unbiased opinions and leadership for specific projects.

The grocery store project involved selling shares in the Blue Mound Store Corporation (BMSC) to local residents and leveraging those funds with a loan from a local lender. The State Bank of Blue Mound supported several local business ventures and development projects in the community and continues to be supportive today. Within two months after forming the BMSC, enough funds were generated to construct a $120,000 building housing both a grocery store and a liquor store. Blue Mound was a "dry" community, but voted in alcohol so those liquor sales could subsidize lower profit margins in the grocery business. Both of the stores were managed by an experienced grocer who moved, with his family, to Blue Mound from nearby Decatur. BMSC's local shareholders did not invest in the corporation intending to reap large financial gains—they simply wanted to avoid driving 15 miles for groceries. However, the BMSC has done so well that by the close of business in 1998, it was expected to begin paying dividends to its (community) stockholders.

IMPROVING PUBLIC SERVICES

Local government in Blue Mound does not use village revenues to repair vacant buildings, manage revolving loan funds, or provide grants to prospective entrepreneurs. Instead, the village board holds fast to the notion that its $325,000 annual budget should be used to enhance local infrastructure and support the improvement of public services. For example, the village expected to resurface many streets adjacent to Route 48 within the next five years. The water department, now fully computerized, had improved its billing procedures and was planning additional improvements to the village's water system (e.g., more than 20,000 feet of new water line, mains, and a storage tower).

The BMDC recently worked with the village board to plan the construction of a senior housing development. However, the Illinois Commerce Commission grant application required that the village's water delivery system be upgraded from its current 231,000 gallon drawing capacity to accommodate the retirement center's sprinkler specifications. Village residents were notified that local water rates would increase 100 percent to put in larger lines, mains, and a new water tower. Interestingly, no one came to a town meeting to discuss the proposal. Apparently, there was no need for further discussion, and the rate increase was implemented without objection. The community trusted that the next big goal was to encourage people to live in Blue Mound, and improving the water system was one step closer to achieving that goal.

Blue Mound's police department is also a success story. State-of-the-art law enforcement departments in rural communities are not common. However, in 1986, the police chief began building a police department in Blue Mound with virtually no resources except his time, his car, much determination, and of course, community support.

With an annual budget of $54,000, the Blue Mound Police Department demonstrated innovative methods for acquiring the necessary equipment and personnel to maintain a high-tech law enforcement agency in a small community. Equipped with a sophisticated communications and data retrieval system that was created with just $5,500 in grants and donations, the Blue Mound force now includes a full-time police chief, two part-time officers, and five auxiliary policemen. The police department installed two main computers with customized software and plugged into a nationwide LEADS (Law Enforcement Agencies Data System) network. One employee who was fully certified to operate the LEADS system staffed the dispatch desk on weekends. Blue Mound officers had access to two laptop computers that could be used in squad cars, or used in the field to generate reports. The LEADS capability in squad cars was made available within another two years, and at least one of the village's two squad cars was fully equipped to respond to nearly every kind of emergency situation at any time. The Blue Mound Police Department, equipped to respond to civil defense and disaster situations, was featured in the June 1992 issue of *Law and Order* magazine as a model for having developed a program called Dial-A-Cop. This new system allowed people to reach a police officer even when no one was at the police station.

A Criminal Justice Authority Grant allowed the Blue Mound Police Department to purchase another computer, two more radios, an assault rifle, and training for high-risk situations and hostage negotiations. Many structural improvements to the building that housed the village hall and the police department were made possible through volunteer efforts. Even local community organizations found new purpose in the development process (e.g., the Lions Club recently constructed a $450,000 civic center in Blue Mound). What does all of this have to do with economic development? In Blue Mound, a "safe" community was defined as a community where people wanted to live, where others visited and shopped, and a secure environment where organizations would invest in the local economy. Quality of life, public services, and economic development were brought together into an integrated approach that yielded benefits for everyone.

KEY INGREDIENTS TO BLUE MOUND'S SUCCESS

Successful communities like Blue Mound have found answers locally, rather than waiting for state or federal government programs to solve their problems. The overriding message from Blue Mound's experience is that successful community and economic development occurred because hard-working people were willing to assume responsibility for their community's economy and systematically improve their quality of life.

Blue Mound leaders indicated that a proactive mind-set may be the most important ingredient of all. Developing a positive state of mind within the local citizenry requires strong leadership, time, and a community's willingness to assume risk and manage change. Blue Mound's success exemplifies how a small community can encourage business development and significantly improve public services with a modest budget, but when occasions arise that require more financial support, the community followed through with a well-planned development program.

In summary, the key ingredients for community and economic development in Blue Mound included:

- *Leadership*: Key individuals who were well respected and considered essential to the community's future were needed to discover new opportunities and bring the local citizenry together.
- *Community Support and Involvement*: Communitywide support for positive change was a basic requirement. Local volunteer efforts in Blue Mound were highly valued.
- *Sound Planning*: Recognizing the community's needs, its vision, and the strengths of the region helped Blue Mound leaders to leverage existing resources and achieve extraordinary results.
- *Organization*: Residents in Blue Mound engaged one another in the development process and organized so those projects were coordinated and managed according to a plan. Blue Mound learned that a large

budget was not necessary, but donations of time, expertise, and interest from local residents were essential for achieving successful outcomes.

- *A Sense of Accomplishment*: Tangible results, such as empty buildings filled with successful businesses, a new library, smooth streets, a new water tower, or a police officer on the corner reminded citizens that their development efforts had paid off. It was all worth it.

DISCUSSION QUESTIONS FROM THE EDITORS

1.   Blue Mound provided subsidies to a metal fabricating firm. The firm was very successful, outgrew its space, and moved away from Blue Mound to another town. Would it be right for Blue Mound to ask the firm to reimburse several of the subsidies it received?

2.   Blue Mound's emphasis appears to have been on assisting existing industry and promoting the overall quality of life in the community, rather than simply trying to attract firms from elsewhere. Discuss the pros and cons of Blue Mound's approach versus industrial attraction.

3.   The author notes the local newspaper's role in creating more business activity and communication in Blue Mound. What do small communities lose when the newspaper can't compete with newspapers from nearby metropolitan areas?

NOTE

With permission from the author and the Illinois Institute for Rural Affairs, this case is an updated version of the original publication: Walzer, Norman C. et al. 1993. "Blue Mound: Achieving A Vision." *Economic Development in Small Illinois Communities* (Macomb, IL: Illinois Institute for Rural Affairs, Chapter 10 by Steven Kline, pp. 103–113).

CHAPTER 13

Developing Agricultural and Nature-Based Tourism in Eastern Connecticut

Norman K. Bender and Nini Davis

INTRODUCTION

This chapter explores a regional tourism development project that used a collaborative approach. It reviews the processes used to identify agricultural and nature-based tourism opportunities formulated from regional and community resources and characteristics. This case study also explores planning and implementation activities designed to strengthen community-based tourism's contributions to rural economic development through active involvement of people from a variety of organizations and situations.

The regional project's purpose and history are discussed, along with its objectives and major activities. Highlighted activities include an agricultural tourism committee, a field survey of tourism enterprises, a regional brochure designed for tourists and residents, and an educational tour of agricultural tourism enterprises in a neighboring state, designed for farmers. Finally, the project's outcomes will be reviewed.

PROJECT PURPOSE AND HISTORY

In 1994, the Northeast Connecticut Visitors District (NCVD) identified a need for the tourism industry to work with farmers and rural landowners in eastern Connecticut to develop and promote agricultural and nature-based tourism. The region's agricultural lands, woodlands, open spaces, and small towns set the stage for a successful rural tourism program. The NCVD believed that increased tourist visits to the region would contribute to rural economic development, while preserving the area's natural attributes, promoting existing farms, and encouraging agri-tourism.

The NCVD initiated formation of the Eastern Connecticut Agricultural Tourism Committee (ECATC). The ECATC brought together representatives of organizations and agencies involved with agriculture and tourism. Members included the Northeast and Southeastern Connecticut Visitors/Tourism Districts, Connecticut Farm Bureau Association, University of Connecticut Cooperative Extension System, Connecticut Department of Agriculture, U.S. Department of Agriculture Farm Service Agency, and local farmers.

A small group of about ten people met regularly for two years (1994–1996), discussing, planning, and implementing a nature-based tourism project. The ECATC organized two workshops, and applied for and received a $22,000 Connecticut Tourism Challenge Grant (Davis 1994). With the financial resource of the grant, the ECATC produced two brochures and promoted two outdoor recreation events. It also administered a survey of farmers involved in nature-based tourism, and encouraged the tourism districts' participation in two tourism "sales blitz" promotions to out-of-state tour operators. Other activities included the organization of an educational bus tour for farmers and the development of a network of farms, tourism businesses, agricultural associations, and tourism organizations.

Eastern Connecticut, as defined in the regional tourism project, consists of Windham and New London Counties and an eastern section of Tolland County. The region extends from the Massachusetts line in the north, down to Long Island Sound and from the Rhode Island line in the east, continuing approximately 30 miles westward.   It consists of upland areas with low hills rising 300–500 feet, woodlands, farmlands, and small rivers.   The region is largely rural, with several small cities and numerous old mill towns. Its combination of rural villages, mill towns, farms, and scenic landscapes set it apart from the more developed areas of Connecticut (Lewis and Harmon 1986).

OBJECTIVES

The members of the ECATC defined the following objectives to guide their activities:

- develop awareness of opportunities for nature-based tourism through a field survey, educational materials, and presentations;
- increase farmers' and other rural landowners' awareness of tourism opportunities;
- promote the region as a family-oriented tourist destination focusing on agricultural and natural resources by developing and distributing a seasonal guide to agricultural attractions;
- coordinate selected outdoor recreational activities in eastern Connecticut; and
- develop a network of local businesses, farms, agricultural and ecological organizations, community officials, and others interested in developing joint ventures designed to increase tourist visits while preserving the area's natural attributes.

Once funding was obtained for a Connecticut Tourism Challenge Grant project, implementation activities began with leadership provided by the Northeast Connecticut Visitors District. Project activities were initiated and implemented through the ECATC.

AGRICULTURAL TOURISM COMMITTEE ACTIVITIES

The ECATC's major role was to bring knowledgeable people together to discuss and develop project activities, divide responsibilities for specific tasks, and review progress being made in accomplishing the tasks. A collaborative approach was used to involve committee members in discussing and agreeing upon goals, methods, and implementation strategies (Bender 1999). Collaboration has been defined as "a process in which those parties with a stake in the problem actively seek mutually determined solutions. They join forces, pool information, 'knock heads,' construct alternative solutions, and forge an agreement" (Gray 1989). This definition applies to the process used by the ECATC. Committee meetings were held monthly at a Cooperative Extension Center with five to ten participants per meeting. The committee started meeting in 1994 and continued into the summer of 1996. The use of a collaborative committee process allowed all committee members to discuss a variety of approaches to accomplishing specific tasks. Individuals responsible for each task would initiate the activity while benefiting from a variety of perspectives and ties related to the tourism and agriculture communities.

Initial committee activities focused upon:

- development of a regional data base of agricultural and nature-based tourism attractions;
- conducting a field survey of selected attractions;
- production of two publications—a guide to tourism attractions and an information sheet for farmers and landowners (Bender 1995); and
- a "sales blitz" promoting the region to several target metropolitan areas in the northeastern United States.

As the project evolved, the focus changed, and committee members worked on:

- an outreach education program for farmers covering opportunities in agricultural and nature-based tourism; and
- plans for two outdoor recreational events (a bicycle tour sampling the region's small towns, village greens, and countryside, and an autumn walking weekend of guided hikes, walks, and presentations highlighting agricultural, heritage, and natural resource attractions).

FARMS AND FAMILY FUN BROCHURE

One of the many projects realized by the committee was the production of a brochure promoting the existing farms in the region open to the public. Representatives of the two visitors/tourism districts researched, contacted, and visited farms in preparation for writing and designing a comprehensive brochure, "Farms and Family Fun." This brochure provided listings and descriptions of agricultural and nature-based attractions. Categories included: animals on the farm, fairs and festivals, fish and the aquatic farm, food from the farm, hayrides and sleigh rides, lodgings, museums, and plants and flowers. Information provided included a regional map with a key to farm locations, telephone numbers, and a brief description of attractions. Also included were brief facts regarding agriculture and natural resources.

Thirty thousand copies of the brochure were printed with 95 percent distributed within two years to tourists and residents. "Farms and Family Fun" was the first brochure in Connecticut to focus upon offering tourists information and opportunities for visiting a wide range of farms and natural resource-based attractions. Never before were milking parlors, pick-your-own farms and orchards, sheep barns, flower gardens, agricultural museums, and farm-related overnight lodgings, all included in one package.

TOURING AGRICULTURAL ATTRACTIONS

Farmers in eastern Connecticut were invited to tour a variety of agri-tourism and direct marketing operations in Massachusetts during July 1996. The bus tour first visited a family-owned and operated dairy farm and retail farm stand. The owners sold their own bottled milk, baked goods, vegetables, plants, and pumpkins. This stop illustrated how a dairy farm in a small town continued milk production, while adding direct marketing to customers, additional products and hayrides, and educational tours for school groups and families.

The bus tour then proceeded to a large family-owned and operated farm in the Boston suburbs that specializes in direct marketing of plants and vegetables. This farm featured a farm market, garden center, bakery, and florist shop. It illustrated a large-scale direct marketing farm serving a densely populated suburban area.

A Christmas tree farm/business with an eight-month season was the third and final stop on the Massachusetts tour. While this farm maintained its identity selling Christmas trees, it had expanded its operations to include weddings, hayrides, sing-alongs, and a site for a variety of meetings, recreational outings, and events. This operation illustrated how some farmers and rural landowners have capitalized upon a farm's scenic beauty to market recreational and event activities that may equal or surpass agricultural activities in providing income to the owners.

This one-day tour of three very different agri-tourism and direct marketing businesses allowed tour participants to explore a variety of agri-tourism operations outside their area with opportunities to exchange information and perspectives with peers from their region as well as a neighboring state.

FIELD SURVEY

An initial project activity was a survey of farmers and landowners involved with agri-tourism enterprises. The survey's purpose was to learn about current agri-tourism operations, issues, and informational needs, which could be addressed in educational workshops, presentations, and a fact sheet.

The ECATC discussed the pros and cons of three different approaches:

- a mail survey to all farmers in the region;
- a survey of a select number of farmers through field visits to their farms; and
- a survey of agricultural and natural resources groups through field visits.

Any of the three approaches could contribute to the information base needed to develop the farmer/landowner section of the project. The ECATC decided to design and carry out a field survey of selected farmers and landowners currently involved with nature-based and agricultural tourism activities. A field survey provided direct contact with a variety of agri-tourism business owners and an opportunity to observe the businesses.

A cooperative extension educator in economic development designed a survey in collaboration with other committee members resulting in a four-page form with 13 questions related to the farms' current and future activities. Farmers were asked to describe:

- the agricultural business;
- agri-tourism activities;
- the accessibility of their farm to people with varying physical characteristics;
- their direct marketing activities;
- their goals relative to agri-tourism;
- advertising and promotional approaches;
- interest in new marketing opportunities;
- future agri-tourism plans;
- concerns and informational needs regarding agri-tourism;
- interest in learning about agri-tourism opportunities and issues;
- membership in trade associations; and
- awareness of other agri-tourism businesses in eastern Connecticut.

Committee members identified a broad range of farmers/agri-tourism business owners to be considered for interviews. Fifteen farmers and business owners were interviewed at their farm or business March–May 1995. Their agri-tourism businesses included: farm or vineyard bed and breakfasts, dairy farms, flowers and everlasting, orchards, vegetables, sheep/wool, vineyards, Christmas trees, buffalo, turkeys, and greenhouses.

The field survey approach provided opportunities to meet with farmers and business owners at their place of business and have in-depth discussions regarding their current situations, future plans, and concerns. Conducting the interview at their place of business established that their experiences and views were important to the success of the project. The use of a qualitative field survey approach allowed the interviewer to collect information concerning a variety of agri-tourism enterprises while observing the enterprises and their locations.

OUTCOMES

An agricultural and nature-based tourism network developed through the meetings and activities of the ECATC. It provided an active forum for agricultural and tourism agencies, organizations, and individuals to discuss and plan the regional tourism project and identify issues to be addressed in future endeavors. Contacts made implementing the project have been maintained as people and organizations continue to work together addressing agricultural, community, and tourism development issues.

The field survey of 15 agri-tourism enterprises provided opportunities for the interviewer to: meet with farmers and visit a variety of attractions, observe successful approaches to agri-tourism, and identify issues to be developed in education programs directed toward farmers, tourism districts, and community leaders.

The tour guide, "Farms and Family Fun in Eastern Connecticut," was the first guide in the state to identify and promote a wide variety of agricultural and nature-based attractions. While its major accomplishment was to provide tourism information to tourists and residents, it was also used to educate farmers about the numerous agri-tourism and direct marketing opportunities available. A second brochure, "Agricultural Tourism: Opportunities for Farmers and Rural Communities," also served an educational role with farmers, landowners, and community leaders.

Approximately 3,000 people of all ages participated in guided weekend walks, hikes, and presentations during the autumn walking weekend. Participants observed and learned about the region's heritage, farms, and resources. More than 100 bicyclists toured eastern Connecticut's rural town greens, churches, farms, and woodlands as part of a steeplechase bike tour.

An educational presentation addressing "Opportunities in Agricultural and Nature-Based Tourism" reached more than 1,000 farmers, landowners, and public officials in Connecticut and the northeastern United States. Presentations occurred before county and state farmers association meetings, tourism districts, a regional economic development summit, and conferences.

SUMMARY

The project developed an awareness of agri-tourism opportunities in eastern Connecticut for farmers and tourists. Though difficult to quantify without formal study, a number of farmers have further diversified their agricultural products to include tourism and direct marketing.

Tourists are more aware of the region as an eco-tourism destination that offers family-oriented activities. While there has been progress promoting regional attractions, there are additional needs to promote specific attractions to target audiences. For example, the Northeast Connecticut Visitors District organized a gardening weekend in May 1998 that highlighted garden centers and greenhouses offering special workshops and gardening demonstrations. Publicity for the event resulted in hundreds of aspiring horticulturists visiting these garden centers and attractions.

An indication of increased communications between the agricultural and tourism communities are two "seats" on the NCVD Board of Directors, one reserved for rural interests and one for natural resources. There is still much to be accomplished. Additional needs include theme workshops for farmers, updating the "Farms and Family Fun" brochure, maintaining a list of the region's farms, and documenting the contributions of agri-tourism and nature-based tourism enterprises to the region's and state's economy. The eastern Connecticut agricultural and nature-based tourism project broke new ground in enhancing agriculture and tourism's common contributions to rural economic development.

DISCUSSION QUESTIONS FROM THE EDITORS

1. Economic development strategies that focus on tourism are often criticized as creating low-wage, low-skill jobs. How does agricultural tourism differ from traditional tourism? What kind of "jobs" does agricultural tourism create?

2. The authors mention joint marketing of unrelated attractions as a key element in the project's success. What would be some of the barriers to doing this kind of marketing, and how would you overcome them?

3. Compare the approach of this community to the Utah case study by Albrecht. Which community has a healthier vision of tourism's place in the local economy? Why?

CHAPTER 14

Recreational and Tourism Development vs. the Decline of Agriculture in Southern Utah

Don E. Albrecht

INTRODUCTION

Throughout most of its history, the United States has been a nation of farmers and farm communities. Since 1940, however, a series of technological developments made it possible for farmers to operate much larger farms. Thus, the size of the average farm increased and the number of farms declined (Albrecht and Murdock 1990; Cochrane 1979). The displacement of human beings that resulted, and the social and economic transformations of farm communities, has been called one of the most astonishing peacetime events of this century (Beale 1993). The raw numbers are striking: the number of farms declined from more than 6 million in 1940 to less than 2 million in 1992; and the farm population declined from more than 30 million in 1940 to about 3.9 million in 1990. In 1940, the farm population comprised nearly one-fourth of the U.S. population; by 1990, this proportion was less than 2 percent.

The mechanization of agriculture and subsequent out-migration of farm families represented the death knell for many farm communities. Population declines were made even more severe because many businesses in these communities were forced to close as their primary clientele moved away. As a result, between 1940 and 1970, there were hundreds of farm communities where the population declined by more than half (Beale 1978; Larson 1981). The problems resulting from the massive population reductions in farm communities are numerous and have been extensively researched (e.g., Rogers 1982). They include a decline in the quality and quantity of community services, the consolidation of schools, a loss of tax base, and erosion of community spirit and morale.

To avoid a gradual slide into oblivion, declining farm communities needed some type of economic revival to replace the jobs lost from agriculture. Some communities were relatively successful in this endeavor, while others were not. Often the factors associated with the degree of success in attracting nonfarm employment were beyond the control of the community. Larger communities, communities located near a metropolitan area or a major highway, and those with plentiful natural resources were more likely to be successful than communities lacking these advantages (Fuguitt 1971; Fuguitt et al. 1989; Smith 1974). Evidence also indicates, however, that aggressive community leadership and entrepreneurial spirit played a significant role in the attraction of nonfarm sources of employment (Adams 1969; Christenson and Robinson 1980).

Most new jobs in communities that successfully attracted nonfarm employment were initially in the manufacturing and more recently in the service sector (Fuguitt et al. 1989; Kassab and Luloff 1993). In these communities, population declines were generally arrested and demographic stability attained. In contrast, most communities remaining dependent on agricultural employment continued to have population declines (Albrecht 1986, 1993; Bender et al. 1985). While a great deal of research has been conducted on demographic patterns associated with farm declines and the degree of success in attaining nonfarm employment, much less is known about what these industrial transformations have meant to individuals and families living in these communities. Community leaders know of the need to attract nonfarm industry, but are generally unprepared to deal with the consequences of the changes brought about by industrial change.

THE SETTING

This chapter will provide a case study of a community that was once farm dependent and has effectively attracted nonfarm employment. While these new nonfarm jobs have halted population declines, they have also had significant consequences for the way of life of community residents. This study will focus on Wayne County, an isolated rural county in south central Utah. The county consists of a few settlements along the Fremont River Valley. High and scenic mountains, some reaching elevations greater than 11,000 feet, surround the valley. The valley eventually descends into a desert partially characterized by sheer red rock cliffs.

The county was first permanently settled in the late 1870s and early 1880s by Mormons, who developed a society based totally on agriculture. The early Mormon settlers found two major obstacles to successful agricultural production—a severe lack of water and a short growing season. Average rainfall in the valley ranges from only 5 to 7 inches annually, and thus agricultural production is almost totally dependent on irrigation, which was initially accomplished by building canals and diverting streams. Later, federally funded reservoirs were built to capture snow melting from the mountains. Despite these advances, however, thousands of level, fertile acres remain uncultivated because water supplies are insufficient to irrigate them. The second major obstacle is a growing season that averages less than 90 frost-free days per year. The short growing season is a consequence of the valley's high altitude; most elevations exceed 7,000 feet.

Settlement in the county is limited to the valley, and less than 7 percent of the land in the county is in privately owned farmland. Most farmland is used for grazing, and less than 1 percent of the land area in the county is in cultivated cropland. The vast majority of the land in the county is under the jurisdiction of the federal government. The U.S. Forest Service manages most of the mountain lands, and the Bureau of Land Management (BLM) manages most of the desert lands, while an area of sheer red cliffs has been designated as Capital Reef National Park and is managed by the National Park Service. Despite water and climate limitations, valley soils are rich, and the cultivated farmland is productive. While limited in its extent, the water supply for irrigation is consistent. Further, extensive amounts of grazing lands are available for cattle and sheep on Forest Service and BLM lands. As a result, a viable agricultural economy emerged soon after settlement.

By 1940, Wayne County was among the most agriculturally dependent counties in the United States. The population of the county was 2,394, and 65 percent of the employed labor force was working in agriculture; this proportion exceeded virtually any county in the country. Most of the nonfarm population consisted of persons operating businesses that served the agricultural industry or were dependent on the farm population for their clientele. The typical Wayne County farm fit the mold of the diversified, full-time, family operation that was prevalent throughout the United States at that time. Nearly all of the farms had a few chickens, milk cows, hogs, and produced a variety of crops. The farm was generally the sole source of the family's income, and family members provided nearly all of the labor on the farm.

THE DECLINE OF AGRICULTURE

Since 1940, mechanization has tremendously transformed agriculture in Wayne County in a manner consistent with changes occurring throughout the country. New machines made it possible for farmers to cultivate and manage much more land. The technology was economically feasible only if the average farm size was increased. As a result, the number of farms declined. In 1940, the average Wayne County farm contained 179 acres; by 1974, the average farm size had increased to 737 acres. During this same period of time, the number of farms declined from 259 to 146. The typical pattern was that when one farmer retired, a neighboring farmer purchased the farm. With the labor needs of agriculture drastically reduced, and with few other employment opportunities available in the county, most young people moved away after completing high school. With fewer farm families to serve, a number of nonfarm businesses were forced to close as well. The demographic consequences of these changes were predictable. The number of county residents declined from 2,394 in 1940 to 1,483 in 1970.

The economic and demographic declines of the 1950s and 1960s meant a reduction in the quality and quantity of community services. With the closing of local businesses, Wayne County residents were forced to make an increasingly larger proportion of their food, clothing, and other purchases in Richfield, a community of about 5,000 residents located some 50 miles away. By 1950, there were no formal medical services in Wayne County. This meant that every dental appointment or visit to a medical doctor meant another trip to Richfield. Community spirit and morale seemed to plunge as each year nearly all members of the graduating high school class left the county seeking employment opportunities in urban areas. With few young families moving to or remaining in the county, the aging of the population became a growing concern.

As the county's fortunes fell during the 1950s and 1960s, community leaders made numerous attempts to attract other sources of employment. A consistent desire was to create jobs so some of the young people could stay in the county. Manufacturing enterprises largely ignored the county because it was isolated from potential markets and far from a major highway that would allow the quick and cheap movement of materials. County leaders were disappointed when the route for Interstate 70 was chosen about 60 miles north of Wayne County instead of a proposed route through the county. In the 1970s, a major coal-fired power plant near the border of Capital Reef National Park was proposed, a development that would have resulted in hundreds of new jobs. However, the project was scrapped because of major opposition from nationally based environmental groups such as the Sierra Club. Environmentalists were concerned that the plant would result in increased air pollution levels in a national park.

A SERVICE-SECTOR ECONOMY

The trend of economic, social, and demographic decline might have continued indefinitely had Wayne County not been blessed with beautiful scenery, and if community leaders and entrepreneurs had not seized the opportunity to take advantage of these resources. While there had long been tourists visiting the county to fish, hunt, hike, camp, or sightsee, this trickle turned into a torrent during the 1970s. Local entrepreneurs constructed motels, restaurants, and other businesses to meet the needs of these tourists, and these developments created numerous employment opportunities for local residents. In addition, many other residents found employment with the National Park Service, BLM, or Forest Service. These agencies added employees because of the increased number of tourists. The service industry also provided a source of off-farm employment for small farmers that made it possible for many of them to earn a livable income and remain in the county. Without nonfarm income, more families would have been forced to sell their farm and move.

The implications of tourism development were soon apparent. By 1990, 27.8 percent of the labor force was employed primarily in the service sector, and service employment far exceeded agricultural employment. In effect, Wayne County communities were no longer farm communities, but had become tourist towns. The county population, which had reached a low of 1,483 in 1970, increased to 1,911 in 1980 and then to 2,177 in 1990 (a 47 percent increase from 1970). The growth resulting from tourism development provided many benefits. There was a definite improvement in the level of community services. For example, a new grocery store is better than any store that had previously existed in the county. A medical clinic was opened where a physician's assistant works each day and a medical doctor drives from Richfield once a week to spend the day examining local patients. In recent years, two dentists have established their practices in the county. Other services have seen similar improvements.

PROBLEMS WITH SERVICE-SECTOR EMPLOYMENT

Some of the changes occurring in the county as a result of the transition from agriculture to service employment were unexpected and unwanted. In this respect, the Wayne County experience was similar to those of numerous communities around the country. A growing body of research has addressed the implications of increased dependence on service-sector employment for rural communities and their residents (Kassab 1992). This research is part of an expanding sociological literature which is making it apparent that the industrial structure of a community is likely to have important implications for the quality and way of life in that community (Edwards 1979; Hodson 1984). Different industries have different wage structures and different work schedules for their employees; they require different levels of education and training; and they vary in the proportion of the workforce that is either male or female. All of these and other factors are likely to impact relationships in families, the strength of community institutions, and numerous other aspects of community life (Albrecht 1998; Lobao et al. 1993). There is a growing concern that, while service-sector jobs vary greatly in quality, many service jobs are low-skill, low-wage, and often temporary and seasonal (Kassab and Luloff 1993; Miller and Bluestone 1987; Noyelle 1986; Smith 1993). As a consequence, a number of problems have emerged in many communities.

Recently found evidence shows that nonmetropolitan counties most dependent on service employment have family structures significantly different from other nonmetropolitan counties. Specifically, evidence indicates that counties most dependent on service employment have higher rates of female-headed households, and a lower proportion of adults who are married (Albrecht 1998; Albrecht and Albrecht 1997). A primary reason for these family structure differences is that service employment tends to be predominately female. According to the 1990 census, less than 20 percent of the workers with primary employment in agriculture were female. In contrast, 62.5 percent of the service industry workers were female. Manufacturing employment was intermediate, with about one-third of the workers being female. The low incomes make men employed in the service industry less attractive as marital partners. Since women are as employable as men in the service sector, the level of economic security for women is relatively greater. Researchers have found that the higher the earning power of women relative to men, the lower the prevalence of marriage (Becker 1981; Grossbard-Shechtman 1985).

The low pay and temporary nature of service jobs leads to additional economic problems. The greater reliance on service-sector employment in rural areas is increasingly acknowledged as a factor contributing to the growing discrepancies in incomes between metropolitan and nonmetropolitan residents (Jensen and Tienda 1989; Litcher 1989). Researchers have also found that service-based counties have higher rates of poverty than either metropolitan counties or nonmetropolitan counties that rely on other employment sources (Albrecht 1998; Garrett et al. 1994; Goreham 1992; Jensen and Eggebeen 1994).

In Wayne County, increased levels of family dissolution, higher rates of poverty, increased crime, institutional decline, and other problems have become more apparent in recent years as the extent of service employment has increased. Many longtime residents have also noted that the sense of closeness and community that once existed has diminished. An example of the institutional declines is that in recent years, little league baseball and boy scouts have suffered from a lack of adult leadership and commitment. In fact, a once thriving little league program has recently ceased to exist. Attributing these problems to the increased levels of service-sector employment would require additional research, but the patterns are consistent with what has occurred in other communities.

Many of these problems have their roots in the type of jobs that tourism has brought into the county. Most of the jobs in the restaurants and motels are near minimum wage, and since the tourist flow slows dramatically during the winter months, many of these jobs are seasonal. Many of the jobs with the federal agencies are seasonal as well, since the agency workload is lower during the off-season. Low-paying seasonal jobs are not attracting individuals who wish to establish deep roots in the community or an educated workforce with the skills and interests to be major contributors to community institutions. Most likely to seek many of the jobs available in the county are persons looking for temporary employment to help them through college or other training, or those without the skills or ambition to seek attractive alternatives. In contrast, research has found that family farm owner-operators have traditionally been widely involved in the community and carried a heavy load in maintaining community institutions (Heffernan 1982). Family farmers hold positions of responsibility in their work and are accustomed to making major decisions. Such experience and responsibility are rare among service workers. Family farmers also are available during evenings to participate in community activities. Many service-sector jobs require evening work.

CONCLUSION

Tourism development has provided badly needed jobs for Wayne County residents, halted long-term demographic, economic, and social declines, and has resulted in improved levels of community services and a sense of hope that young people will be able to find jobs close to home. However, a number of problems have also emerged as a result of the unique aspects of tourism employment. Since many of the jobs are low-wage and low-skill, increased family dissolution, poverty, crime, and institutional decline are apparent. Community development specialists need to be aware of both the positive and negative changes that accompany various types of development. Such awareness will allow them to make informed decisions about the types of development to pursue. Likewise, as development occurs, they will be in a position to enhance its positive aspects while diminishing the negative.

DISCUSSION QUESTIONS FROM THE EDITORS

1. It is clear that the shift from agriculture to tourism in Wayne County just "happened." It was not the result of strategic initiatives by the local leaderships. What steps could local leadership have taken to make the most of the county's high amenity setting?

2. The author notes that with the shifts to large-scale agriculture many rural towns face population loss. Nationally, are there long-term negative consequences associated with having a greater concentration of population in cities? Why should the nation worry about population decline in the rural areas?

3. Imagine that you are the newly hired economic development director of Wayne County. You have a three-year contract and a mandate to improve the county's economic performance. What would you do? How would your approach be different if you had only a one-year contract?

CHAPTER 15

Agricultural Processing Facilities as a Source of Rural Jobs

F. Larry Leistritz

INTRODUCTION

This case study addresses agricultural processing facilities as a development option for rural communities. Expanded processing of agricultural products in rural areas has been widely pursued as a strategy for rural economic development (Barkema et al. 1990; Leistritz and Hamm 1994). Expansion of value-added agricultural processing in rural areas is generally seen as a positive development; cooperatively owned, value-added processing plants may allow producers to integrate forward and capture potential profits from processing and marketing their products. Also, whether locally-owned or part of a large, integrated agribusiness company, new processing plants may create new employment opportunities in rural areas previously hard-hit by the farm crisis of the 1980s and subsequent farm consolidation (Sommer et al. 1993; Murdock and Leistritz 1988). As a result, the expansion of agricultural processing in rural areas receives broad-based support from commodity groups, rural development interests, and state political leaders. This case study summarizes recent experiences in North Dakota, where several new agricultural processing plants have recently been created.

The expansion of value-added processing in rural areas, while widely supported, has not been without its problems. First, many rural areas have been disappointed in their efforts to attract or develop such facilities, often because of the distance between these rural farm areas and major consumer markets (Barkema et al. 1990). Even when communities have succeeded in developing or attracting new processing plants, some host communities have found that the new plants offered more jobs than the local labor supply could fill or at wages lower than local workers would accept (Broadway 1994; Allen 1995).

Commuters and in-migrants filled many of the jobs, changing the age and racial/ethnic composition of some towns (Broadway 1994; Stull et al. 1992). An influx of newcomers, many with racial/ethnic backgrounds different from those of long-term community residents, has led to social disruption in some communities (Allen 1995).

VALUE-ADDED AGRICULTURAL PROCESSING IN NORTH DAKOTA

During the 1990s, several new agricultural processing facilities were developed in North Dakota. These plants process a number of the region's agricultural products, including durum wheat, corn, potatoes, oilseeds, and bison. Most, but not all, have been organized as grower-owned cooperatives. Selected characteristics of six of these projects are summarized in table 15.1. The six plants represent an initial investment of about $378 million and employed about 420 workers at their initial level of capacity. Three of these plants have subsequently been expanded substantially, and by the third quarter of 1998, the plants employed almost 700 workers.

Table 15.1
Recently Initiated Agricultural Processing Projects in North Dakota

Project	Form of Initial Organi- zation	Date Started		Operating Employment		Initial Investment
		Construction	Operation	Initial[1]	Current[2]	$ million
Dakota Growers Pasta	Cooperative	1992	1993	100	275	43
North American Bison	Cooperative	1993	1994	9	46	1.6
ProGold	Cooperative	1995	1996	120	120	260
Farmers Choice Pasta	Cooperative	1996	1997	17	18	9.8
Avico USA	Investor- owned firm	1995	1996	160	220	70
AgGrow Oils	Cooperative	1997	1998	16	16	8.5

Notes:
1. Employment after one year of operation
2. Employment as of third quarter, 1998

The six projects summarized in table 15.1 are the result of substantial development efforts over a period of several years. Among the motivations for developing these projects were farmers' desire to add value to their crops and livestock and state leaders' goal of diversifying the rural economy. Both of these interests were intensified by the economic hardships that agriculture and rural communities endured during the 1980s. In an effort to encourage expanded processing of agricultural products, North Dakota established an Agricultural Products Utilization Commission (APUC) in 1979. The APUC has played a key role in predevelopment financing for several agricultural processing initiatives, and APUC grants have funded numerous feasibility studies.

The effort to expand North Dakota's agricultural processing sector received a boost in 1991, when the state legislature enacted a comprehensive economic development program called "Growing North Dakota". Growing North Dakota provided subsidized interest rates for loans to primary-sector (basic-sector) ventures, such as agricultural processing facilities, as well as additional funding for APUC. These economic stimulus programs in turn helped to energize rural development efforts statewide. In particular, the North Dakota Association of Rural Electric Cooperatives took an active role in promoting economic development and the potential of cooperatives to provide local ownership and control of new projects (Torgerson 1994). The association hired a small staff led by a professional economic developer, and is seen to have played a key role in catalyzing a number of new development projects.

When North Dakota producers have considered new agricultural processing ventures, they have often chosen to organize their company as a *closed cooperative*. This form of cooperative (sometimes referred to as "new generation cooperative") differs from other types in that membership is restricted (i.e., to those growers who purchase shares). In addition, the grower members are typically obligated to deliver specified quantities of product (e.g., X bushels of wheat) to the plant for processing each year. One reason that this form of organization has been popular in the Upper Midwest is past experience with closed cooperatives, particularly in the sugar beet industry of the Red River Valley (North Dakota and Minnesota). American Crystal Sugar and Minn-Dak Farmers Cooperative have both been operating as closed cooperatives for more than 20 years, and both have excellent records of producing significant financial returns to their members.

DAKOTA GROWERS PASTA COMPANY

The process of developing one of these new agricultural processing projects can perhaps best be illustrated by briefly tracing the development of Dakota Growers Pasta Company. North Dakota is the nation's leading producer of durum wheat, accounting for 66 percent of national production in 1997. Durum wheat is used almost exclusively in the production of a variety of pasta products (e.g., spaghetti, macaroni, noodles). As a result, agricultural leaders in North Dakota have long been interested in the concept of locating durum-milling/ pasta-processing facilities in the state. As early as 1974, North Dakota State University conducted a study on the economic feasibility of processing pasta products in the state (Fraase et al. 1974). Interest in agricultural processing grew during the 1980s as low returns in agriculture stimulated farmers' desire to integrate forward into processing and depressed economic conditions throughout the state's rural areas heightened state leaders' concerns to create new job opportunities (Murdock and Leistritz 1988). In particular, several farm leaders who were also durum producers became convinced that they should attempt to create a durum-processing venture organized in the closed cooperative format that had been successful for the sugar beet industry.

The initial board of directors of Dakota Growers came together early in 1991. With funding from APUC, they commissioned a feasibility study, which indicated that a plant processing durum wheat into finished pasta products could potentially add $1 to a farmer's return on a bushel of durum. Encouraged by this result, the organizers incorporated the cooperative on December 16, 1991, and early in 1992 they began holding informational meetings for potential members (Zeuli 1998). Interested growers were asked to purchase one share of membership stock for $125 plus at least 1,500 shares of equity stock at a cost of $3.90 per share, for a minimum total investment of $5,975. Each farmer received delivery rights of one bushel of durum wheat per share (i.e., they had both the right and the obligation to deliver the grain).

Dakota Growers' goal was to sell 3 million shares, and this was accomplished in less than a month. By February 7, 1992, a total of 1,040 durum growers had purchased 3.1 million shares (2,997 shares per farmer). This equity drive provided about 30 percent of the initial capital for the project, with the remainder coming from loans from the St. Paul Bank for Cooperatives, the City of Carrington, the Tri-County Electric Cooperative, and Dakota Central Telecommunications. The St. Paul Bank was the major lender and obtained a first lien on all plants and equipment.

Carrington, North Dakota (county seat of Foster County) was chosen as the plant site in June 1992. It was chosen over 28 other site proposals, based on a number of factors including excellent highway and railroad access, an adequate water supply, a good strategic location, and community support (Zeuli 1998). Community support included the loans from local entities mentioned previously, as well as local tax abatements. Construction of the plant began in 1992, and production began in 1993. Today, Dakota Growers has 1,084 durum growers as members, with about 96 percent in North Dakota and the remainder in Minnesota and Montana. Since beginning operations, the company's average annual growth rate of 38 percent has made Dakota Growers one of the five largest pasta producers in the United States.

SOCIOECONOMIC EFFECTS

The effects of the processing plants on the communities where they are located will depend in large measure on their success in the marketplace, which in turn will be reflected in expanded sales and employment, and (for the cooperatives) dividends to their grower-owners. Because some of the North Dakota agricultural processors have only recently begun operations, it is perhaps premature to evaluate their effects. However, several of the projects have already demonstrated encouraging evidence of growth and profitability.

Dakota Growers Pasta has more than doubled its production capacity and employment since beginning operation in 1993. After a substantial expansion in 1996, the mill now has the capacity to grind about 7 million bushels of durum annually (compared to an initial capacity of 3.2 million bushels). The pasta plant's production capacity has been expanded twice, going from 120 million pounds to 270 million pounds annually. Since the 1996 fiscal year (August 1995 through July 1996), Dakota Growers has paid annual dividends to its farmer-owners. The dividends distributed for past fiscal years were: FY '96—$.30 per share, FY '97—$.485, and FY '98—$1.00 (Zeuli 1998).

The North American Bison Cooperative members received their first dividends in 1998, for animals delivered to the plant in 1997. The 1997 dividend was $41.06 per share (one share - one animal). Producers who purchased the original shares paid $250, but those shares are now worth about $500. The cooperative processed about 8,000 animals in 1997. The co-op is planning to build a second plant (Johnson 1998).

The experience of the ProGold corn-processing project, on the other hand, illustrates some of the problems that can affect new enterprises. The plant was completed on schedule and within budget in the fall of 1996, and produced its first commercial-quality high fructose corn syrup (HFCS) in December 1996. However, the plant experienced difficulty in marketing its corn sweeteners because several other major firms in the industry had recently increased their production capacity, resulting in an oversupply in the HFCS market. HFCS prices fell to all-time lows, and the grower co-op sustained a net loss of $11.7 million in fiscal year 1997. To reduce losses and improve the likelihood of future dividends to members, ProGold management negotiated an agreement to lease the plant to Cargill, Inc., effective November 1997. Since the lease went into effect, the plant has been operating with stable employment (Golden Growers Cooperative 1998).

The Avico USA plant, which processes potatoes into frozen french fries, appears to be off to a good start. The plant's production and employment have expanded substantially since it began operation in the fall of 1996. One effect of this project has been a substantial expansion of irrigated potato acreage in south central North Dakota. The plant uses the production of more than 8,000 acres per year (Campbell 1998). Farmers Choice Pasta and AgGrow Oils both began operation quite recently; it is too early to assess their success.

All the processing plants have created new jobs in the communities where they are located, but the magnitude of job creation has varied widely in both absolute and relative terms. The operating employment at the plants ranges from 275 for Dakota Growers Pasta and 220 for Avico USA to 18 at Farmers Choice Pasta and 16 at AgGrow Oils (table 15.1). Farmers' Choice Pasta accounts for less than 1 percent of total employment in Benson County. ProGold represents 1.3 percent of total jobs in Richland County. Avico USA provides about 2 percent of the total employment in Stutsman County, and the North American Bison Cooperative provides about 3.8 percent of all jobs in Eddy County (tables 15.1 and 15.2). Foster County is the site of two projects (Dakota Growers Pasta and AgGrow Oils), which together account for almost 14 percent of total county employment.

Recent changes in employment, population, and taxable sales in the plant site counties are summarized in table 15.2. Three of the five counties registered increases in total employment from 1990 to 1996, and the five counties had an increase in employment of 3.5 percent overall. This is slightly higher than the 3.4 percent growth recorded for North Dakota's nonmetro counties overall during the same period. Four of the five site counties lost population from 1990 to 1996, with an overall decrease of 2.6 percent. This is a smaller decrease in population than the 3.4 percent drop registered by North Dakota's nonmetro counties overall. All five counties recorded increases in taxable sales (adjusted for inflation) from 1990 to 1996, with the increases ranging from 4 percent to 39 percent and averaging 12.7 percent overall. This was a slightly smaller increase than the 13.7 percent gain posted by North Dakota's nonmetro counties. Overall, these changes suggest that the new processing plants have made a substantial economic contribution in some counties, while in others their contribution to date has been less significant, or in some cases the economic growth associated with the processing plants may have been offset by declines in other sectors.

Table 15.2
Changes in Selected Socioeconomic Indicators in Plant Site Counties, North Dakota, 1990–1996

| County | Employment | | |
	1990	*1996*	Percent Change *1990–1996*
Benson	2,679	2,514	-6.2
Eddy	1,354	1,207	-10.9
Foster	1,872	2,120	13.2
Richland	8,229	8,897	8.1
Stutsman	10.879	11,145	2.4
Total	25,013	25.883	3.5

| County | Population | | |
	1990	*1996*	Percent Change *1990–1996*
Benson	7,198	6,905	-4.1
Eddy	2,951	2,875	-2.6
Foster	3,983	3,859	-3.1
Richland	18,148	18,266	0.7
Stutsman	22,241	21,211	-4.6
Total	54,521	53,116	-2.6

| County | Taxable Sales 1996 $ (million) | | |
	1990	*1996*	Percent Change *1990–1996*
Benson	7.2	10.0	38.9
Eddy	7.5	7.8	4.0
Foster	25.4	31.4	23.6
Richland	87.1	98.5	13.1
Stutsman	139.0	152.4	9.6
Total	266.2	300.1	12.7

CONCLUSIONS AND IMPLICATIONS

Expansion of the agricultural processing sector has been a major rural economic development initiative in North Dakota. During the 1990s, this strategy has resulted in the development of several new processing plants, most of which are organized as farmer-owned cooperatives. Efforts to organize such projects have been supported by state development programs, including an Agricultural Products Utilization Commission, which has funded feasibility studies for many potential agricultural processing ventures, and a program that provides subsidized loans for qualifying projects. While all of the plants studied have begun operations within the past five years, several have already demonstrated considerable success in the marketplace, which has been reflected in expanded operations and dividends for their farmer-owners. On the other hand, at least one of the plants experienced significant marketing problems during its first year of operations, pointing out that risks are inherent in such ventures. On balance, the experience of North Dakota suggests that expanded agricultural processing can be a viable economic development strategy for some rural communities in agricultural areas. State efforts to support such ventures can enhance their development. However, because of the inherent risks, the feasibility of each potential project should be carefully evaluated.

DISCUSSION QUESTIONS FROM THE EDITORS

1. What advantages does the closed cooperative business model discussed in this chapter offer over more usual forms of financing and ownership (i.e., stock or partnership)? What might be the disadvantages?

2. The author states that North Dakota accounted for 66 percent of national durum wheat production in 1997. Why do you think there was not a significant pasta production facility in North Dakota before the cooperative venture was begun?

CHAPTER 16

Educating for Industrial Competitiveness and Rural Development

Stuart A. Rosenfeld

INTRODUCTION

In 1988, Ireland's Galway-Mayo Institute of Technology[1] (GMIT) and Connemara West, a rural community development organization in the village of Letterfrack, embarked on an innovative path to jointly establish and operate a furniture college for youth. The heady goals of this ambitious project were no less than to expand economic opportunities for youth, stimulate the local economy, and, by infusing creativity, design, and entrepreneurial energy into the industry through these young workers, invigorate the Irish furniture industry. Thus, the alliance represented lofty hopes for both the region and the Republic of Ireland.

Connemara, a scenic but remote area on the western side of county Galway, had virtually no industry and few job opportunities for its youth. The best hope for enterprising local youth was to migrate to Ireland's urban areas, where employment was expanding, fueled by an influx of foreign-owned branch plants. What led Connemara West and the Galway-Mayo Institute of Technology to believe that the furniture industry, which was not a strong or growing cluster in Ireland and not located in the vicinity of Letterfrack, could become a catalyst for economic development? What conditions led to this unlikely alliance, unlikely choice, and more unlikely national support, and what benefits have been realized during its first years of operation?

Map 3
Location of Case Study: Educating for Industrial
Competitiveness and Rural Development

CONNEMARA WEST, GALWAY-MAYO INSTITUTE OF TECHNOLOGY, AND THE FURNITURE INDUSTRY

For much of the twentieth century, Ireland was economically disadvantaged. Few youth entered higher education, unemployment was high, and the population was poor and declining in numbers. That was particularly true in county Galway and the adjacent western and rural counties of Mayo, Leitrim, and Roscommon. Prospects improved in the late 1950s, when a new international airport combined with low wages, surplus labor, and reduced corporate tax rates began to attract branch plants of foreign-owned, multinational corporations, especially from the United States (Industrial Development Agency 1996). The new branches, however, imported their supplies, technology, and key managerial and technical staff, and the jobs available to local youth were mostly low skill and low wage. Thus, until the 1990s, Ireland remained poor compared to European Community member countries. Today, Ireland is undergoing a remarkable recovery, its growth outpacing nearly all of Europe (*Economist* 1997). Between 1980 and 1991, the nation's manufacturing output grew faster than in any other Organization for Economic Cooperative Development (OECD) country, including Japan (Sabel 1996a).

Yet, despite its recent success, policymakers are concerned about the staying power of foreign investment as wages and costs rise, and about the persistence of unemployment and poverty in many rural areas. The village of Letterfrack in the rural outreaches of Connemara, is one such place. Its population in 1972 was about 1,800, but declined rapidly as most young people left. Many left school early and few achieved third-level education. Although the official unemployment rate was 22 percent, local officials placed the true rate closer to 50 percent. Poor roads and transportation, inadequate public services, and infertile land all stymied attempts at economic development. It was these conditions that led the community to take action. Citizens had formed their own community development organization in the 1970's, the Connemara West Centre (CW), as a first step towards rebuilding their economy.

At first, CW's efforts focused on the area's natural attractiveness, developing the self-catering[2] industry, shellfish farming, and recreational opportunities. Then CW turned to the area's root problem—education. In 1978, CW purchased the Letterfrack Industrial School which had been established by Quakers in the mid-nineteenth century. The Industrial School was converted into an industrial and reform school in 1886 to produce more "useful citizens and prevent social disorder." Finally it closed in 1974, after a national study found it to be inadequate.

To Connemara West, however, this abandoned school building was an asset and opportunity. Connemara West renovated the drab buildings and began planning to transform them into an industrial training center that might be a stimulus for the economy. In 1980, the Irish Development Authority helped the school purchase a number of craft centers, including one for woodworking and furniture restoration. Two years later, as a result of research documenting high school dropout rates and youth unemployment, the fledgling Irish Youth Employment Agency (YEA) established a craft training center there—ostensibly to generate interest in, and provide potential school leavers with skills for the construction industry. Connemara West began a three-year pilot project in woodworking and cabinet making, and in 1984 and 1985, Letterfrack was chosen as the site of the Wood Turner's Guild annual seminars. But in 1988, when support from YEA ended, the CW, building on the craft traditions, decided to expand into programs that might lead to employment as well as improved performance in Ireland's larger furniture production industry.

IRELAND'S FURNITURE CLUSTER

The community realized that moving from furniture making as an artisan craft to a manufactured product would be a risky challenge. First, the industry, though located in the northern part of Ireland, is not particularly close to Letterfrack. Second, government had almost given up on the industry. One official commented that "getting technology into furniture would be a waste" (interview conducted on site, April 14–18, 1997). Since the mid–1980s, the furniture industry had received little support from Ireland's sector-based assistance programs.

Though important in the domestic economy, furniture was not considered to be globally competitive. Most furniture companies were managed by owners with some manufacturing but little management or marketing expertise. Many plants were quite old and cold, not an environment to operate new and expensive equipment, achieve high productivity, or attract youth to jobs. Further, the industry was not noted for its aesthetic design or innovation, and few companies employed professional designers or engineers. One study reported that "the use of designers in the furniture industry is almost non-existent." Consequently, the bulk of output was for mid- and low-price market segments and customers who had their own designs and specifications.

The industry clearly lacked the traits—interdependent companies, social infrastructure, flow of information and innovation, and sense of common purpose and vision—which characterize successful clusters. Irish firms typically view each other with caution and suspicion based on a history of copying one another. Instead of cooperating and networking, they rely on their own internal capabilities to meet market opportunities, but younger owners and managers seem to be more willing to look for opportunities to cooperate[3].

Yet, the CW was convinced that this industry was important to the nation because of its relative size within the Irish economy. The industry consists of about 600 companies and 5,000 employees, has a high incidence of local ownership, and a large number of rural plants. In an economy heavily dominated by foreign-owned branch plants, furniture represented a refreshing contrast, an Irish industry loyal to its home communities. The CW believed that better-educated workers might help turn this industry around, that remoteness could be turned into an advantage by highlighting the natural beauty of the area, and that furniture could become an economic development niche for the community. Realizing that the community could not do this alone, Connemara West began to search for partners. The first and, as it turned out, most important partner, was the Galway-Mayo Institute of Technology.

This institution, founded in 1972, was the first of eight regional technical colleges[4] established to develop technical, scientific, and management expertise needed to attract and place Irish youths in higher value added and higher wage industries. Galway, then an economically depressed city of about 28,000 serving a predominantly rural region, initially aimed its programs at rural development, and thus emphasized agriculture and tourism. But in the 1980s, it expanded its programs and added customized training to meet the needs of the newly imported high-tech companies that subsequently became the county's largest employers.

ESTABLISHING THE FURNITURE COLLEGE AT LETTERFRACK

After considerable analysis and discussion, CW and Galway-Mayo Institute of Technology formed a partnership to design and deliver a high- quality, two-year, tertiary degree program in furniture design and manufacture and work toward making the college a nationally, and perhaps even internationally, renowned center for modern furniture design and technology. Subject to state approval and support, GMIT would certify the program and take responsibility for academic content, quality, and management in cooperation with CW.

The aim of the first national certificate program was "to provide a seed ground for the development of an indigenous furniture industry in Ireland which will be committed to quality products." Goals included:

- providing for the local community, region, and nation a base for the development of the Irish furniture industry, and creating a market awareness of quality furniture made in Ireland;
- enabling its graduates to contribute to and influence the design process and manufacture of modern furniture in ways that are innovative, creative, and responsive to social and economic need; and
- laying the foundation for an indigenous approach to furniture making and enhance the influence of Irish design.

Objectives were to:

- select both local and national students who would develop skills and generate ideas necessary to enhance the furniture industry;
- provide conditions whereby graduates and the college could successfully use their skills and expertise;
- create a physical and educational environment with the resources necessary to nurture and support the aims; and
- promote interaction with the local and regional community and so disseminate the ideas generated to a wide audience.

With start-up funds from the European Union's Social Fund, one full-time person, and a second person assigned part-time from the main campus at Galway to help with more theoretical content, the program began in January 1987. By 1988, the curriculum had been developed and validated for certification, and 15 people were selected from among 37 applicants for the first class. The application process included a trip to Letterfrack and a presentation to demonstrate the applicant's creativity, such as a crafted product, sketchbook, writing, or art portfolio. In 1990, the first national certificates were conferred at Letterfrack, and by 1992 the college had received 380 applications from all over Ireland for 15 annual places in the program (at least five were reserved for local students). In 1997, over 400 applied for 27 openings. The students selected (based on interviews and surveys) were drawn from all over Ireland and a few from other nations. Only 24 percent were from Galway County, 69 percent came from the rest of Ireland, and 7 percent from other countries. In 1995, the college added a bachelor of science degree to equip students with more advanced work in theory and practice and enable them to function as professionals in the furniture industry. Total enrollment in 1997 was 97.

The college is operated by a full-time staff of three and a panel of 20 part-time specialists, including lecturers from Europe's most prestigious schools. It has well-equipped workshops and design studios with facilities for laminating, veneering, bending, upholstering, assembling, and using computer-aided design. The college also teaches graphics and office management. The library contains more than 2,000 volumes, videos, and an electronic information center with specialized software and computer-based access and retrieval systems, including computer links to GMIT. Students also have full access to all of the resources and courses at GMIT. A newly instituted bus service (to accommodate the college's growth) between the two institutions reduces the impact of isolation and of the commute.

STRESSING ENTREPRENEURSHIP AND INNOVATION

One of the special features of the program is an emphasis on entrepreneurship and design. Students are expected to not only understand the materials and processes, but also how to manage an enterprise and sell goods. Design is a cross-cutting theme running throughout all work, and students are encouraged to be creative and innovative. Although wood is the basic material students use, they also learn about and integrate a wide range of materials into their furniture, including copper, steel, plastics, and fabrics. But students also learn to apply the computer-based technologies, including computer-aided design that will enable them to take craft products to high-volume production.

The goals expressed by students underscore the entrepreneurial bent of the program. In the short term, 22 percent expect to start their own businesses, and more than 16 percent anticipate continuing on to higher education programs. In the longer term, 69 percent expect to own their own businesses. Some disturbing news is that only two students expect to work in the region (within 100 kilometers) after graduation, and, therefore, the region will not directly reap the benefit of the new companies.

Table 16.1
Immediate Goals of Students

Goal	Number	Percent
Employment in locality	2	3.6
Employment elsewhere in Ireland	14	25.5
Employment outside of Ireland	8	14.5
Self-employment	12	21.8
Apply for higher education	9	16.4
Travel/break from work	5	9.1
Other	5	9.1

Figure 16.1
Long-Term Aspirations of Students, Percent

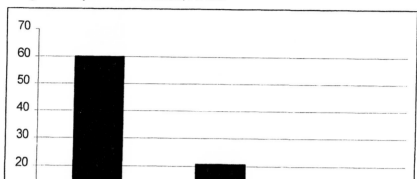

EXPANDING THE ALLIANCE

As the college developed, staff saw an opportunity to add research and development and more directly diffuse the technologies being taught to their students into the industry. This, they anticipated, would solidify Letterfrack's claim as the furniture skills and technology center of Ireland. The key agency in this process was Forbairt, Ireland's agency for science and technology, which already supported specialized technology centers, many connected to similar institutes of technology. CW and GMIT began to explore the possibility of applying for an additional Forbairt technology center. Connemara West contracted with an expert from the Danish Technological Institute to carry out a study of the industry and potential for a technology center at Letterfrack. It found, among other things, that "In production/technical areas, workers with detailed understanding of the properties of materials used and their reactions to each other, tools, machinery, safety, etc., are just not available to employers" (Bülow 1996).

As a result of the consultant's findings that education and technology adoption were intrinsically related, he recommended that a furniture technology center be established at the college in Letterfrack. Forbairt funded the center in 1997. It was located at the college, managed by Connemara West, and advised by Galway-Mayo Institute of Technology and a group of furniture companies. This was quite an achievement, since both Limerick and Dublin—both more easily accessible to the industry—had previously proposed such a center and were rejected. The center is currently staffed by four full-time furniture technologists, a part-time senior technologist, an administrator shared with the college, and a half-time consultant from Denmark. It offers technical consulting and information, courses, seminars, technology demonstrations, and research and development.

ACCOMPLISHMENTS AND IMPACTS

Given the Furniture College's ambitious and multiple goals of serving students, revitalizing a weak industry, and creating rural development and economic opportunities, what has it accomplished during its first years?

The college has had a remarkable record to date in attracting and selecting good students and helping them find employment. Applicants far outnumber openings, and the fact that students are drawn from all over Ireland and abroad is testimony to the reputation of the college and the community. Students are easily placed after graduation. The new bachelor's degree program gives students earning certificates an opportunity to continue their education, and many now do. One in six certificate students expect to go on to further education. How the additional education will affect their future is still unknown since the first class has not yet graduated.

The entrepreneurial spirit that pervades the program has shown results. Since 1990, graduates have successfully started 15 new businesses that incorporate design and innovation into niche products. By integrating management, marketing, and administrative skills with technical and design skills, the Furniture College enhances its graduates' entrepreneurial capabilities.

It will take more time for the college to build productive links with industry, largely because Ireland's furniture companies still lack any collective vision or the social fabric that might produce such a vision. The Furniture College and Technology Center and the new young skilled workers and artisans, however, may eventually change industry attributes and attitudes.

How quickly the industry accepts and uses the resources of this college and center will be a test of the effectiveness of its programs. The full impact will only be known as more students join the industry and eventually move into management positions. Currently the number of graduates is too small to discern an impact. With the expected quadrupling of enrollments by the end of the decade and the new technology center's potential to catalyze modernization, this ought to change, and strong entrepreneurial aspirations of the students may be the long-term salvation of the industry and region. If they receive support to achieve their goals, the industry may experience significant growth in the future.

The effects on the local economy are, thus far, mainly attributable to the college itself, rather than the students it produces. All but one of the students surveyed expect to leave the immediate area—not surprising since there are few local companies to employ them, and young people often seek an environment with more social amenities. The real test, however, is whether some will later choose to return. As the new furniture technology center grows, it may create opportunities for new businesses in the Connemara region. Nevertheless, there have been several immediate effects on the community. For example:

- For the first time, there is a regularly scheduled bus service to Galway.
- The average age of the community dropped from 57 to 27, and with new sports events, music, and recreational activities, there are more incentives for young people to remain in this area—which had been losing 70 percent of its youth population on average each year.
- Housing has been renovated and improved to accommodate the growing student body and the area is now more appealing to tourists.
- New full-time and part-time teaching and administrative jobs at the college and new service jobs have been created to cater to the student body.
- Isolated elderly people who rent to students feel more secure.

By expanding employment, increasing the population of young people, and enhancing the visibility of the village, the college has given the community hope and a basis for economic growth. Further, the furniture industry has broad appeal and long-term potential for the nation because it is largely an Irish-owned industry that could provide a stable source of income and jobs, is likely to use local suppliers, and is also likely to invest its profits in the Republic of Ireland.

PROSPECTS AND CHALLENGES FOR THE FUTURE

Since the college has three sets of customers—students, the community, and the industry—prospects are mixed. The students have the brightest future. There are sufficient economic opportunities, though not necessarily in the region or even in Ireland, and many students have already set their sights on other locations and countries. Yet many may leave to acquire new skills and contacts and, as many Irish youth are now doing, return to Ireland.

The college is currently formulating a new five-year plan that will include an ambitious expansion of current offerings. In May 1997, the minister for agriculture, food, and forestry approved a $6.6 million grant for expansion[5] that will include a certificate in conservation/restoration and a postgraduate diploma in furniture manufacturing (intended to make the field attractive to high-quality graduates from other fields). The college also is developing courses that can be delivered via distance learning to people working in industry who want to pursue a degree on a part-time basis. These new programs, combined with growing enrollment in current programs, are expected to boost total student enrollments to 160 within the next four years.

The talent in the program and the immediate and long-term desires to become entrepreneurs—as some 15 graduates already have—is significant. The college is planning to form its own local furniture company in the community, and in the near future, the CWC may want to consider a new business incubator to give students a chance to share start-up risks and establish markets.

The community is likely to experience more rapid growth as college enrollments grow. The challenge will be in locally meeting the entertainment and purchasing needs of the influx of youth and in avoiding becoming completely dominated by a nonlocal student population, which could change the nature of the Connemara West region. At its current levels, the student population is a tremendous asset and source of new wealth. A student body multiplied by four, however, may qualitatively alter the community ecosystem.

The prospects for the industry may depend on the degree to which the industry eventually becomes a full partner along with the college and technology center. At present, a partnership exists between the college and the community development organization—with strong industry representation but not participation, largely because there is still no industry organization that can speak on behalf of the furniture companies. Key challenges will be to convince Irish industry of the value of the expertise of the college, center, and students, and to retain more of the production in the region.

DISCUSSION QUESTIONS FROM THE EDITORS

1. The author states, "A student body multiplied by four, however, may qualitatively alter the community ecosystem." What negative effects can a large influx of students have on a small community? How would the impacts of students be different than the impacts of tourists?

2. The author expresses concern over the fact that very few of the students intend to work in the region after graduation, and mentions plans for a business incubator to help students start their businesses. What other steps might be taken to encourage students to stay in the region?

3. Does it make sense for a national government to invest in a new training program located in a region that is lagging, but is not a center of activity for the industry the training program will serve? Why or why not?

NOTES

This chapter is based on research conducted during 1997–1998 for the Community College Research Center at the Institute on Education and the Economy, Teachers' College, Columbia University.

1. Although known as Regional Technical Institute Galway when the project began, in February 1998 all technical colleges officially were renamed "Institutes of Technology" and the college became Galway-Mayo Institute of Technology.

2. Bed and breakfast businesses and renting of cottages.

3. Much of the information about the industry is based on a background paper prepared by Patrick Tobin, lecturer at Galway Regional Technical College, in March 1997.

4. Prior to February 1998, the institutes of technology were known as regional technical colleges.

5. Connemara West Annual Report 1996/97 (Letterfrack: Connemara West Centre, 1997): 3.

Attracting Large-Scale Industry

CHAPTER 17

Introduction: Attracting Large-Scale Industry

Peter V. Schaeffer

Industrial attraction is the form of economic development that receives the most attention in the popular press. When a new firm enters a community, the addition to the number of jobs is evident in a way rarely experienced when existing firms expand by adding a few jobs. Maybe it is because the results are so visible that industrial attraction seems to enjoy strong public support. It is both the most widely used and the most controversial economic development tool (Bartik 1991; Loveridge 1996).

The case studies in this section illustrate both the promise and problems associated with industrial attraction. Some of the cases reflect support for the strategy, while others are skeptical about its results. To some extent, the outcomes associated with industrial attraction depend on the approach used. We distinguish between three different approaches to industrial recruitment (for a different classification, see Isserman 1994)[1].

1. *Self-improvement.* Examples of this strategy include infrastructure investments ("build it and they will come"), site preparation, and labor force training.

2. *Industrial recruitment.* Self-improvement is a passive approach that relies on firms to make a choice. Industrial recruitment includes the pursuit of firms, often with the promise of financial incentives if they locate in the community.

3. *Creating a favorable business climate.* This approach is more effective when used by state rather than local governments. State governments can

influence the business climate through their income tax code and through labor, safety, and environmental laws and regulations. Local governments have a limited ability to affect the business climate.

Although we list the approaches to industrial attraction individually, they are often used in combination. In the pursuit of large firms, industrial attraction is also very often a cooperative effort between state and local governments. The involvement of state government, although it may be necessary, is not without risk, as the goals of the state and the community may not coincide. Because of the greater resources of state governments, small communities may end up as "limited partners" in the attraction effort. The case study of the location of the Mercedes Benz plant in Vance, Alabama, provides an example of the lead role of the state and the limited role of the community. Without the assistance of state government, however, small local governments, may be unable to offer incentives that are competitive with those available in large communities.

In a large urban area, a new employer is hardly noticed. This is not the case in a small town or rural area. The addition of a large new employer may strain the capacities of infrastructure, schools, and the housing market. It may take some time before bottlenecks are removed. Small-town residents are often willing to accept the disadvantages associated with strained infrastructure because they hope that the added employment will enhance the long-term economic health of their community. This hope is not always fulfilled, however. Some of the positive developments associated with industrial growth—expansion of retailing, new residential construction—may occur outside of the community. Two of the case studies in this section provide examples of communities that "won" plants that provided new jobs, only to see many of the benefits accrue to neighboring communities.

Map 4
Location of Case Study Sites: Attracting Large-Scale Industry

NOTE

1. All three approaches are represented in the case studies in this section.

CHAPTER 18

Industrial Attraction: The Experience of the Crawford County (Ohio) Development Board

Greg Davis and Jerold R. Thomas

This case study explains how a rural community in north central Ohio initiated the development of a successful industrial attraction organization in 1989, and how that organization created a 270 acre industrial park which boasts the creation of more than 400 new jobs and more than $90 million in new property investment. The case study approach describes how local leaders, in an effort to alleviate persistent double-digit unemployment figures, have developed successful industrial attraction strategies, raised more than $300,000 in local funds from private citizens, business, industry, and other community groups, and successfully leveraged nearly $2 million in state and federal funding. In addition, the various qualities and characteristics of the development organization and the community in which it operates that have enabled this effort to achieve this high level of success are also detailed.

COMMUNITY HISTORICAL BACKGROUND

Crawford County (population 47,000) is an agricultural and industrial community located in north central Ohio. Bucyrus is the county seat, and the most central municipality. Until the 1980s, the county had a large manufacturing base with more than 50 percent of the nongovernment and nonagricultural workforce employed in manufacturing. However, as a result of the economic downturn of the eighties and the subsequent plant closings and economic restructuring, manufacturing employment in the county decreased substantially. Concurrently, the unemployment rate rose to double-digit levels.

In an effort to improve the local economic situation, community leaders in Bucyrus began to discuss ways of revitalizing the economy. In the late 1980s an attempt was made to attract a manufacturing company. For various reasons, however, the company chose another location. According to the company's site selection consultant, the most notable reasons for not locating in Crawford County were the lack of a prepared industrial site possessing the necessary water, sewer, roads, storm water control, and the lack of community control over the selling price of the property. The consultant was not interested in dealing with "speculative sellers."

To maintain the community's economic viability, it was becoming clear that Bucyrus would need to attract outside industry, and to attract any industry, the community would need to develop and control a property suitable for industrial development.

THE GRADUAL DEVELOPMENT OF A FOCUSED PURPOSE AND ORGANIZATION

To this end, when roughly 270 acres of farmland beyond the corporation limits of Bucyrus became available for purchase, the local community improvement corporation entered into an option to purchase. The land was unimproved, containing no public infrastructure, and ironically, there was no plan on how to extend infrastructure to the site or whether or not the land was even suitable for industrial development. Despite this, local leaders viewed this site as the future industrial park for Bucyrus, and consequently, one of the local utility providers, American Electric Power, offered to conduct a site feasibility study for the board. Local leaders then raised $115,000 in loans as a down payment for the acreage.

In 1990, the board of county commissioners hired the county's first countywide economic development professional through Ohio State University Extension. Unbeknownst to him at this time, this county agent would spend considerable time during the next several years assisting in the development of the park.

Local leaders in Bucyrus also decided to create a separate, nonprofit organization to develop and market the land. This organization, the Crawford County Development Board, Inc. (CCDBI), would be volunteer driven, with some input from paid professionals. The organization's founding members made what turned out to be a critical decision in selecting a local retiree, a former industrial plant manager, as their board president. This individual proved to be a highly effective president, organizer, and catalyst for the board.

In retrospect, the board approached the industrial site development process from the wrong direction. Instead of conducting a study to determine the best site, the board selected what appeared to be a good site (and this was good judgement, since the site location was excellent). They then purchased the site without any plan on how much it would cost to extend infrastructure to the potential industrial park. These are *not* recommended steps in developing sites suitable for industrial development.

However, what the board lacked in industrial park financial planning, it more than made up for in industrial park vision, which proved to be powerful in the years ahead. Their contagious vision spread, and many in the community bought into the concept. This "buy-in" enabled the community and the board to expand their capacity to overcome the various hurdles that would come before them. Interestingly, one of the unique things about the vision of the industrial park was that no one called it a vision; in fact, the term was not in vogue at the time. But it was a vision, and a shared one at that. Community members understood the need for an industrial park, where the park would be, and held a general consensus that this was an appropriate and necessary economic development strategy for the community.

STEPS LEADING TO THE DEVELOPMENT OF THE INDUSTRIAL PARK

Due to space considerations, the major steps, activities, setbacks, and problems associated with the development of the park are outlined in the brief format below. The reader should be reminded that most of these steps were complex and time consuming.

1990

- The board was organized to represent various stakeholders (i.e., county, city, township, school district, etc.) and to bring broad leadership to the board.
- A fund drive was initiated by the board with a goal of $250,000 in donations over a four-year period. Because of the strong, shared vision, the board was able to raise $283,000.
- Ohio State University Extension's community economic development agent began to work with the board on developing funding scenarios for the park. The agent and board president began to contact various public agencies about funding. The Economic Development Administration (EDA) proved to be an excellent asset and provided most of the funding for the park. However, EDA funding required match funding from other sources.
- A preapplication for EDA funding was started.
- Because of an existing gas transmission line, it was discovered that the layout of the park required revision (a typical "setback" experienced by the board, requiring perseverance to overcome).

1991

- A wetlands study for the property was started.
- The EDA preapplication for $1,041,000 was submitted.
- The Board of County Commissioners agreed to fund part of the project.
- The Board of County Commissioners applied for $966,000 in water and sewer loans from the state. This was a no-interest, no-term loan that is repaid as land is sold in the park.

- With the park in two townships, neither of which were zoned, the board developed protective covenants for the park.
- To meet EDA requirements, five local banks agreed to supply an unsecured loan for the project.
- The county received $866,840 in water and sewer loans.

1992

- The Board of County Commissioners applied for and received $184,416 from the Ohio Department of Development for roadway development.
- A final Economic Development Administration application for $1,129,570 was submitted to EDA. County, sewer, and water loan money, and Ohio Department of Development road monies were used as matches.
- An archeological study of the park was undertaken costing the board $6,000 and about one-half acre of land. In 1994, an additional study costing approximately $7,000 was completed and enabled the board to develop the half acre in question.
- An enterprise zone was expanded to include the industrial park area.

1993

- Formal EDA approval was obtained for $1,087,200 representing 60 percent of the total on-site costs of the project.
- Ohio Governor Voinovich conducted an official groundbreaking for the site.
- Local investors decided to construct a 70,000-square-foot speculation building at the park.

1994

- Infrastructure for the park was completed.
- The speculation building was completed.
- The board met with their most serious prospect; however, the prospect chose another site because the land could not be provided for free.

1995

- In December, Bucyrus Precision Tech (BPT), a Japanese Honda supplier, announced plans to locate its first American facility in the industrial park.

1996

- The industrial park was annexed from the two townships in which it resided.
- The board requested to amend the enterprise zone boundaries to reflect the annexation.
- Two more companies selected the industrial park for their new site location.

1997

- The board worked with the city of Bucyrus to purchase 12 acres of the industrial center that could not be developed (a pond).

1998

- Two automotive suppliers announced plans to expand operations, one involving the purchase of more land.
- The speculative warehouse was signed for a ten-year lease. The construction of another speculative building was discussed with local investors and developers.

THE FIRST TENANTS

The industrial center's first construction involved a 72,000-square-foot speculative building/warehouse. The facility was the product of a local partnership developed with the assistance of the president of the development board. Approximately $1.4 million was invested in the project, which was initiated in July 1994, completed in July 1995, and provided warehouse space for several years before becoming home to a local expansion in late 1998.

Soon after the completion of the One Bucyrus Warehouse, the development board experienced three industrial announcements and groundbreakings within a six-month time period.

In early 1996, Bucyrus Precision Technology (BPT), a start-up company incorporated in 1995, located a 92,000-square-foot manufacturing facility in the Crossroads Industrial Center to produce rear wheel suspension spindles and transmission shafts for the Honda Accord. BPT is a subsidiary of Kaneta Kogyo Company Ltd., a Japanese corporation established in 1949 that produces frame parts for automobiles and motorcycles (Honda Motor Company Ltd. is Kaneta's largest customer). BPT was the first Kaneta subsidiary to conduct any business in the United States.

Kaneta invested approximated two-thirds of the $30 million required to start up the BPT operation. BPT projected 89 full time employees by 1999, with a payroll of more than $2.2 million. Total sales for 1999 were projected to be approximately $19 million.

Shortly after the announcement and groundbreaking ceremonies, which were coordinated by Honda of America associates from Marysville, Ohio, two more companies initiated efforts to locate facilities in the industrial park.

Approximately 200,000 square feet of warehouse/distribution space was constructed in 1996 by Arctco Sales Incorporated, a division of Arctic Cat. Arctic Cat manufactures snowmobiles, all-terrain vehicles, and personal watercraft and related accessories. The Bucyrus site location was the result of a consolidation of warehouse/distribution centers in several locations in Minnesota and Wisconsin. Employment levels projected by 1998 included 160 full-time and 30 part-time associates with a payroll of more than $2.7 million. The building, equipment, and inventory represent a new investment of approximately $31 million.

In May 1996, Imasen Bucyrus Technology (IBT is a subsidiary of Imasen Electric Industrial Company, Ltd., a Japanese Corporation) announced plans to construct a 52,000-square-foot facility to employ approximately 130 employees by the end of 2002. Groundbreaking ceremonies were held in June 1996 for the $12 million investment. IBT currently manufactures seat-related component parts for the Honda and Acura automobiles and has initiated plans to expand its operations to include a total of 173 positions by 2002 and an additional real and personal property investment of approximately $14 million.

Upon finding a long-term tenant for the One Bucyrus speculative building in 1998, the owners of the industrial park set the wheels in motion to have another speculative building constructed, preferably a 50,000-square-foot facility with the ability to expand.

THE CURRENT SITUATION

The Crawford County Development Board's forming membership originally involved 15 volunteers. Those trustees included three representatives from county and local government, two utility representatives, and one each from the financial institutions, chamber of commerce, industry, communication, and law. Eight years later, the board's membership has changed somewhat, reflecting the issues that it has confronted and the changing needs of its leadership.

Today's board involves fewer trustees and more consultants (both paid and unpaid). The board, heavily utilizing tax incentives in the attraction of new industry over the past six years, now includes a board member of the affected local school district. Furthermore, consultants serve the specialized needs of the board, involving issues of law, finance, engineering, state tax incentives, labor availability and skill levels, and others. In short, the board's membership has been adaptive to the needs of the board's leadership.

While the board has evolved partly as a result from the experiences and activities of the past eight years, the committee structure has remained essentially unchanged. An executive committee of four individuals exists to handle matters of day-to-day interest. Several ad hoc committees, most often led by the board's consultants, exist at any given point in time to address the changing concerns of the board's leadership. The board's president continues to administer the daily operations, relying on the guidance of the executive committee to make decisions regarding concerns that do not require the attention of the full board, which meets on a quarterly basis to hear ad hoc committee and financial reports and offer guidance to the executive committee and board president.

Since its inception, the board has utilized the assistance of part-time clerical help on occasion. In all but one instance, this support has been a compensated position involving an employee of an area utility company, chamber of commerce, or county office. At present, the board employs a part-time secretary 20 to 24 hours per week.

With the exception of receiving prospect leads via the Internet, normal day-to-day operations of the board today are similar to those of eight years ago. The president continues to assume responsibility for coordinating individual efforts of the consultants and members of the executive committee, communicating with area utility company and state development representatives with regards to particular prospect inquiries, and coordinating site selection efforts with potential industrial center tenants.

The board's financial situation is of primary importance to the success of the Crossroads Industrial Center. At the current funding levels, with current liabilities at approximately $1.4 million, the board will be required to sell the remaining 137 saleable acres over the next 4-6 years at no less than a $9,700-per-acre average. As a result, efforts are currently under way to improve the board's long-term financial position so that per-acre land prices can remain competitive.

The success of the board in developing an industrial center, however, is readily apparent. A brief look at its impact in terms of jobs and revenue generated illustrates the following: nearly 450 new full-time positions will have been created generating additional new annual payroll of approximately $7.5 million. This new payroll will generate additional municipal income tax of $110,000. The industries that have located in the industrial center will have invested more than $15.7 million in new real property improvements, and more than $74 million in new personal/tangible property improvements, which will provide in excess of $1.5 million to Crawford County in new tax revenue annually.

CONCLUSION

When asked what, if anything, would have been approached differently in the development of the board and the industrial center, the board's president noted that more attention should have been given to understanding basic storm water infrastructure development costs. In particular, a site development cost comparison study should have been undertaken involving the chosen site and other potential industrial sites. It was noted that after purchasing the property and beginning site development, approximately $900,000 of unanticipated storm water infrastructure costs were incurred. Furthermore, the development organization has been made aware by many outside sources on many different occasions that considerable more forethought should have been given to selecting a site for industrial development before purchasing one.

Further, the initial board's size was difficult to manage, which accounts for the current board's smaller membership and increased use of consultants. The board's president noted that empowering consultants to lead the committees was proven to be an effective means of achieving results somewhat insulated from the "politics of the trustees."

The extension agent involved in the development of the site recalled the importance of the local leadership in creating the industrial center. He emphasized the critical role of elected and volunteer community leadership in keeping a project of this magnitude on track and warns other communities to take this vital element into account before initiating such a project. Moreover, the agent noted the considerable amount of time that was involved in acquiring the various funding and approvals for the development of the site. He cautions others to carefully consider the time commitment necessary for an endeavor of this magnitude.

DISCUSSION QUESTIONS FROM THE EDITORS

1. The authors note that land for the industrial park was purchased before an overall plan was developed, and without proper study of the property. Yet such preparation would be time consuming, and taking more time might translate into the available 270-acre site being sold to someone else. How would you balance opportunities with careful study in an industrial recruitment effort?

2. Given the absence of zoning, the board developed "protective covenants" for the park. Can you guess why?

3. The authors note that 50 percent of the nongovernment, nonagricultural employment is in manufacturing in Crawford County. What does that tell you about Crawford County's suitability for new manufacturing firms? Would a county with less manufacturing employment have better or worse odds of attracting companies to an industrial park? Why?

4. List the direct costs and other expenses (in dollars) of the industrial park. Have the costs been worth the results?

CHAPTER 19

Is the City Really a Growth Machine?
A Case Study of Forestville, Alabama

Andrew A. Zekeri

INTRODUCTION

In a provocative discussion of the relationship of power holders to economic development and population growth that has attracted much attention among sociologists, Molotch argues that the key to understanding local politics is to conceptualize the city as a growth machine, proposing that the "political and economic essence of virtually any given locality, in the present American context, is growth" (1976, 309–310). Thus, the city may be viewed as a "growth machine" which reflects an overriding common interest among some local residents, especially those active or influential in local politics, in development and expansion.

Molotch (1976) uses the concept of a "growth machine" to describe the process whereby local power elites actively promote and directly benefit from local economic development. Land is considered the basic market commodity that provides wealth and power to those controlling it. He asserts that local elites with vested interests in the use of land and buildings, such as developers, landlords, and savings and loan officials, build their own fortunes by managing urban governments and cultural institutions and promoting growth. The positive impact of intensive land use on land values and property rents provides incentives for these elites to promote economic growth and development. While this group of local elites may remain divided on other local issues, economic growth is the main issue that binds them into a coalition (Molotch 1976, 314–315). In other words, Molotch is arguing that the desire for growth creates consensus among a wide range of elite groups, no matter how split they might be on other issues. Therefore, disagreement on some public issues does not necessarily indicate any fundamental disunity, nor does change in the number of actors on the scene affect the basic matter.

Molotch (1976, 318) argues that the burdens of local development are borne by the community at large, while the benefits tend to be highly concentrated. He claims that beyond the elite, very few residents benefit from their community's growth. For example, the direct economic gains derived from local housing and commercial development go almost exclusively to landowners and particular local business elites. Community residents may also benefit from the availability of housing and services, but these benefits are diffuse and may be unavailable to many. The costs, however, are generally spread throughout the community in the form of increased taxes to cover higher infrastructure costs and public debt. Thus, the local elite has convinced residents that the quality of life improves with growth when, in reality, it decreases (1976).

One of the most frequently cited justifications for local growth is that benefits will be generated in the form of reduced unemployment. In a later work, Logan and Molotch (1987) assert that the claim, however, is rhetoric. Local growth does not create jobs; it merely distributes them from a finite pool of national employment opportunities.

The purpose of this case study is to examine selected aspects of the growth machine hypothesis as presented above. Since Molotch's work is of a logical-deductive form, with few empirical examinations from urban areas (see Bridger 1992, 1989; Bridger and Harp 1990), further testing of the hypothesis with data from rural communities is needed.

THE COMMUNITY

Forestville is strategically located in the south-central part of the state and served by five state highways. The city is located 124 miles south of Birmingham and 134 miles north of Mobile. Montgomery, the state capital, is 75 miles northeast of Forestville. Forestville's 1990 population was 13,568; 31 percent of which was white and 69 percent African American. Since the early part of the century, the population of Forestville has been declining. During the period 1980–1990 the city lost 8 percent of its population, and from 1970 to 1980 the loss was 9.5 percent. About 51 percent of the residents who were at least 25 years old were high school graduates; 10.3 percent had completed college and 3.3 percent had graduate/professional degrees.

THE ECONOMIC DEVELOPMENT EFFORT

In the mid–1960s a multimillion-dollar forest products manufacturing plant was recruited from British Columbia, Canada, by the Forestville Industrial Development Board and a group called Pine Hill Associates. The Forestville Industrial Development Board and Pine Hill Associates promoted the forest and water resources of south Alabama, which resulted in a decision by company officials in British Columbia to establish a branch in Forestville. Forestville local officials, business leaders, and the Industrial Development Board arranged a $70 million municipal industrial bond issue that financed the major portion of the company's original construction. At the time of the bond issue in 1966, this was the largest municipal industrial development bond sale ever made in the United States by any municipality. To get public support, residents were persuaded by the recruiting groups that the company would make the community grow and would also improve the economic environment by generating local employment. In short, they argued that growth would benefit everyone. This is similar to Logan and Molotch's contention that "a key ideological prop for the growth machine, especially in appealing to the working class, is the assertion that local growth makes jobs" (1987, 88). Manufacturing began in December 1967, when the plywood and sawmills started production of lumber and plywood. The first paper machine began production of lineboard (the strong smooth paper used in the inner and outer part of corrugated containers) on September 10, 1968. The first saleable tons of lineboard were produced on October 1, 1968.

Today, the company dominates the private economic sector and is rated as one of the top industrial companies in Alabama based on the number of employees (Alabama Development Office 1996). Company officials in British Columbia had originally planned to invest $90 million in the complex in Forestville; but in 1983, there was a $250 million expansion to the complex. In 1991, another expansion doubled the paper mill's recycling capacity, making the company's old corrugated container facility the largest paper recycler in Alabama. The company's shares are traded on the NASDAQ Stock Exchange and other financial markets. Of the company's 1,027 employees, 381 are hourly workers in the pulp and paper section, 299 are hourly workers in the wood products section, and 31 are hourly workers in the woodland unit. Only the remaining 310 employees are salaried workers.

METHODS

The data used for the analysis are from an ongoing study of Forestville. The methods used in collecting the data are participant observation, personal interviews with local officials and residents (key informants), and data from secondary sources. A total of more than 40 field trips ranging from two to four days were made to the community for observation and participation in community activities.

Through initial contacts with influential people in the community (the probate judge, tax collector, and tax assessor), knowledge of the community was obtained, and contact persons knowledgeable about the community were identified through the snowball technique of sample identification. Community officials were contacted because they usually have acquired broad knowledge of their community. Interviews were held with all six county commissioners, the tax collector, the tax assessor, the probate judge, the district judge, the circuit court clerk, the sheriff, two bank managers, an attorney, a police officer, three business owners, and 20 other community residents. In Forestville, there were approximately 40 informants, many of whom were interviewed multiple times. Interviews were semi-structured and typically lasted about one hour. Most of the interviews took place in homes, offices, local restaurants, and less formally on main street, in local businesses during working hours, or while attending community events. Most of the interviews were taped and transcribed verbatim for analysis. In the semi-structured interviews, I asked informants about employment benefits from a multimillion-dollar forest products plant recruited into the community in the 1960s, and social and economic changes that occurred since the company's establishment in Forestville. Other sources of data were tax records and several federal, state, and local documents in the tax collector, tax assessor, and probate judge offices. These sources were used to supplement the description provided by the informants.

FINDINGS

The first issue examined is that of employment benefits, because according to the growth machine hypothesis, "a key ideological prop for the growth machine, especially in appealing to the working class, is the assertion that local growth 'makes' jobs" (Logan and Molotch 1987, 88).

When public officials and influential community residents were asked about the promised local employment benefits from the Forest Products Company, many of them expressed the opinion that their community has not benefited from the company. One public official replied:

I don't think they give a better share back to the community like they should. For example, a lot of our people are not being employed by the company. The industry is in our community and does not pay taxes but the bulk of the people that are employed at the mill are from other counties surrounding us. They are tax-free and we are poverty stricken. Though we've got 40 to 50 percent of our people on welfare programs, the company officials care less to employ them. So, a majority of the residents do not benefit from the company except the privileged landowners.

Available data from the Alabama Department of Economic and Community Affairs showing where employees live support this resident's contention. In 1993, 881 citizens of Forestville were receiving financial assistance, 659 were receiving Aid to Dependent Children (AFDC) and 5,499 were food stamp recipients. In comparison to Alabama, Forestville does not fare well.

The above narrative illustrates a major theme embedded in the case study data. Regarding employment benefits, most of the residents interviewed believed that the majority of the Forestvillians have not benefited from the company, though they support the company with their local taxes. Some long-term Forestville residents, particularly older persons and people who managed to become a part of the white-collar economy, lamented during interviews that, in their opinion, many of the younger people have not benefited from the company's presence.

The tax collector explained that:

Even when it comes to the percentage of the employees at the plant and, you know, when you look, about 80 percent of their work force is out of the county and the plant is here. They're not paying their fair share back to the residents. I think that we should have more citizens of our county employed within the mill. They get away with a lot of tax money. For example, they have ad valorem tax exemption.

Another resident put it this way, "we cannot dream of being employed by one of the largest companies in Alabama located in our community. Yet, the company has many tax exemptions."

Research on employees of the company by place of residence revealed that of the 1,027 employees, 325 (32 percent) are from Forestville. Only 78 (25 percent of Forestville workers) are salaried workers. The remaining 75 percent are hourly workers. Data available from the U.S. Department of Commerce, Bureau of the Census for 1990 commuting patterns show that 1,870 workers commute to and work in Forestville, while 908 Forestvillians commute to work elsewhere. This finding supports the contention of Molotch (1976) and Logan and Molotch (1987) that the assertion by landholding elites that local growth generates jobs is little more than empty rhetoric. In Forestville, local growth has not generated a large number of jobs, but merely distributed them from a finite pool of national employment opportunities as claimed by the growth machine hypothesis (see Molotch 1976; Logan and Molotch 1987, 89).

To some extent, there is an agreement among residents that the forest products company in their community has not been effective in helping to employ citizens and in improving the community's economy and way of life. One elderly Forestville native, when asked about employment benefits from the forest products company in his community, replied:

Well, the fact is that a lot of us have never benefited from the company. They do not employ our own people. Furthermore, they built a big apartment building, a shopping center, and a golf club in the neighboring community where many of them live but nothing in our own community where their plant is located.

The other major consequence of growth predicted by the "growth machine" hypothesis (Molotch 1976, 315) is that there may be a tendency for growth to be associated with a high rate of unemployment. The data (the unemployment rates from 1980–1994) support the contention of many residents that they have not benefited from the company. Since 1980, the unemployment rates for Forestville are higher than those of Alabama and the United States.

There were clear benefits to landowners and housing and property development agents. A company official explained some of them:

When I first saw this site, the road was unpaved, but there was a little area cleared with ten acres of cotton and twenty acres of corn. From this land the owner grossed about six thousand dollars a year. That's gross. He has to pay his wages, seed, and fertilizer. Today this same property is grossing over forty million dollars.

Some of the citizens complained that elected officials, such as the mayor, are taking advantage of their position for their own gain. Some of the informants believe this complaint to be true. One woman informant had this to say about the mayor, who was influential in recruiting the company:

Our mayor is a realtor and an appraiser. He has his own business and he takes care of that and tries to look over that and protect it when things come in that matter to his business.

He owns houses that he rents out to some of the people working at the mill. The general impression is that officials work for themselves, it's me first and then the people of Forestville. We have major problems here. I hope that we can work together and get them ironed out so that we can make things better.

Concerning housing and property development, one young informant said "white people within the clique always develop properties and they make money off the development. For example, when the industry came here, the inner clique was involved in the development of the property and they made money off it." In a similar vein, another knowledgeable male resident argued that:

People try to bring things that will be of their own gain to Forestville and so they can make the money. Now, the mayor is a realtor. He is the owner of a realty company and he is also a licensed Alabama appraiser. When he helped in bringing the industry from Canada he gained in housing development and things like that. He owns the housing on Highway 28. You know, people in power, and I can't say how I'd do if I was in power and could stop something that was going to benefit me financially.

One informant thinks that there is too much corruption among elected officials because, he believes, officials always do things that will have immediate benefit for them. He said, "they do not want any development or growth that will benefit all or most of the community residents. They seek personal gains and interests." Lending support to this contention, the editor of a newspaper said:

We have some totally incompetent public officials. Ninety percent of them are concerned only with their own little agenda and that agenda is to stay in office and keep drawing the check for whatever office they hold and other benefits from any development they support in the community such as the industry they recruited a long time ago.

CONCLUSION

This case study tests some of the contentions of the growth machine hypothesis regarding economic development. Findings from Forestville, Alabama, support Molotch's contention that the community can serve as a "growth machine" for segments of the local elite. For example, consistent with Molotch's (1976) prediction, ideology was used by elected public officials and some powerful residents to recruit the forest products company to this rural community. Benefits from the economic development efforts promised by public officials and some groups in this rural southern community are exclusionary. The development effort was aimed at generating profits for the elite with the promise of jobs used as justification for economic growth. The Pine Hill Associates sold their 750 acres of land to the company. This supports Molotch's (1976, 309) assertion that "land is a market commodity providing wealth and power, and that some very important people consequently, take a keen interest in it." In an extended discussion, Molotch argues that growth profits those who control land in the community and that they have a common interest in promoting and gaining the rewards of growth. This seems to be true in Forestville. Pine Hill Associate members who owned land sold their land to the company and some of them were also employed when site clearing and construction began in July of 1966. One of them later became the president of the company. Today, some of the original members of the Pine Hill Associates are still employed with the company. Some of them celebrated 25 years of employment with the company at the end of 1993.

A firm recruited with tax and other incentives from local residents created jobs and other benefits; however, the majority of the beneficiaries are not local residents but live in neighboring communities. In Forestville, community is an arena of self-serving action rather than a cohesive acting unit. Public resources were used for the development of private gain. Thus, growth promotion may be suspect as a development strategy because it may reflect elite interests rather than the interests of the community as a whole (Molotch 1976).

While Molotch's (1976) contention that community mobilization tends to be class action, serving only the interest of those in the community who control key resources such as land without regard for the costs to the local community, is supported by the findings of this research, there is an alternative explanation. It is possible that the relatively small size of Forestville prevented it from capturing the majority of the benefits. Regardless of the reason or reasons behind the relatively small beneficial impact, this case illustrates that when small communities pursue large employers, many of the benefits may accrue in communities that did not contribute to the costs of attracting the firm.

DISCUSSION QUESTIONS FROM THE EDITORS

1. Was the Forestville industrial recruitment project a success? Why or why not?

2. How might Forestville residents who work elsewhere or who are unemployed benefit from the presence of the wood products firm?

3. What steps might Forestville have taken to ensure that more of the benefits of having the plant were felt by residents of the city?

NOTE

This research is supported by a grant from Tennessee Valley Authority Rural Studies Program (Competitive Research Contract No. UKRF 433441-98-19). The author wishes to express appreciation to Yetunde Williams and Mamo Abeye for research assistance.

CHAPTER 20

Economic Development Agendas and the Rhetoric of Local Community Action: Locating Mercedes Benz in Vance, Alabama

Ralph B. Brown, Clark D. Hudspeth, and Janet S. Odom

INTRODUCTION

In a global economy dominated by multinationals, to what extent can rural towns *act* to foster local economic development? Community development theories generally hold that collective action at the local level along with infrastructure development are key elements in attracting new business and/or industry to an area (Castle 1991). On September 30, 1993, Mercedes Benz announced the site for the auto maker's first U.S. factory——Vance, Alabama, located 30 miles east of Tuscaloosa. The state of Alabama expects more than 9,500 new direct and indirect jobs in the first year, resulting in direct and indirect wages as high as $294 million. Further, tax receipts are projected to increase $16 million the first year (Tuscaloosa News [TTN] October 1993).

Mercedes could have built the new plant elsewhere. What was it about Vance, population 226, that put it above all other places being considered? Who were the players involved in the effort to locate the Mercedes facility in Vance, and what was the role of the community itself?

RURAL TOWNS AND THE GLOBAL ECONOMY

Rural areas have moved beyond an insular local economic base to places with a genuine stake in the global economy. Extensive national and global markets provide consumer products to even the most isolated rural resident (Brown 1993). These global economic forces have dramatically reshaped the face of rural America, and new obstacles constantly present themselves to rural residents attempting to gain or maintain some degree of control over local development processes. About one-half of America's labor market areas are rural (Flora et al. 1992). During the 1970s, manufacturers began leaving urban areas, taking advantage of cheaper rural labor and land. Thus, by 1979, manufacturing had become the largest employer of the rural work force. Therefore, one way rural towns have tried to remain economically viable is through attracting manufacturing industries. Attracting industry to a specific locale implies a deliberate organized effort at some level to "sell" the site and distinguish it from among all other possible suitors.

How well this local activeness model actually applies to contemporary rural places whose immediate economic fortunes have long been removed from the locale itself has not been extensively examined. Therefore, the role of community organizing is examined in the case of Vance, Alabama, and the siting of the Mercedes Benz plant. Understanding why Vance was selected as the site for the Mercedes plant will facilitate a greater understanding of how large-scale economic development in rural locales often works in a global economy and to what extent rural communities act to bring about its development.

VANCE

Vance was founded around 1830. Timber and agriculture have been main contributors to the economic base of the area. After a century of slow growth, by the late 1950s, established businesses began to "die off," largely due to improvements in transportation and changes in the local economy. The result has been to further tie the residents' economic fortunes to neighboring Tuscaloosa. Thus, most residents who lived in and around Vance have found employment in the surrounding larger cities.

THE RHETORIC OF LOCAL ACTION AND MERCEDES BENZ

In 1992, a new mayor, along with two other council members, began taking an active role in the Tuscaloosa County Industrial Development Authority (IDA). They felt that IDA involvement would afford the best opportunity to attract more industry or businesses to their town. It appears they got much more than they bargained for. Indeed, residents from the Vance area generally saw the Mercedes deal as a process external to them. They were also of the opinion that the IDA was primarily responsible for Mercedes Benz locating in Vance. A former Vance official remarked that:

The IDA and, to a lesser extent, a state senator were the key people who put the Mercedes deal together. Primarily two members of the IDA executive board were handling the negotiations with Mercedes and had already decided on the Vance site. Vance has representatives on the IDA board—two council members and the Mayor— who knew about the Mercedes deal but due to their positions, were sworn to secrecy until its official announcement. Consequently, Vance representatives had only a very small active voice in the Mercedes deal and were excluded from the upper-level negotiations.

Economies of scale were in favor of the IDA, which could afford to finance larger projects and thus do more to promote economic development than could the much smaller Vance. As one interviewee explained, "It was really all cut and dried before hand; it was a big boy's game and Tuscaloosa was the pros playing in that ball game and we [Vance] were just a high school team." It appears community action in Vance was nonexistent (both for or against Mercedes). This changed, however, when a battle between Vance and Tuscaloosa began as a result of a proposed annexation of a 14-mile corridor along Interstate 59/20 by Tuscaloosa. Certain Vance officials began to be more proactive and fairly unified in their opposition activities. Yet these activities have been directed toward Tuscaloosa, not Mercedes Benz. To date, the only organized opposition in Vance remains strictly the mayor and town council. They have rightly viewed this 14-mile corridor as the location where many of the spin-off industries will locate. With Tuscaloosa annexing the corridor, Vance City has lost any opportunity to tax potential enterprises that locate there. Consequently, Vance has tried to secure other spin-off potential (they have invested in sewer and water lines for the area) and to challenge the legal basis of Tuscaloosa City's annexation of the corridor. These strategies and tactics by Vance City in an effort to save a piece of the "pie" in this annexation war are clearly more reactive than active. Therefore, the organized community endeavors occurring in Vance have been community reaction, not community action.

Because it appears Vance officials and residents had a minimal role in securing the Mercedes plant, who were the major actors? Key informant interviews point to the political leadership of the state of Alabama, officials from the Alabama Development Office (ADO), and the IDA. Each played their own part in bringing Mercedes to Vance. However, they also show that two IDA officials were the primary actors in securing Mercedes. As for either promoting the Mercedes project or opposing it, "There was no individual or group in Vance that was active in promoting the Mercedes Benz deal besides the town officials on the IDA and they only had a small voice. Though some individuals would speak out against Mercedes Benz coming here, no action was ever taken by them other than to make plans to leave."

Informants stated that although, initially, Billy Joe Camp of the ADO was responsible for Mercedes locating in Alabama, two IDA officials did all of the "legwork" and put together the package. They knew of the Vance site and had previously shown it to other corporate prospects — Stress Creek and Saturn. Again, Vance was only involved in the project in so much that it had IDA membership.

So, was it Tuscaloosa that "advanced" Vance? Interviews from key actors in Tuscaloosa show that the economic development system (e.g., the ADO and IDA) that has been in place in the state for decades was primarily responsible for Mercedes Benz locating in Alabama. The ADO (namely, Billy Joe Camp and Glenn Pringle) and the IDA (specifically, Dara Longgrear and Chairman

Anthony Topazi) met with Mercedes officials, enticed them to visit Alabama, entertained them once they arrived, set up the itineraries, and planned the strategies to bring Mercedes to Vance. "Tuscaloosa played a very critical role in this: Tuscaloosa would have to be one of those 'why we got its.' "

The IDA had developed an experienced group of people who also had very good governmental continuity with the speaker of the senate and other representatives in Montgomery, as well as a four-term probate judge and a four-term mayor (both in Tuscaloosa) and Billy Joe Camp as ADO director. Vance's role was simply confined to having members on the IDA who apparently had little or no voice in the decision. The members of the IDA from Vance "were not instrumental in any way in meeting with Mercedes representatives and selling this project."

In addition to interviews, numerous articles published in the *Tuscaloosa News* (TTN) between October 1993 and January 1995 were examined. Information gathered from these was supportive of that gleaned from the interview data. Newspaper data indicate that, for all practical purposes, a total of seven people were responsible for bringing Mercedes to Vance, Alabama: Governor Jim Folsom, ADO Director Billie Joe Camp, ADO Director of Industrial Development Glen Pringle, IDA Chairman and Vice President Western Division Alabama Power Company Anthony Topazi, IDA Executive Director Dara Longgrear, IDA Vice Chairman Tom Joiner, and IDA Treasurer Bryan Chandler. Moreover, it affirms that Topazi and Longgrear were responsible for practically all negotiations with Mercedes. The majority of IDA board members described their personal involvement as minimal as they authorized Topazi and Longgrear to proceed autonomously with recruitment efforts.

The articles also indicate that the major reasons for Mercedes Benz locating in America, in Alabama, and particularly in Vance, were: in-place infrastructure, available land in proximity to urban areas and amenities, the economic atmosphere in the United States (as compared to Germany), and the incentive package offered Mercedes by the state of Alabama that was four times the amount of some states' offers and exceeded the second-place bidder by $104 million.

Joab Thomas, president of the University of Alabama 1981 to 1988, commented that "road, rail and even river transportation modes were in place and framed the area perfectly for such a development" (TTN 10 October 1993).

Despite the activities of the key people and organizations identified above, and in addition to the in-place infrastructure of the area, the extremely lucrative incentive package offered by the state of Alabama was very important. The Alabama legislature set up a plan that allowed Mercedes to keep 5 percent of its workers' wages to pay off construction debts of $300 million (the workers will get a matching tax break) and approved a 25-year corporate tax holiday for the company. The state paid the workers while they were in training, the trainers, and for construction of the training facility. In addition, in December 1993, the Alabama Department of Economic and Community affairs approved a grant for improvements to the site and surrounding area for $426.3 million. According to TTN (1994), this grant was used as follows:

- Site acquisition, $5.3 million
- Site preparation, $12.4 million
- Site improvement, $10 million
- Plant facility, equipment, and other expenses, $30 million
- Railroad extension, $4 million
- Job training facility, $30 million
- Service center building, $5 million
- Fire station, $.6 million
- Interstate interchange and access roads, $50 million
- Water and sewer, $11 million

Relative costs of labor between Germany and the United States also played a role in locating a plant in the United States. Mercedes Board Member Dieter Zetsche explained that not only is the German auto worker a generation older than his or her American counterpart, he or she averages between 300 to 400 fewer hours of work per year and earns up to $15 an hour more (TTN 10 October 1993). "It's cheaper to do business here [in the United States]." Mercedes also expects the largest percent of sales of its new SUVs (Sport Utility Vehicles) built at the Vance site to be to the American public, therefore another "important reason for coming to the U.S. was the market." By building in America, Mercedes is able to dodge a 25 percent import tariff. Thus, the savings on production and labor costs also add to the list of reasons for locating the facility in the United States.

The various aspects of the incentive package have been largely downplayed by both Mercedes and the state of Alabama, which is understandable given the unprecedented size of the package and the negative publicity it has generated. Others, however, have not downplayed incentives as a reason to locate in Alabama. Fieldcrest Cannon Company Chairman James M. Fitzgibbons stated that the economic incentives were instrumental in his company's decision to locate in Alabama rather than Georgia: "Economically, it was more feasible to locate in Alabama" (TTN 15 February 1994). Supporting this declaration was an article revealing that 11 other firms were also to receive sizable tax breaks if they located in Alabama (TTN 17 February 1994). It is apparent that significant cost reductions due to both location factors and the incentive package also contributed greatly to the decision to locate in Vance.

MAKING SENSE OF THE FINDINGS

There were essentially four entities involved in the decision process of choosing Vance, each with its own particular goals in mind: Mercedes Benz, the state of Alabama (specifically, the governor and the ADO), the city and county of Tuscaloosa (specifically, the IDA), and in a minimal role, the town of Vance (specifically, city officials of Vance).

Mercedes Benz had made a decision to go into the lucrative new SUV market as part of the Daimler plan to be one of the top multinational corporations in the global economy (TTN 10 October 1993). There were three overriding issues that influenced Mercedes' decision-making process: the market, tariffs, and production costs. All of these were facilitated by a significantly cheaper American labor force and an enormous reduction in capital outlays as a result of Alabama's incentive package, estimated to have been worth between $253 million and $500 million.

Alabama's reasons for pursuing Mercedes extended beyond expected immediate and direct revenue increases for the state. They were looking at two main objectives with the Mercedes deal: (1) Long-range economic gains; and (2) positive social and economic image. Not unlike other southern states, Alabama has an image problem state officials were trying to overcome (Billings 1988; TTN 10 October 1993). Government officials and industry promoters in the state believed that hanging the Mercedes "star" over Alabama would result in immediate revenue increases and destroy the view of the state as a "red-headed stepchild," moving them up to "world-class" status (TTN 10 October 1993).

The IDA's motivations for persuading Mercedes to locate its new SUV plant in Vance parallel those of the state. Revenue gains and publicity windfalls were expected to make Tuscaloosa County in general, and the city of Tuscaloosa in particular, the leading economy in northwest Alabama (TTN 10 October 1993).

Vance's initial interests in economic development, however, were not so lofty. Vance officials were looking for ways to achieve a slower, more controlled growth for their small town. For them, the winning of Mercedes was more a matter of "being in the right place at the right time" than deliberate action on their part. Since they had decided to put active board members on the IDA as a means of facilitating the city's growth effort, they can ultimately claim participation in the courting of Mercedes. However, the IDA had shown the site to other industries before these Vance City members joined the IDA (in particular the Saturn plant that finally located in Tennessee) and was continually seeking a large industry to locate there. Therefore, it is more than likely that the Mercedes plant would have been located in Vance whether or not town officials were involved in the process.

CONCLUSION

In the case of Vance, there are several implications to the issue of effectiveness of local community action and development. First, top-down development efforts based on supply-side, trickle-down economic philosophy assures that the lion's share of economic gains will accrue at the top. Second, intervention into the process (i.e., community/economic development in an attempt to capture gains which do not accrue at the top) is at the intermediate level (e.g., Tuscaloosa [City and County] in concert with the state of Alabama) and not at the specific local level (e.g., Vance). Finally, large-scale economic development at the local level is more likely to be the result of actions by players in the global market than of efforts at the grass-roots level. In fact, as the experience of Vance illustrates, local efforts are often a reaction to changes imposed from the outside and not directly targeted at the development project itself.

Vance's experience also shows that there is a conflict of ideology between a global market economy and its articulation at the local community level. Vance demonstrates that in the global economic context, extralocal actors (i.e., Mercedes Benz) will by-and-large determine the parameters within which the event could occur. The large influence of "global actors" therefore determines what options are available to participants at the local level (Logan and Molotch 1987; Offe 1985). Local-level actors (e.g., residents of Vance) would therefore have a limited range of options from which to formulate a strategy and thus are forced primarily into a reactionary posture. Therefore, by its very nature, organizing for action in such a context becomes reactionary as residents must first organize to legitimize an opposing view to the existing norms of the global market economy.

The Mercedes Benz project was "signed, sealed, and delivered" before any but three residents of Vance even knew anything of it. Additionally, Tuscaloosa with its existing legal infrastructure and superior financing, not to mention advanced knowledge of site location and negotiations, was able to legally annex a 14-mile corridor to the gates of the plant, thus capturing potential spin-offs from the expected Mercedes induced growth. At this point, Vance could only react from a position of weakness vis-a-vis Mercedes Benz and the city of Tuscaloosa, as it is left with very little in its power to organize in light of the changes facing it. Consequently, residents of Vance have begun the process of organizing the only thing they have some modicum of control over—their own sense, identity, and definition of community. This they can achieve; they cannot block the construction of the plant or the Tuscaloosa annexation, as these events have already transpired external to them.

DISCUSSION QUESTIONS FROM THE EDITORS

1. Representatives of Vance who were members of the Industrial Development Authority were "sworn to secrecy" about the new plant. Why would people want to keep the project secret?

2. The state of Alabama gave Mercedes a 25-year tax holiday and provided other incentives that cost it money? Why?

3. What are some of the benefits other than jobs and tax base that might accrue to Vance because it is home to a Mercedes-Benz plant?

CHAPTER 21

The Development by a Community and Its Part Ownership of an Investor-Owned Manufacturing Plant

David Zimet

"There's an old saying, 'Heroes come along when you need them.'"
John Street

INTRODUCTION

This case study tells the story of an investment of approximately $180,000 that created a major industrial plant. It is unlike many other industrial attraction projects in that it did not rely on large incentives offered to a firm. The investment discussed included some public funds and a good deal of work and initiative by community leaders. It took more than ten years, much hard work from a variety of community leaders, some originality, some help from an array of public institutions and agencies, community support, and at least one false trail before a good idea resulted in a major investment. This chapter tells the story of the effort required. Other authors have reported unsuccessful attempts to develop major projects (for example, Ramsay 1996).

This case study describes the development a medium-density fiberboard plant (MDF) in Clarion County, Pennsylvania. Although individual leaders are highlighted, the reader must realize that those individuals viewed (and still view) themselves as part of a team. The acknowledged leader of that team was John Street, the executive director of the Clarion County Economic Development Corporation. He coordinated the efforts of other individuals and facilitated their work to make sure that things got done in a timely fashion. Strong community support was also an important factor in the successful completion of the project described here.

The chapter is organized as follows: First, economic and institutional settings of Clarion County are presented in the introduction. The organizations that created the situation for the development of the medium-density fiberboard plant are also discussed to a limited extent. In the next section, the history of the planning and collaborative efforts that led to the establishment of the MDF plant are presented. Finally, the present situation is described. In the words of one of the community leaders who worked to make the MDF plant a reality, its establishment shows "what a community can do if it supports an idea. You need a sound idea, but the community must get behind it." The goal of this chapter is to relate the story of Clarion County's success.

This chapter is based upon interviews conducted by William K. McAllister and this author in the fall of 1994, within weeks after the U.S. Forest Service pledged $50,000 for the development of a detailed business plan (McAllister and Zimet 1994), and interviews conducted in the summer of 1998. In 1994, we learned of the process that led to the establishment of the plant. At that time, however, some of the critical events were too recent to allow for adequate perspective or thought. In addition, the plant had yet to be constructed—that required almost two more years. The 1998 interviews have the advantages of historical perspective and the experience of establishing the medium density fiberboard plant. By 1998, the long-sought project had become a reality, employed 100 people, and produced a high-value product.

ECONOMIC AND INSTITUTIONAL SETTING

Economic Setting

Clarion County is located in the wood basket of the Allegheny National Forest. Its economic history is not dissimilar to that of other counties in the area. Its economy, like that of nearby counties, has been natural resource dependent (primarily coal mining and timber). The region suffered from the decline in the importance of mining and other extractive industries. The following numbers illustrate the dramatic decline of mining. In the late 1970s, a local bituminous coal surface mine employed some 1,000 people. During the 1980s and into the 1990s, employment declined steadily, to only 125 in 1994. The unemployment rate in the county rose to more than 16 percent. Six thousand jobs were lost in a three-year period and prospects for improvement were not good. During the same time, Pittsburgh (some 100 miles to the southeast) also lost much of its traditional industrial base. The only positive development was that demand for the principal products of the area—manufactured housing and hardwood products such as veneers and furniture—increased during the 1980s. Thus, the region's hardwood sawmills continued to operate. Byproducts were sawdust and other wood waste materials.

Institutional Setting

In the early 1980s, four county economic development organizations existed in Clarion County. The organizations reflected the recognition by local public officials that there was a need to plan for economic diversification and an acknowledgment that flexibility was required for success. The four institutions were:

- The Clarion County Industrial Development Authority (IDA), a five-member public body with the authority under state law to issue industrial revenue bonds. Its members are appointed by the Board of County Commissioners.
- The Clarion County Economic Development Council (EDC), an advisory public body of 11 members with the goal of generating ideas for economic diversification. The EDC members are also appointed by the Board of County Commissioners. The EDC has three committees; their focus areas are natural resources, education, and tourism.
- The Clarion County Economic Development Corporation (EDCorp), a private, nonprofit organization which had the responsibility of assembling public and private funding for specific projects. Like the EDC, it started in 1982. Its membership is private. In 1989, it became a private not-for-profit corporation to increase flexibility. The EDCorp evolved into the lead development organization after it won 501(c)(3) status from the U.S. Internal Revenue Service. The offices of the IDA, EDC, and the EDCorp were located in the same building in Shippenville.
- In addition, there was the Chamber of Commerce, to promote the county and assist retail businesses in the borough of Clarion. The chamber was located in Clarion, the county seat.

That these entities were able to work together demonstrates that, in spite of the multiple levels of local government in Pennsylvania, Clarion County is a special place. The number of local governments makes collaboration difficult. In Clarion County there are seven school districts, each with its own elected board, 20 townships which have three elected supervisors each, and 13 boroughs which are governed by a mayor and a council. County residents are exposed more to fragmentation than they are to unity. Although the large number of jurisdictions sometimes hampered the project, the county government and at least two townships were able to collaborate to develop the MDF plant.

EVOLUTION OF THE MDF PLANT

"You need a sound idea, but the community must get behind it."
Larry Heasley

In 1984, Larry Heasley, a businessman and resident of Shippenville in Clarion County, chaired the Natural Resources Committee of the Clarion County Economic Development Council (EDC). He believed that wood waste materials could be used to produce fiberboard, particle board, and two new products, oriented-strand board and medium-density fiberboard. He approached the EDC with the idea. The council championed the idea to establish a plant that would utilize wood residue and wood waste. It acted in the conventional way by organizing a search to recruit an outside firm.

Industrial Recruitment

The industrial recruitment effort was initiated with a feasibility study to clarify production options by estimating the availability of raw materials required for each of the four product alternatives (fiberboard, particle board, medium-density fiberboard, and oriented-strand board). Such a study was necessary because different proportions of hardwood and softwood are necessary for each product. Medium density fiberboard requires a relatively large proportion of hardwood (in the form of sawdust), while conventional fiberboard and particle board requires relatively little hardwood. The EDC commissioned Columbia Engineering Company of British Columbia, Canada, to perform the study for $20,000. The consulting company reported that the wood residue of Clarion County included sufficient hardwood waste to consider the production of MDF.

Failure

Eight firms were identified as potential producers of medium-density fiberboard or other similar wood products, but only one particle board producer responded to initial contacts. This producer decided to locate a new particle board plant one hour north of Clarion. Overall, about three years passed between the first public discussion of Mr. Heasley's idea and the company's decision. No other formal marketing or prospecting effort was put forward. Because of a rift in the community, the idea of an industrial plant was not pursued for several years after the initial failure, and Columbia Engineering Corporation's feasibility study languished on the shelf.

The failure of the recruitment effort taught the individuals involved that they could not depend upon the location of Clarion County to "sell" a project. They came to realize that Clarion County was not unique. There were other counties that were also located in the "wood basket of the East." Thus, Clarion County had to do more than just promote its location. The failure also convinced some of those involved that, if the county was to derive benefit from the raw materials feasibility study (a positive and assertive step on its own), it should become entrepreneurial. The promotion of the potential to produce medium-density fiberboard , a product well suited for the waste stream of the area, was a step in this direction. The EDCorp developed the idea into a fundable business project, complete with site and business plans and financial alternatives.

Participants in the effort also realized that more public funds would have to be used to develop the business plan for an MDF plant because MDF was a new product. Because it was a new product, some participants believed that MDF was inappropriate for their development efforts and that trying to establish such a plant was poor use of public funds. After several years and much public discussion, the rift was healed. The public discussion or education about the plant was to be an important factor several years later, however. Community leaders realized that the promotion of an MDF plant would require more information for prospective producers. A comprehensive business plan would generate such information.

Further Studies and Community Participation

A consultant capable of performing the complete study or business was identified in the original feasibility study. According to that study, $200,000 was required to develop a complete business plan. There were sufficient funds to perform the initial material feasibility study, but not to develop complete plans, which required a set of tests (such as wood quality and adhesive compatibility tests), labor availability information, and a development plan, including financing for the plant. Dr. Tom Vernon of Clarion University informed the EDCorp of the possibility of obtaining funding from the Center for Rural Pennsylvania, a state program. An application was submitted, and the center provided the $50,000 match required by the U.S. Forest Service (USFS), yielding a total of $100,000. The EDCorp contributed $10,000. No other funds were available from either the community or the state. Ron VanDenHeuval, owner of Spirit Construction, the firm that was recommended by the original consultant, added approximately $90,000. In addition, the College of Business of Clarion University, in the person of Dr. Joseph Grunenwald, agreed to participate in the development of the plan at a much-reduced price by having students perform some of the analysis. Thus, the equivalent of more than $200,000 was obtained.

Through community support, a site for the MDF plant was made available. At the time the funds for the comprehensive study were being sought, a local landowner offered an option on a property of 170 acres, with a rail spur through it, to the EDCorp. The option price was $1.00. The property is located between the cities of Shippenville and Clarion. A local engineering firm signed a contract to carry out the site design and develop cost estimates for an access road and water and sewer services.

A Different Kind of Ownership

"Certainly the twists and turns in terms of the key players, that was surprising,"
Joe Grunenwald

In 1994, the EDCorp initiated work on the comprehensive plan. While the EDCorp prepared the plan, the EDC helped garner community support for the project. The development of the plan revealed many complexities and complications to the EDCorp. While organizing the original tests and surveys, the EDCorp realized the need for speed and flexibility when negotiating contracts. The realization of the complexity of the project, the need for flexibility, and the experience with the failed effort to recruit a company, convinced the EDCorp that it would have to participate actively in the development of such a plant. Thus, in late 1994, the EDCorp created Clarion Fiber, Inc. to manage the financial aspects necessary for the establishment of the new industrial plant. The EDCorp owned 26 percent of Clarion Fiber. The remaining 74 percent of stock was owned by Ron VanDenHeuval, who was interested in constructing the plant.

Despite the fact that a company was created through local and outside investments, many steps had to be performed before an industrial plant could be built. None of the parties from outside of Clarion County were committed to develop such a plant, only to determine the feasibility of doing so. As evidenced by their investments, however, all concerned believed that there was a high probability that a successful plant could be developed. The natural resources, an appropriate site with rail access and water, and labor were available. The county was willing to promote financing by issuing industrial revenue bonds.

The Comprehensive Planning Study

The EDCorp, in the person of John Street, coordinated the comprehensive planning study for Clarion Fiber. To satisfy the bond underwriting company, a series of studies were performed. It often seemed that one study gave rise to the need for one or more ancillary studies. For example, the soil physics study revealed that the abandoned strip mine on the site had created large pits of organic debris, such as tree trunks. These pits would not provide a suitable base for a foundation that had to support heavy machinery. Addressing this concern required additional studies and tests. In addition, many sawdust samples were sent to Europe to verify compatibility with adhesives. Other studies included due diligence to assure the absence of potential Native American archeological sites. The EDCorp had to provide further evidence of labor availability and quality. The financial or economic plan or study, including market evaluations, was also of critical importance. Because medium-density fiberboard was a new product, the economic analysis was highly sensitive. The viability of the entire project often rested on the results of a single test.

Financing the MDF Plant

Finally, all tests were completed satisfactorily, and the time to sell bonds arrived. The Pennsylvania Department of Environmental Protection (DEP) had classified sawdust as an environmental hazard.[1] Because the MDF plant was to use sawdust as a raw material, the plant would be eliminating an environmental hazard. The plant owners were therefore eligible to sell tax-free bonds to support the plant. Even eligibility under this program was not always secure, however.

When the MDF plant was still only an idea, sawdust had no value and was viewed as a relatively costly waste. The development of the plan to establish the plant caused the value of sawdust to increase to as much as $22 per ton. According to the Pennsylvania DEP, such a value implied that sawdust was not a hazardous waste. The case had to be argued that sawdust was indeed a waste and that it was the possibility of establishing the plant that generated the value in the first place. With the support of State Representative David Wright, the EDCorp prevailed.

McMillan-Bloedel (M-B), a major Canadian wood products company, announced its intention to establish the MDF plant. EDCorp could not guarantee the bonds and also be an owner of the plant, so it sold its share to Ron VanDenHeuval for approximately $180,000,[2] a greatly reduced price, to avoid further delay because of price negotiations. Market value was not truly established until $99 million in industrial revenue bonds sold in 17 minutes. This result made it clear that the market valued the project very highly.

The work of EDCorp and EDC was not over when the bonds were sold. The EDCorp worked to overcome or circumvent a variety of problems, including rail accessibility and water availability. In addition, although the high quality of the labor force was attractive to the outside owners, the labor force was untrained in the use of the specialized machinery used in the plant. Thus, when the plant was ready to become operational, $500,000 was needed to train the employees. The EDC helped to locate the resources, and the Clarion County Career Center (the county's vocational technology school) did the training. For a temporary outlay of approximately $180,000 in public funds, a plant valued at more than $100 million was established.

Current Situation and Ownership

Clarion Fiber, Inc., started operations in July 1996, under the joint ownership of M-B and Ron Van Den Heuval, with 100 employees; it employs approximately the same number today. There is a significant learning curve for those who operate an MDF plant because the equipment is very sophisticated and each product order is distinct. Specifications concerning hardness and shape vary with each order. To meet specifications, each batch of MDF must be formulated, using varying proportions of hardwood (and species of tree) and different combinations of resins and glues. According to Mike Barnes, the production manager of the plant, it takes from three to five years for an MDF plant to reach production capacity. Product quality is generally lower during the starting period than after a plant has been fully operational for a period of time. In this regard, the MDF plant in Clarion County is above the norm; the plant will reach capacity within three years. More impressively, it is already known as a quality producer of MDF and therefore its product is in high demand.

The importance of early outreach efforts or extensive discussion at the community level cannot be overstated. Because questions were addressed in that early stage, there has been little opposition to the heavy industrial plant. Owners of property that borders the industrial park on which the MDF plant is located, have protested the dust generated by the plant. The plant already has purchased some of those properties and has agreed to purchase others. The protest continues, however. It is noteworthy that Protect Environment and Children Everywhere (PEACE), an active local environmental group, has not supported that protest because the plant removes a hazardous waste while generating jobs and income in Clarion County, the dust is not a hazard to the vast majority of county residents, and the operation of the plant does not stimulate tree harvest.

WHY CLARION? CONCLUDING REMARKS

> *"The key players spent many, many hours . . . trying to make it work."*
> *Valerie Decorte*

There is not much to differentiate Clarion County from its neighbors. Clarion University is perhaps the only tangible difference between the city of Clarion and other cities in Clarion County, and between Clarion County and other counties in northwestern Pennsylvania. Other positive characteristics of Clarion County are not as objective, but there is an abundance of evidence that they are real. The entrepreneurial attitude of the EDCorp is the primary intangible factor. There would be no MDF plant in Clarion County if the EDCorp had not taken bold steps trying to create an industry. County residents take pride in the work ethic and skill of the labor force. As a result of those characteristics, according to Mr. Barnes, the plant has been noted as the best MDF start-up in North America. Valerie Decorte, the current executive director of the EDCorp, stressed the role individuals played in organizing the resources necessary to establish the plant. In sum, it is an attractive, vibrant county with forward-looking jurisdictions in which residents take a great deal of pride.

This project was based upon a good idea of a community leader. It took several years for the initial idea to become the basis for an industrial recruitment effort. The failed initial recruitment effort led to a community-based industrial development project. The transitions occurred through hard work and persistence over almost ten years. Clarion County was able to attract outside investors because the EDCorp and associated institutions created a set of necessary information, including complete business plans, for the development of a medium-density fiberboard plant. The EDCorp started with targeting an industry that matched the county's natural and industrial resource base. The plant depends upon those resources. It was not attracted to the county by offering spectacular financial incentives. Instead, the county raised a high-tech industry out of the dust of common industry because of pride and belief in its ability, and through great effort by many people associated with the EDCorp. The pride shines through in the words of Karen Pope, director of the Clarion Borough Chamber of Commerce and self-proclaimed cheerleader of Clarion County: "This is the only place I would ever want to raise my family."

DISCUSSION QUESTIONS FROM THE EDITORS

1. The author notes that the number of local governments made the process of establishing the new plant more complex. Would the public in Clarion County be better served by a unified government that covered all local government functions in the county? Why or why not?

2. How would a local landowner benefit by offering an option to sell 170 acres at a fixed price in exchange for $1? How would this option help the local Economic Development Corporation?

3. The author states in a footnote that sale of the bonds established market values of the 26 percent share in Clarion Fiber at $10 million. This 26 percent share was sold at cost to a local entrepreneur for $180,000. Was this a fair return on the entrepreneur's risk?

NOTES

1. The classification was made because as it decomposes, sawdust releases an acid that, unless the sawdust is handled as a hazard, leaches into the soil and eventually into the water table.

2. Cost was determined as the cost plus value, including grants, of conducting the various tests that were performed. The bond sale established an approximation of market value of the 26 percent at approximately $10 million.

CHAPTER 22

Local Capacity and Industrial Restructuring in the Periphery of Belgium and France

Bruno Henry de Frahan,
Pierre Dupraz, and Béatrice Van Haeperen

INTRODUCTION

Some European Union (EU) member countries have been much more successful at creating rural job growth than others. There are 195 regions designated as "rural" in the European Union. Almost one-third of these rural regions have a nonagricultural employment annual growth rate .5 percent above the national growth rate, while 49 regions are .25 percent below the national growth rate (Esposti et al. 1999). The capacity of local leaders to design and implement employment growth strategies has been shown to be particularly relevant (Von Meyer et al. 1999) in explaining some of the differences among these regions. This case study explores the specific role of local capacity in generating and sustaining employment growth.

This case study starts with a comparison of two contiguous rural regions similar in terms of resource endowment and rural amenities. Both regions were faced with industrial restructuring in the 1980s; one region's employment grew much faster. To contrast the two rural regions, a territorial approach and a "strengths, weaknesses, opportunities, and threats (SWOT)" analysis are used. The territorial approach views the rural region as a geographic and socioeconomic entity with relatively low population density. The SWOT analysis lists strengths and weaknesses of the rural regions in sustaining employment growth, and also examines the opportunities and threats within or outside the rural regions that may affect employment growth in the near future. Section 2 provides an overview of the two regions, with special emphasis on

Map 5
Local Capacity and Industrial Restructuring in the Periphery of Belgium and France

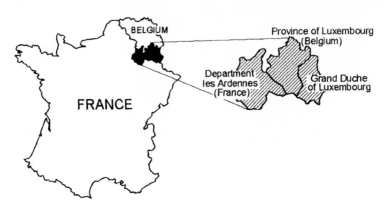

employment trends. Section 3 compares the strengths and weaknesses of the strategies used by local leaders to restructure their manufacturing sectors, as well as their capacity to implement these strategies. The final section draws some lessons and discusses some challenges for these two regions. More details can be found in Dupraz, Henry de Frahan, and Faucheux (1998) and Dupraz and Henry de Frahan (1998).

BASIC FACTS ABOUT THE CASE STUDY REGION

The Province of Luxembourg is in southeast Belgium and the Département Les Ardennes is in northeast France. Both regions are similar in terms of population and population density (about 55 persons per square kilometer). Les Ardennes has only one town with more than 30,000 inhabitants; Luxembourg has none (table 22.1). Despite sharing some common geographic, historic, and economic features, they have significantly diverged in terms of gross domestic product (GDP) and employment growth during the last two decades. They have also significantly diverged from the GDP and employment growth of their mother countries. While one region was outperforming the GDP and employment growth of its country, the other region was far below the national level of GDP and employment growth of its country.

The forest plateau of the Ardennes crosses both the Province of Luxembourg and the Département Les Ardennes. The fringes of the Ardennes forest have traditionally been devoted to meadows and pastures, while flat areas have been cultivated. On and around this plateau, both regions have specialized in forestry products and livestock breeding and, to a greater extent in the Département Les Ardennes, in milk production. The large fertile plain in the southern part of the Département Les Ardennes has been cultivated with cereals, sugar beets, and industrial crops. The industrial crops spawned a related processing industry. The two regions are similarly endowed with historic sites and beautiful countryside attractive for recreational purposes.

Both regions have a tradition of iron and steel manufacturing, and this industry modernized and expanded after World War II (between 1950 and 1970). Many of the workers in the iron and steel sector also maintained small farms. The expansion of the iron and steel industry was concentrated in the extreme south of the Province of Luxembourg and, to a larger extent, along the Meuse River in the northern part of the Département Les Ardennes. Along this river, an automotive industry has developed. In the late 1970s, a European crisis in the iron and steel industry struck both regions. In the Province of Luxembourg, the southern iron and steel site was abruptly closed in 1977, with its remaining 1,665 workers put out of work. In the Département Les Ardennes, the iron and steel crisis started later and extended over a much longer period than in the Province of Luxembourg. The crisis in Les Ardennes culminated in 1983, with the closure of two large state iron and steel plants along the Meuse River. The two plant closings put about 5,000 workers out of work; several family-owned, medium-size subcontracting firms also closed.

Table 22.1
Basic Socioeconomic Indicators

Regional Indicators	Luxembourg	Les Ardennes
Population, 1993	237,500	293,500
Annual Population Growth, 1981–91 (%)	0.5	-0.25
Size (square miles)	1,714	2,027
Density, 1993 (inhabitants/square miles)	139	145
Population of Largest Town, 1990	23,325	67,213
Number of Municipalities	44	421
Agricultural Area (1,000 acres)	339	823
Forest Area (1,000 acres)[a]	514	378
Number of Farms[a]	5,348	4,285
Nominal Annual GDP Growth, 1980–93 (%)	6.4	5.3
Per Capita GDP, 1993 (US$)[b]	17,241	19,124
Unemployment Rate, 1985	9.5	13.9
Annual Employment Growth, 1980–92 (%)[c]	0.89	-0.60
National Indicators	**Belgium**	**France**
Nominal Annual GDP Growth, 1980–93 (%)	5.9	6.4
Per Capita GDP, 1993 (US$)[b]	21,506	22,358
Unemployment Rate, 1985 (%)	11.3	9.8
Annual Employment Growth, 1980–92 (%)[c]	0.12	0.06

Notes:
[a] in 1992 for Luxembourg and 1995 for Les Ardennes
[b] 1 US$= 0.83 ECU (European Currency Unit) in October 1998
[c] between 1980 and 1993 for Les Ardennes
Source: de Schrevel (1994), EUROSTAT, INS, and INSEE

The traditional textile industry in the eastern part of the département also enjoyed a short postwar revival. However, competition from synthetic textile products hurt the once-flourishing textile industry of the département and led to its disappearance in the 1970s, creating unemployment for unskilled female workers. The cumulative result of these changes meant that the manufacturing industry of the département Les Ardennes lost about 8,500 jobs between 1981 and 1993. Since 1993, the food-processing industry in the département has been hit by closures. Most of the food processors in the southern part of the region closed as corporations located facilities elsewhere.

To recover the region's lost employment, officials from the Province of Luxembourg adopted a strategy of industrial recruitment. The governor and local business support agencies succeeded in attracting eight subsidiaries of multinational companies. Companies received financial incentives and investment subsidies that added up to 20 percent of the total investment; services to facilitate start-up operations for branch plants in the province; and assistance in helping foreign managers and their families adapt to their new environment. This concerted action generated more than 2,000 jobs between 1977 and 1990. In the mid–1980s, the governor of the Province of Luxembourg, the prime minister of the Grand Duché of Luxembourg, and the head of the French region of the Lorraine, initiated a multicountry European Development Pole (EDP). The EDP's objective was to generate 8,000 new jobs on the former sites of the iron and steel industry in the three bordering regions. Due to national and European investment subsidies amounting to about 30 percent of the total investment and the active role of local business support agencies, 1,443 more jobs were generated between 1988 and 1995 in the Belgian part of the region. Authorities in the Province of Luxembourg also improved the road network dramatically. This restructuring, as well as the improvement of the overall economic situation, helped the revival of the provincial economy since 1987, with the private sector now taking the lead in employment creation.

In the Département Les Ardennes, some existing small and medium-size enterprises (SMEs) of the iron and steel industry were able to adapt to the industrial crisis and remain competitive. These SMEs used national assistance funds either to specialize in some metallurgy, foundry, and steel works or to diversify in intermediate goods for the automotive and other industries. Some other SMEs were bought by larger ones or disappeared. In the late 1980s, several high-technology subsidiaries from multinational automotive companies specializing in plastics also settled in the département thanks to national investment subsidies amounting to 12 percent of the total investment. These large plants now form a dynamic, capital-intensive industrial pole of plastic manufacturing employing some 6,000 workers. Because they did not have a unified territorial strategy towards employment, the département's officials did not take full advantage of the available European recovery programs for creating jobs.

During the industrial restructuring period of 1980–1993, the GDP in the Province of Luxembourg grew at a slightly faster rate than in the Département Les Ardennes (table 22.1). At the end of this period, the economy and employment of the Département Les Ardennes continued to depend largely on a capital-intensive manufacturing sector characterized by a per-worker gross value added (GVA) higher than in the Province of Luxembourg (tables 22.2 and 22.3). However, with a smaller variation in per-worker GVA across sectors and a smoother population distribution, the Province of Luxembourg showed smaller income differences between urban and rural populations than the Département Les Ardennes. The Province of Luxembourg also maintained continuous population growth, with immigration and natural rates significantly higher than national rates (table 22.1). In contrast, after 30 years of continuous high growth, the population in the Département Les Ardennes started to decline in 1975, reaching an annual decline of 1,000 persons in the early 1990s due to emigration.

Table 22.2
Sector Shares in Domestic Income and Employment (%)

Sector	Luxembourg		Les Ardennes	
	Income (1993)	Employment (1992)	Income (1994)	Employment (1992)
Agriculture	7	8	4	8
Industry	18	19	39	35
Services	75	73	57	57

Source: EUROSTAT

Table 22. 3
Sector Per-Worker Gross Value Added (US$), 1992[a]

Sector	Luxembourg	Les Ardennes
All Sectors	49,578	55,280
Agriculture	42,533	32,306
Industry	49,429	61,264
Services	50,288	54,699

Note: a. 1 US$ = 0.83 ECU (European Currency Unit) in October 1998
Source: EUROSTAT

During the restructuring period, total employment grew at an annual rate of .9 percent in the Province of Luxembourg, but declined at an annual rate of .6 percent in the Département Les Ardennes. During this period, the rate of farm expansions due to labor productivity increases was faster in the Département Les Ardennes than in the Province of Luxembourg. As a result, employment loss in the agricultural and forestry sector was greater in the Département Les Ardennes than in the Province of Luxembourg, respectively 29 percent and 20 percent (table 22.4). The Province of Luxembourg was able to maintain its employment in the industry and construction sectors, while the Département Les Ardennes lost 19 percent of its jobs. Employment in the service sector increased much more in the Province of Luxembourg than in the Département Les Ardennes, respectively 20 percent and 8 percent. Between 1985 and 1995, the total unemployment rate declined from 9.5 percent to 7 percent in the Province of Luxembourg, but increased from 13.9 percent to 14.4 percent in the Département Les Ardennes.

Table 22.4
Employment Change in the Province of Luxembourg and the Département Les Ardennes between 1980 and 1992

	Luxembourg		Les Ardennes	
Sector	*Employment*	*%*	*Employment*	*%*
Agriculture and Forestry	-1,700	-20%	-3,100	-29%
Industry and Construction	-100	-1%	-7,800	-19%
Services	+9,800	+20%	+4,200	+8%
All Sectors	+8,000	+11%	-6,700	-6%

Source: EUROSTAT

More disaggregated data show that about half of the net increase in jobs actually occurred in public services (administration, education, health, entertainment, etc.) in both regions. Significant net increase in jobs occurred in sectors characterized by limited exposure to global markets, relatively stable prices, and rather labor-intensive production: trade and catering in the Province of Luxembourg, and other private services to households and enterprises in both regions. Only in the Province of Luxembourg was there a net increase in jobs in sectors exposed to global markets and price fluctuations: manufacturing, transport, communication, and financial services. The job losses in the Département Les Ardennes occurred not only in the manufacturing sector, but also in the trade, transport, and communication sectors.

Moreover, compared to the Province of Luxembourg, job losses in the Département Les Ardennes were greater in the agricultural sector, but fewer in the construction sector.

The public sector apart, new firms contributed the most to job creation in both regions. In the Province of Luxembourg, enterprises of either less than ten or more than 100 employees created relatively more employment than medium-size enterprises. In the Département Les Ardennes, small and medium-size enterprises created more employment, while large manufacturing enterprises experienced most of the employment loss. The labor participation rate, female share of the labor force, and the share of part-time jobs in total jobs progressed similarly in both regions during the restructuring. Average labor cost was about 10 percent higher in the Belgian Province of Luxembourg than in the French Département Les Ardennes.

Multiple factors made the growth of employment easier in the Province of Luxembourg than in the Département Les Ardennes. First, the manufacturing sector in need of restructuring at the end of the seventies was a smaller part of the regional economy and was concentrated among fewer firms in a smaller area in the Province of Luxembourg than in the Département Les Ardennes. With a sector mix already largely diversified into services, restructuring was therefore more manageable in the Province of Luxembourg than in the Département Les Ardennes. Second, the proximity of a growing economy localized in the neighboring Grand Duché of Luxembourg in need of labor for its dynamic manufacturing and service sectors was equally favorable for the Province of Luxembourg. Not only did this across-the-border dynamic economic area absorb some extra labor from the Province of Luxembourg, but it also stimulated immigration to the Province of Luxembourg from other parts of Belgium. Because of a growing population, private and public services in the Province of Luxembourg continued to grow and hire labor. Third, a regional institutional framework concentrated among fewer municipalities and business supporting agencies made it easier for the Province of Luxembourg to design and implement a territorial approach to job creation. Access to relatively higher investment subsidies supported this approach. Despite this more favorable economic and institutional context for employment growth, the attitude of the local leadership was the real key to the success of the Province of Luxembourg.

STRENGTHS AND WEAKNESSES IN THE INDUSTRIAL STRATEGIES OF LOCAL LEADERS

The ability of local leaders such as regional authorities and administrators, heads of professional associations and business support agencies, and trade union representatives to implement conditions for successful regional strategies is a key factor explaining the difference in employment growth of the two regions. The organization and role of local leaders, as well as other actors such as entrepreneurs, have already been underlined in the growing field of economic research on industrial districts as surveyed in Benko, Dunford, and Heurley (1997) and Barré (1998). The industrial district is a system of SME organized locally for the supply of both goods and services. The development of these industrial districts is generally endogenous, based on the capacity of the local actors rather than on natural resources, and rooted in an institutional and political environment. As shown below, the Province of Luxembourg shares several characteristics of industrial districts, such as a strong local identity, a consensus on the defense of collective economic interests among local leaders, and a dense network of associations. This social capital is much less well developed in the Département Les Ardennes.

In the Province of Luxembourg, the collapse of the iron and steel industry spurred a strong regional strategy of economic and employment development. At that time, the leaders of the province had a defensive strategy: their main goal was to replace the 1,700 jobs lost in the steel and iron industry and diversification of investments. To do this, they tried to attract foreign investment to the province, and were successful. Even if the role of exogenous forces in recovering the previous employment level was essential, this process actually was the result of a strategy coordinated at the level of the local leaders as a bottom-up strategy—and so, endogenously determined.

Thanks to general political and social consensus, local leaders were able to stimulate development and employment growth in the province by creating or enhancing the conditions that favor enterprise settlements and endogenous development. They encouraged the institutional development of organizations representing local actors: the municipal league (IDELUX), the provincial Chamber of Commerce and Industry (CCILB), and the regional interest group *Fondation rurale de Wallonnie* (FRW). The strong cooperation between the provincial authorities and IDELUX during the restructuring period stimulated cooperation among other institutions. Elsewhere, competition and discord is common among municipalities, as well as with the provincial administration, the public employment and vocational training institution (FOREM), the training institution for SME (IFPME), trade unions, and business organizations. This cooperation allowed targeted, coordinated efforts, facilitated the exchange of information and services, and reduced social conflicts to the point that strikes have been avoided. Thanks to this cooperation, provincial officials have been able to anticipate business needs. Some initiatives by local officials have included finding and lobbying national and European subsidies for local businesses, orienting professional training to business needs, and providing information on labor availability. The effective cooperation among the public and private institutions of the province enabled a considerable reinforcement of networks of local actors. These strongly cooperative internal networks translated into a new positive image of the region, which helped attract new firms to the province. A successful lobbying effort by the FRW and provincial authorities to achieve parity in financial support between rural and urban areas was also helpful.

This well-developed networking proved to be an efficient way to understand the problems encountered by the enterprises, to respond properly to these problems, and to disseminate information. One problem encountered by most of the local enterprises in the Province of Luxembourg that became noticeable after the restructuring period, was their small size. Due to insufficient managerial skills, lack of managerial training, a risk-averse attitude towards investment, and high costs of collecting information, these small enterprises seldom expanded beyond five employees. To overcome these difficulties, the municipal league and the provincial Chamber of Commerce and Industry have been involved in advising and training managers from SME. Local leaders have since refocused their economic and employment strategy to create or enhance the socioeconomic conditions favoring endogenous development. The shift has been to supply services to small enterprises to improve their managerial skills. There is also emphasis on better horizontal and vertical coordination among local firms. The regional strategy also continues to emphasize natural comparative advantage, like the quiet and green environment of the province.

External networks developed considerably, both in the public and private spheres at the regional, national, and European levels. Political and economic leaders from the province usually worked together in networking activity. Consequently, the provincial authorities were able to negotiate with the national and regional authorities on the basis of a political consensus reached at the provincial level. They coordinated efforts for the infrastructure investments, such as the road network, and for the land use plan identifying potential sites for enterprises. They were able to impose a territorial approach to solve their problems and exploit fully regional, national, and European investment and employment measures. Among them, the most frequently used measures included investment subsidies with their associated premium for employment creation. The provincial authorities were also able to innovate by negotiating subsidy packages from national or European sources on a case-by-case basis. They also developed a positive image of the province symbolized in a digitized green wild boar representing enthusiasm for work, modernity, and verdant beauty of the province. The strong presence of subsidiary businesses in the province, the multicountry EDP scheme strengthening links among local actors of the province, the Grand Duché de Luxembourg and the French Lorraine region, as well as other cross-border initiatives provided the province with many economic opportunities.

In the Département Les Ardennes, the main goal was to foster regional competitiveness and economic growth, but without a specific focus on employment growth. A large part of new investments were in capital-intensive, high-technology automotive and plastic industries. This choice was mainly made by large enterprises, rather than resulting from a regional consensus. Some measures designed at the national level for regions facing industrial restructuring were adopted in the Département Les Ardennes. However, due to a lack of leadership in the Département, ineffective lobbying at the national or European levels, and poor internal organization, the available subsidies did not give rise to a general and coordinated territorial strategy. As a result, restructuring was mainly sector-based, and only a few broad territorial projects emerged. Due to their small scale—they generally involved only a few municipalities—and their competitive nature, these small initiatives can hardly be called a territorial strategy.

Compared to the Province of Luxembourg, the Département Les Ardennes proved incapable of designing an effective territorial strategy of development. Weak representative organizations and insufficient networking activities were a handicap in attaining consensus about regional development and may, at least partially, explain this difference. Despite a strong regional identity, the image of the département has not improved either inside or outside the region and is still associated with several historical military defeats, industrial decline, and rural backwardness.

In the département, there was no political consensus among local authorities. One reason may be the high number of municipalities. The department has ten times the number of municipalities as the Province of Luxembourg. While both regions have roughly the same population and area size. Several groups of municipalities have tried to create associations for a variety of purposes, but no actual territorial policy has emerged. Moreover, the département had no political influence at the national level. Local entrepreneurs and policymakers were unfamiliar with European Union programs designed to assist with industrial restructuring. This impeded the expansion of road infrastructure and full exploitation of measures offered at the national and European levels for fostering employment. For example, the highway network that the département planned in the sixties has not yet been completed. The resulting poor internal road connections are considered by many companies specialized in intermediate goods as a major handicap. To cite another example, while European structural funds for rural areas were available, the authorities of the département decided not to apply for these funds, but only for European structural funds for industry restructuring. Moreover, the poor coordination between local leaders resulted in insufficient efforts to provide potential investors from outside with customized aid. As a result, the available European structural funds were not fully used.

LESSONS AND CHALLENGES

When the restructuring of its manufacturing sector began at the end of the 1970s, the Province of Luxembourg had several natural advantages over Les Ardennes. These advantages included a more favorable sector mix of agriculture, industry, and services; closer proximity to a dynamic economic region lacking labor (the Grand Duché de Luxembourg); and a more uniform spatial distribution of population. The Département Les Ardennes also had some advantages over the Province of Luxembourg. The principal advantages were a more skilled manufacturing labor force and relatively lower costs. What made the difference in employment growth was the capacity of local leaders in the Province of Luxembourg to design and implement purposeful economic and employment strategies beginning in the late seventies.

The importance of strengthening the capacity of local leaders to play an active role in developing and implementing together a common employment strategy is the primary lesson from this comparative analysis. This lesson was also learned from the other cases examined in other parts of the European Union in the RUREMPLO (1998) study. The way in which local leaders cooperate not only with each other, but with leaders outside the region to design and implement specific projects in line with the strengths and opportunities of their region, is a critical component to regional success. In the case of the Province of Luxembourg, there are many tangible signs of regional cooperation. Some examples of cooperative projects include: persuade national authorities to invest in the road network; marketing the rural amenities of the region to potential investors and skilled managers from outside; exploiting every source of regional, national, and European funds; building equipped industrial sites to facilitate the conversion or creation of firms; and, more recently, providing risk capital and managerial training for managers of small firms.

The capacity of local leaders can be strengthened by:

- providing local officials with training and assistance in conceiving, planning, managing, monitoring, and evaluating regional development policy and assessing labor market development;
- reorganizing relationships between vertical and horizontal layers of local officials to stimulate coordination and bottom-up initiatives;

- redistributing local and regional responsibilities among public and private institutions to avoid overlap, and implementing the development operations at the relevant level;
- organizing the private sector into a few trade unions and business associations to encourage public-private dialogue and cooperation; and
- providing local entrepreneurs of small firms with training and assistance in management, market analysis, and technology assessment and financing.

Both rural regions studied in this comparative analysis face several challenges. Much employment growth in the Province of Luxembourg since industrial restructuring has revolved around public services responding to population growth and low-skilled, labor-intensive activities dependent on subsidized investment. With public financial flows drying up and competition from low-wage countries increasing, the sustainability of the employment growth observed in the Province of Luxembourg is at risk in both the private and public sectors. Although employment in the Département Les Ardennes relies less on public financial flows, it has increasingly relied on capital intensive manufacturing activities requiring skilled labor but less of it. In the longer term, employment in Les Ardennes will depend on the extent to which the managers of high technology enterprises are able to maintain a competitive edge in their activities. Employment growth in the Province of Luxembourg will rely on enabling small entrepreneurs to expand their firms into larger enterprises with more employees. The phasing out of the European structural funds and the reform of the European Union's Common Agricultural Policy as planned in the Agenda 2000 in preparation for the integration of additional member countries from central Europe will add stress to employment in both regions. The development of tourism, a positive avenue for both regions considering the increasing demand for rural amenities from urban regions, may, however, partly counterbalance this stress.

DISCUSSION QUESTIONS FROM THE EDITORS

1. The Province of Luxembourg successfully used funds from a larger governmental unit (in this case, the European Union) to create incentives to locate there. What are the advantages and disadvantages of this strategy from the perspective of local people living in the Province of Luxembourg? What are the advantages and disadvantages of this strategy from the perspective of the European Union?

2. The Province of Luxembourg has lower productivity per worker than the Département Les Ardennes. Yet people are moving into the Province of Luxembourg; Les Ardennes, in contrast, is experiencing out-migration. Why do you think this might be happening?

3. The authors state, "Average labor cost was about 10 percent higher in the Belgian Province of Luxembourg than in the French Département Les

Ardennes." What might lead to such a large difference between two regions that border each other with similar resources and industries? Are markets working well in this case?

4.   The European Union constitutes one of the world's biggest markets. It negotiates international trade agreements with other parts of the world, and is therefore known as a "trading block." If, as the authors state, the national and European Union subsidies amount to "up to 30 percent of the total investment" for certain firm relocations, does this subsidy constitute a distortion of free trade?

5.   While both the regions in this case study were similar in terms of the size of their population, their share of the mother country's population was quite different. In 1998, France had an estimated population of 58.8 million, while Belgium had an estimated population of 10.2 million. How might size of the mother country affect a rural region's ability to respond to changing world markets?

6.   The authors mention that the subsidized investments have been in low-skill, low-wage industries that are facing increasing competition from less-developed nations. What might this mean for the long-term payoff on the public investments?

7.   The authors conclude that tourism may be a future growth area for both regions. Is industrial development compatible with tourism development?

Public- vs. Private-Sector Roles

CHAPTER 23

Introduction: Public- vs. Private-Sector Roles

Peter V. Schaeffer

Public-private cooperation is a necessity in many economic development projects because the private sector is responsible for most of the profit-oriented activities that contribute to job growth. The public sector's roles are usually limited to the provision of shared services such as infrastructure and education, and the creation and enforcement of rules and regulations. Nonprofit organizations are interesting because they can be both entrepreneurial and engage in business activities and serve as providers of public goods. Because of their role, they sometimes function as intermediaries between the private for-profit and the public sectors. A good example of the intermediary role is provided in the case study of a microloan program in West Virginia (chapter 27). In the case study of a community festival in Hawaii (chapter 24), nonprofits play similar roles. A somewhat different role is that described in the case study of public-private partnerships in Nordic countries (chapter 28), where nonprofit organizations act on behalf, and with the financial support of, the government in the provision of selected public services.

Public-private cooperative efforts are often referred to as partnerships. Unfortunately, the widespread use of this term hides variations between different forms of public-private cooperation. The extent and form of cooperation can be critical to the success or failure of a project. Using the same term for all forms of cooperation may lead us to overlook some of the causes for success or failure. The term "partnership" has the further disadvantage of emotional connotations. It evokes an image of friends or close colleagues who share goals, responsibilities, and rewards and who work together on the basis of trust that has been built over time. Almost all public-private efforts, however, are between organizations that have very different goals and may never have worked together before. This is particularly true in economic development where the for-profit sector is interested in market share and profit potential, while the public sector is interested in creating jobs or enhancing the tax base. While the goals of the public and private sectors are often compatible, a necessary condition for any collaboration between them, they are almost never identical. Whenever goals differ, there exists the chance for conflict.

To bring more clarity to this issue, we provide a characterization of a partnership as the strongest form of cooperation.

The ideal-typical partnership satisfies the following criteria, listed in their order of importance:

1. Partners share the same goals and objectives.
2. Partners share all risks and rewards.
3. Partners share decision making.
4. A partnership is long-lived.

We believe that the first criterion is the most important one, because it tends to influence the other criteria. A partnership where partners share all risks and rewards is unlikely to form unless their goals and objectives are well aligned, if not identical. Shared risks and rewards are a strong incentive for all partners to assume some responsibility for decision making. The fourth criterion is the least important, but is listed for practical reasons. A true partnership takes time to form because it is based on mutual trust. Without trust, sharing of risks and ceding decision-making power to the partnership is not possible. It therefore makes no sense to take the time to form a partnership that lasts for only a short time.

The criteria suggest that a true public-private partnership is more likely between the public sector and the nonprofit sector, than between the public and the for-profit sectors. The reason is that, by law, the nonprofit sector is required to benefit society. Since the public sector also serves society, it is much more likely that nonprofit and public sector organizations share goals and objectives than is the case for the public and the for-profit sectors.

We define cooperative efforts as successful if all participants get significantly closer to their goals. In their eagerness to attract jobs, communities sometimes assume that their goals and those of the firm they are pursuing are the same. This is rarely the case. The following example illustrates how a lack of attention paid to the goals of all partners may result in unintended outcomes.

A community is recruiting a firm in the hope of gaining a significant number of jobs. The community has as its goal to increase the number of "good" jobs by as much as possible. The firm's goal is to create a profitable business. The community offers to issue industrial revenue bonds so as to make financing available at below-market costs. However, by lowering the cost of capital expenditures relative to the cost of labor, the community has created an incentive for the firm to substitute capital for labor beyond what might have been the case without the incentive.

The lesson from this introduction is that goals define what forms of public-private cooperation are suitable. The case studies that follow provide examples and illustrations of this important but often overlooked lesson.

Map 6
Public- vs. Private-Sector Roles

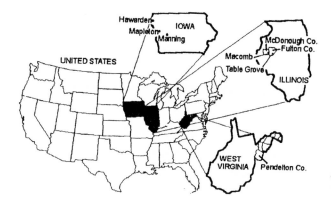

Ua Mau Na Po'e 'O Wai'anae Community Cultural Festival: An Experience in Community Collaboration

Linda J. Cox, Dolores Foley, and Joseph Lapilio

INTRODUCTION

This case study examines a collaborative project in a rural Hawaiian community. The community was interested in economic development, and this project was seen as a way to encourage private and public sector collaboration to begin building the social infrastructure needed by the community. While the academic community has debated the exact definition of and parameters associated with the term "social capital" (Castle 1998), the importance of the concept in community development has wide acceptance across disciplines (Oakerson 1998; Kraybill 1998; Salmon 1998; Summers and Brown 1998). Flora et al. (1992, 234) offer a definition of social infrastructure as the "social capacity and the collective will of local communities to provide for their social and economic well being." The terms "social capital" and "social infrastructure" appear to be synonymous concepts. The model of social infrastructure put forth by Flora et al. (1997) details its three fundamental elements as: (1) legitimization of alternatives, (2) networks, and (3) mobilization of resources. These are the elements on which this case study will focus in analyzing the project's outcomes.

BACKGROUND

In 1996, Hawaii's economy had been in an economic downturn for six years, with the two largest industries—tourism and military services—showing no growth. Agriculture is the state's third largest sector, but with many sugar and pineapple plantations closing and diversified agriculture faltering, this sector was also struggling. With urban and tourism development competing for land with agriculture, land prices had risen and water availability had become a major issue. In the past, the plantation system provided a comprehensive management system which supplied and maintained housing, water and sewer systems, roads and other infrastructure, but the visitor industry had outgrown it and the state's fiscal crisis delayed improvements.

While many U.S. communities complain of political isolation, the challenges associated with a lack of local access to governmental decision making in Hawaii are readily apparent. Modern Hawaii has never had political subdivisions below the county level, and most governmental functions that are municipal responsibilities elsewhere are handled by the state. One party has dominated both the executive and legislative branches for almost 40 years. These factors have in the past stifled local decision making and created barriers for community-based development.

Map 7
Ua Mau Na Po'e 'O Wai'anae Community Cultural Festival

HAWAIIAN ISLANDS

A resurgent interest in native Hawaiian culture and a concern for the state's fragile island ecosystem have introduced a new social dynamic in many communities. The economy of ancient Hawaii was organized around a highly structured hierarchy which managed resources collectively at the community level. Islands were sectioned into ahupua'a or land divisions that go from the mountain to the ocean, often following watershed divisions. Thus, collaboration ensured that each ahupua'a had all the resources a community needed to thrive. Communities across the state are recalling this traditional ahupua'a system to help provide physical, economic, and political infrastructure as a means of pushing decision making down to the community level.

The economic concerns that exist throughout the islands are exacerbated in poor rural communities like the Wai'anae Coast. The coast, a rural area with about 43,000 residents on the leeward side of Oahu, has a native Hawaiian population of 45 percent. Nearly a fifth of the population have annual incomes under $15,000, more than a quarter rely on some form of public assistance, and only 7 percent have college degrees. The coast has an estimated 29 percent unemployment rate and is a sizable distance, by local standards, from Oahu's employment centers.

The coast has a scenic beauty that is not commonly enjoyed by visitors to the state. The Wai'anae Mountains provide a backdrop to some of Hawaii's most unspoiled beaches. Sites of cultural and historic significance abound along the coast, although little exists in terms of visitor infrastructure and site interpretation. A common perception is that visitors, especially out-of-state residents, are not welcome on the coast.

Although the coast's socioeconomic indicators are among the lowest in the state, in terms of social infrastructure, the coast fares better than many other communities. The state's most populated island, Oahu, has many bedroom communities with few neighbors knowing each other or organizing around issues. Wai'anae, in marked contrast, has many community organizations and its residents are known for their activism.[1] The Wai'anae Coast Coalition (WCC), a collection of more than 200 community associations, civic organizations, and business groups, has assumed the role of catalyst for change on the coast. This case study describes a partnership that was formed in 1996. The partnership included the WCC, the Hawaii State Department of Business Economic Development and Tourism (DBEDT), a local foundation called the Queen Lili'uokalani Children's Center (QLCC), and the University of Hawaii (UH). These organizations worked together to create a community cultural festival entitled Ua Mau Na Po'e 'o Wai'anae, which means The Steadfast People of Wai'anae (Ua Mau).

THE PROJECT

Since 1992, the Wai'anae Coast Coalition has convened an annual community summit to gather resident input on the direction of the organization. These summits have resulted in the following key policy shifts:[2]

- Reducing the emphasis on human services and increasing activity in the economic development, education, and culture of the community, and shifting emphasis from the needs of individuals to the strengths within families and their communities.
- Increasing the community's control over its affairs, and restructuring the distribution of public funds into the community to shift resources from human services to an investment in the community's strengths.
- Focusing on the long-held values of the community and articulating these through five key activity areas:
  - Education and lifelong learning
  - Health education and activities that promote wellness
  - The promotion of intergenerational activities and interaction.
  - Family strengthening

- Increasing opportunities for social and cultural interaction and providing activities for families to have fun within their respective communities
- Organizing and developing the community through the traditional ahupua'a concept of land division, and sustainable development using the resources within each valley

In 1996–1997, the WCC focused on the Ua Mau festival as the main instrument to achieve these goals. Many partners, including businesses, universities, and foundations were part of this effort providing more than $120,000 in funding or in-kind contributions. In addition, there were thousands of volunteer hours donated by local residents. As one of the key partners, QLCC donated extensive staff time and financial support to assist with organizing because QLCC saw the festival as complementing its goal of community building.

To further the WCC's policy to organize the community using the traditional ahupua'a system, monthly council meetings of the four primary coast ahupua'a—Nanakuli, Lualualei, Wai'anae, and Makaha—were started immediately after the Ua Mau collaboration was formed. Each council took ownership of an Ua Mau event, giving the groups immediate activities on which to focus. The first Ua Mau was held over eight days in June 1997, and its success set the stage for the development of a long-term, community-based tourism effort on the coast. The annual community summit that followed in November 1997 provided a forum to facilitate the development of a long-term vision for community-based tourism. In the meantime, Ua Mau was expanded to an eight week festival for the summer of 1998, and short-term planning efforts continued.

Using information gathered at its annual summit and from surveys of community residents, the WCC identified a strategy to help community members gain the skills and knowledge they need to accomplish their economic goals.[3] WCC identified four key areas that will establish an infrastructure for economic development activities throughout the community. These areas include: (1) the creation of a business and entrepreneurial development training and business assistance program to increase the number of locally owned enterprises, (2) the development of a microloan program to assist local entrepreneurs, (3) the development of a promotional structure to assist local businesses in marketing their products, and (4) the identification and reduction of economic leakages from the coast.

At the request of the WCC, University of Hawaii students helped develop a concept paper for a business center. As part of the Ua Mau collaboration, the Wai'anae Coast Community Business Development Center (business center) opened as a "virtual" organization.[4] It offers workshops and short courses using QLCC and Legal Aid staff as facilitators, and UH faculty, DBEDT staff, and other business assistance providers as trainers.

The business center's microloan program was established in 1997, and includes a training component staffed and funded by QLCC. Its first ten clients included artists, crafters, and cultural practitioners that were among the vendors at the 1997 Ua Mau events. The Ua Mau vendors' survey for 1997 measured how business goals were met by vendors' experiences at the festival. Thirty-nine percent of the 28 vendors responding were pleased with the money they earned. Respondents reported total gross sales of $15,927. Seventy-two percent of the respondents wished to participate again in the following year, but 57 percent wanted more promotion and 28 percent asked for different festival dates. The vendors surveyed felt the festival was a success and that more attention should be given to staging large events that bring in more customers. The results of the 1998 Ua Mau evaluation have not been completely analyzed yet, but the response generally seems to indicate that the 1998 festival was a great success. The festival has catalyzed a group of artists and crafts people to explore the development of a cooperative. The Wai'anae Mall, one of the partners of the festival, has donated empty space for the group to exhibit and sell their works.

In 1998, the business center acquired space in Waianae Satellite City and obtained a Honolulu City and County community development grant to hire staff and expand the microloan program. Additional staff support came from Americorps volunteers. Fourteen new loans were disbursed, and Alu Like Inc., a statewide nonprofit organization that offers educational programs for native Hawaiians, provided an entrepreneur training program for start-up small businesses and the expansion of micro-enterprises. More than 400 coast residents have completed classes covering topics such as how to start a business, accounting methods, pricing products, and how to conduct interpretive tours, aimed at helping participants launch businesses during Ua Mau. In addition, more than 60 residents have completed training in home-based child care and are currently working on state certification. The WCC's involvement with a business assistance organization institutionalizes its links with the business community. In 1998, the business center formed an advisory group with members from the local business community and businesses and institutions outside the community.

Another social institution was formed when the WCC collaborated with QLCC and the University of Hawaii to create the Wai'anae Coast Community Development Institute.[5] The Institute offered classes for residents in 1997 and 1998 that were eventually linked with one or more aspect of Ua Mau. A series of courses focused on assessing community assets and the development of a resource directory of cultural practitioners, artists, and crafters that was distributed throughout the community. Another course examined community building and brought coast residents together to plan and deliver a summer session course during the 1998 festival, entitled Ua Mau Na Po'e 'O Wai'anae, that is, Building Community Wai'anae-style. All courses received positive evaluations from participants, with the summer session course having large enough enrollment to exceed break-even enrollment.

In 1998, the Hitachi Foundation awarded a $200,000 grant over a three-year period for a community-based planning initiative in Wai'anae. The grant was made to a group of community-based organizations and other institutions that included all of the Ua Mau collaborators except one (DBEDT). The grant will enable the collaborators to facilitate a community-wide vision for tourism, to further develop the business center, and to provide for an ongoing community-based evaluation of these efforts. The grant from the Hitachi Foundation will help further the goals of the business center by providing a more comprehensive program to assist community members and local businesses, to collaborate with the local schools, and to develop the capacity of local leaders.

The members of the WCC are cognizant that the well-being of the community and thus the success of any project requires full participation and contribution from all sectors of the community's citizenry. The 1993 Wai'anae Coast summit focused on community governance issues and recommended increasing community control over the destiny of the Wai'anae Coast using the ahupua'a model. The Ua Mau planning group has representation from each council and assisted the councils in various ways.

An evaluation of the 1997 Ua Mau found that the planners agreed that the festival was a success and that the councils were stronger as a result of working together. Some events overlapped because planning had emphasized a decentralized approach, which resulted in capacity building at the ahupua'a level, but also created tensions between the ahupua'a councils. The group concluded that (1) future events should be scheduled with no overlap so that cooperation along the coast can occur, and (2) that efforts to develop the ahupua'a councils need to continue to enable the planning committee to focus more on marketing the entire festival.

The WCC has also articulated the importance of extending the social networks to include youth. A variety of Ua Mau activities, including the annual community health summit, the ahupua'a councils, other community groups, and the emerging cultural tourism industry, encouraged youth involvement. Although the summit usually takes place during a school day, students are encouraged by their schools to attend and participate. They are delegates with voting and decision-making power, and many have been chosen to present their ahupua'a's decisions and action plans in plenary sessions. Some students have multiple roles and also assist summit organizers with group facilitation and recording, and asset mapping, while others provide entertainment such as traditional chanting and hula dancing.

The future vision involves young people in planning the summit, and the development of a youth summit as a preconference activity. Each of the community ahupua'a councils has established an 'opio (youth) delegate position, with voting rights, on their executive committees. Each 'opio is asked to assist in activities designed to promote intergenerational cultural exchanges, specifically between young and old. In addition, the youth delegate insures that some facet of cultural activities, including events staged as a part of Ua Mau, have a component that is attractive to the young generation.

CONCLUSION

The Ua Mau project has given Wai'anae Coast residents a project that helped bring them together to build community cohesion and celebration, while at the same time, pursuing economic development. Networks both within the coast and to outside groups have been strengthened, and new complementary relationships have developed. While social institutions are plentiful on the coast, the development of networks that facilitate dynamic community adjustment to challenging issues are a key element to increasing the area's social infrastructure. The centralized nature of the political system seems to make change overwhelming for Hawaii's disadvantaged communities, reinforcing the need for private and public sector collaboration.

This case study outlines how a single project involving private and public sector collaborators assisted in developing the social capital of the Wai'anae Coast. As efforts continue to mandate or promote economic development, more care must be given to promoting the development of social infrastructure, including defining the role of outsiders. As people come into a community from the outside, focusing their efforts to emphasize facilitation and the discovery of community assets is likely to prove more successful at building sustainable social capital. In the case of the Ua Mau project, formal partnerships were formed with the University of Hawaii and the Wai'anae community through an agreement with the QLCC and four departments at the university. These relationships were qualitatively different from past arrangements. In the past, professionals worked in the community as researchers or as experts. In this case, the community demanded a different role and as a result, the relationships between community organizations and external organizations emphasized a facilitative role rather than a "helping" or expert role. The assistance of outside professionals is important, but in an assets approach, professionals build on existing strengths and help community members to empower themselves.

DISCUSSION QUESTIONS FROM THE EDITORS

1. In this case study, planning a tourism event is the basis for improving local capacity. Would planning a festival always help build local social capital?

2. One of the initiatives in this case study had to do with encouraging making and selling crafts. People rarely get rich selling crafts. Why should this kind of activity be subsidized?

3. Most participants in the festival come from nearby. Is it still tourism when participants are local? Why or why not?

4. Compare the approach to tourism in this community to the discussion of tourism in Utah by Albrecht.

NOTES

1. In other words, there are strong social networks present.
2. These policy shifts can be considered as the legitimization of alternatives.
3. In other words, these are efforts to mobilize resources.

4. By "virtual" we mean that in 1996 the business center had no permanent office space or staff.

5. In terms of the model of Flora et al. (1997), this can be described as a strengthening of networks, whereas the next paragraph describes more efforts at mobilizing resources.

CHAPTER 25

A Small Town Creates New Alliances for Community and Economic Development

Steven Kline

INTRODUCTION

There are many factors that contribute to the long-term success of any community, and some of those factors are certainly more controllable at the local level than others. Planners and futurists often suggest that education, health care, telecommunications and other public services, cultural diversity, transportation, housing, economic vitality, leadership, environmental stewardship, and many other socioeconomic factors will be important for creating a higher quality of life in the twenty-first century.

Although not every community is prepared to deal with such a range of topics, leaders in at least one small town in west central Illinois recently concluded there were only two options available to them: (1) observe change and let the future happen to them, or (2) take charge of their community's future and become participants in the process. For Table Grove, Illinois (pop. 408) residents, it became evident that the future was happening to them and that it was time to obtain the help they needed to start doing something about it.[1]

SETTING THE STAGE FOR A NEW PLAN OF ACTION

Table Grove can be described as a western Illinois Mayberry. Everybody knows everybody. However, things were not going well. Between 1980 and 1990, Table Grove experienced a 17 percent decline in population. The population's median age (38.1) was 16 percent higher than the median age of Illinois. More than 25 percent of Table Grove's citizens were over 65 years and per capita income was 27 percent below the state average.[2] Despite these unfavorable statistics, local leaders managed to formulate a plan to address the issues of a weakened farm economy and an aging population, while maintaining Table Grove's small-town charm. The results of their efforts have stimulated new and exciting partnerships between public sector and private sector leaders who share a bold vision for managing change.

STARTING THE PLANNING PROCESS

In December 1993, a group of Table Grove leaders consisting of a few residents, village board members, and trustees of a local endowment fund requested assistance from the Illinois Institute for Rural Affairs and Mapping the Future of Your Community, a community-based strategic visioning and planning program. Subsequent to meeting with local steering committee members, institute staff recommended a planning process involving three stages: (1) assessment of community attitudes and interests through written surveys, focus groups, and town hall meetings; (2) three, three-hour visioning sessions in Table Grove involving 30 to 40 residents; and (3) ongoing technical assistance and customized training programs to develop a volunteer base and implement high-priority projects in the community. The University of Illinois Extension accepted an invitation to co-facilitate the Mapping process in Table Grove with the Illinois Institute for Rural Affairs.

Through the Mapping process, Table Grove participants reached a consensus on many long-range goals. The ultimate vision for the community focused on the needs of a growing number of elderly residents and the potential exodus of many young people who might be permanently lost to job markets in other areas. Local leaders recognized that the growing number of elderly residents provided an opportunity to develop Table Grove as a bedroom community. Residents could live independent lifestyles, enjoy rural America, and still have access to essential conveniences associated with larger communities (e.g., a local grocer, financial services, health care services, reliable public services, and good schools). As a bonus, high-quality housing alternatives would eventually offer options for new families interested in relocating to a quiet farming community. With population increases, the community would eventually be able to support a grocery store and a restaurant—two items high on the wish list of current residents.

Mapping participants realized early that for the general citizenry to share in this vision, people would need to see valuable results before committing to the long term. In spring 1994, volunteers initiated their first major project—a health care project that has since proved to be a critical step toward achieving the community's vision of the future and establishing mutual trust among local residents. Leaders believed that attracting a physician to Table Grove would not only benefit residents, but it would also improve access to health care services for people living within ten miles of the village and make Table Grove more appealing to seniors or families interested in moving to the community.

DEALING WITH REALITY WHILE BUILDING THE DREAM

While attracting a health care professional to the community was an admirable objective it was generally accepted that efforts to attract a physician to a relatively remote community of less than 500 people were unlikely to succeed. It was at this critical juncture that the Illinois Institute for Rural Affairs and University of Illinois Extension staff intervened to suggest that Table Grove citizens consider creating their own small health care facility, certified as a rural health clinic and staffed with a midlevel practitioner.

Table Grove Mapping participants were not at all familiar with the health care industry. None had ever heard of a nurse practitioner or a physician's assistant. The Table Grove Development Group was formed as a not-for-profit, tax exempt organization. It charged its first standing committee with the task of learning all that they could about midlevel health care professionals. Meanwhile, town meetings and focus group discussions were scheduled to keep residents engaged with the project. The community's response was overwhelmingly in favor of pursuing the clinic. Support was so positive that the Table Grove Development Group began a fund-raising campaign for construction of the clinic's building, start-up operating costs, and expenses associated with recruiting a midlevel practitioner. Within six months, the group collected more than $30,000 from local residents, and the fund amounted to more than $70,000 by fall 1995. A local bank agreed to provide the Table Grove Development Group with gap financing secured by a guarantee from the community's local endowment fund (a $500,000 trust that was established many years ago as a vehicle for managing philanthropic donations to the community).

A sign was erected in Table Grove to mark the site where the new health care clinic would be built. Shortly thereafter, local leaders purchased a modular building they found more than three hours away from Table Grove, loaded it onto a flatbed truck, and moved it to a vacant lot in the center of town. Volunteers quickly began renovating the structure as a medical facility (i.e., residents remodeled, painted, wired, and plumbed the structure to meet specifications obtained from interviews with staff at other similar clinics in the state and area health care professionals).

ASSESSING MARKET POTENTIAL

While the Table Grove community prepared the building for the health care clinic, the Illinois Institute for Rural Affairs and the University of Illinois Extension staff began collecting secondary data to more precisely determine what Table Grove would have to do to create a sustainable health care practice. The technical assistance was important because information of this type was otherwise unattainable in Table Grove.

Confidence in the project was bolstered after the Illinois Department of Public Health Center for Rural Health indicated that Table Grove was designated as a health professional shortage area. This was a significant turning point because it was clear that the rural health clinic stood a greater chance of remaining financially solvent if it qualified for higher Medicare and Medicaid reimbursement rates. In addition, figures from the Illinois Health Care Cost Containment Council indicated that a significant patient base existed in the Table Grove area for the McDonough District Hospital (MDH) in Macomb. This was a key factor, since MDH was the closest hospital to Table Grove and a physician's assistant must be supervised by a licensed physician.

With technical assistance from the Center for Rural Health and the institute and extension staff, Table Grove leaders prepared a market study showing that the Table Grove clinic could expect to exceed 4,000 patient visits during its first year of operation. This projection assumed a 25 percent capture rate from the nearly 17,000 potential visits from residents in Table Grove and nine ·surrounding townships. Information exchanged with other Medicare-certified rural health clinics in Illinois indicated that the clinic would be of special importance to Table Grove's elderly population and area residents with annual incomes below poverty thresholds (14 percent of the population). These two groups are traditionally at a disadvantage for accessing health care services located a long distance away from their residence.

By May 1996, MDH accepted the Table Grove Development Group's proposal and agreed to help make the clinic fully operational. A physician's assistant was hired to provide primary health care services and to coordinate patient care with doctors in surrounding areas whose patients lived in Table Grove. Table Grove's certified physician's assistant was required to earn 100 hours of continuing medical education every two years and pass a recertification exam every six years. In addition to the physician's assistant, the clinic created a second full-time staff position to take calls, make appointments, and otherwise accommodate the needs of the patients visiting the clinic five days a week or after hours as necessary.

After opening the clinic, the physician's assistant immediately began providing intermediate treatment for a variety of illnesses and injuries. Within a very short time she had been all but adopted by local residents and was regarded as something like a "mom" to everyone who visited the clinic. Although capable of handling serious cases, the physician's assistant always referred patients with complex conditions to their personal physicians or sent them to facilities with medical personnel able to provide more specialized treatments. The physician's assistant's main responsibilities included recording individual medical histories, conducting physical examinations, treating minor wounds, performing and interpreting laboratory tests to diagnose and treat common illnesses, and counseling patients about a variety of health-related issues. With supervision of a licensed medical doctor, the physician's assistant was authorized to dispense medication at the Table Grove Rural Health Clinic. In a community where prescription drugs were not otherwise available, this service gave residents more convenient access to medical treatments and supplies, including prepackaged, pre-labeled prescriptions and over-the-counter medications—all available with personalized instructions and guidance.

POWERFUL RESULTS INSPIRE A BRIGHTER FUTURE

The Table Grove community is an inspiration for small towns throughout rural Illinois because the residents assumed responsibility for achieving their health care goal. Although no government funding (local, state, or federal) was needed for the health care clinic project; Table Grove leaders accessed a variety of resources and established a broad base of support for their project. For example, the McDonough District Hospital helped the community recruit a physician's assistant, establish a management structure, and secure the interest of a sponsoring physician. The Macomb Area Industrial Development Corporation, the McDonough County Board, and Central Illinois Public Service Company publicly endorsed the project and offered their support. Residents were especially impressed by McDonough County's willingness to help because Table Grove is located in neighboring Fulton County. Clearly the county line, which had been perceived by so many people in the past as a somewhat impervious border for economic development was no longer seen as an impediment for enhancing the area's quality of life.

Over and above statistical evidence supporting the Table Grove Health Care Clinic, this community's success is strongly based on intuition, tenacity, and dedication to the long term. Community leaders and volunteers absorbed much information before finally going with their instincts and making something happen. Roles played by the community development practitioners, change agents, counselors, and technical assistance agencies were often more similar to expediters and cheerleaders than educators. Assistance from the Illinois Institute for Rural Affairs, University of Illinois Extension, Illinois Department of Public Health Center for Rural Health, and McDonough District Hospital increased confidence levels among leaders in Table Grove and helped raise the standards for what local citizens expected their community to accomplish.

Although efforts to increase patient visits are ongoing, approximately 200 patients per month visit the Rural Health Clinic in Table Grove. The clinic has helped to stabilize the village's population and provides valuable services for the very old and very young—two groups which most often need medical services, but are least able to travel. While the residents of Table Grove actually own their clinic's building, the McDonough District Hospital has continued to provide professional support in many areas such as public relations, housekeeping, engineering, human resources, physician recruitment, and business management services. In 1998, the Table Grove Development Group was presented a special award of merit from the Illinois Rural Health Association for the group's efforts to create better access to primary health care services for residents living in the Table Grove area.

ON TO THE NEXT VENTURE

Residents in Table Grove were extremely proud of the success they experienced during the last five years. However, as of December 1997, the development group decided it was time to begin focusing on the next segment of their action plan. The strategy of creating the health care clinic and maintaining other existing "Mayberry" features was expanded to include housing. Again, the Table Grove Development Group formed a team of local residents who agreed to work as diligently on creating new housing opportunities as did the team that worked on health care.

After nearly 11 months of research, consultation with university staff, regional planners, and private consulting firms, the Table Grove Development Group obtained an innovative agreement between local government officials, schools and other taxing districts, local property owners, a developer/consultant, and a private contractor. As a result of the agreement, six new single-family homes will be constructed every year for the next ten years. The specific strategy involved the creation of a tax increment financing (TIF)[3] district.

The TIF plan calls for the village of Table Grove to contract with a professional consulting firm and designate a specific area for housing and redevelopment. In that area, the following activities would occur: (1) the current assessed value of the properties would be frozen for a period of 23 years, giving existing taxing districts the same tax base as in the previous year; (2) the village would issue bonds as necessary to pay for new streets, sewer and water extensions, sidewalks, curbs, lighting, etc. in the new small residential development; (3) a builder/contractor would agree to begin building new homes in the redevelopment TIF district; and (4) as new homes are built on previously vacant and unimproved lots, the increase in the assessed property value is taxed by the TIF district. These TIF revenues would be used to repay the village's debt incurred when it installed the initial infrastructure for developing the area.

This approach was chosen because it would cost $15,000 to $18,000 to prepare a lot for construction of a new home, but the market value of the improved lot would be only about half that amount. Using TIF, the development of a three-bedroom home would generate enough TIF revenue to amortize $20,000 to $25,000 of TIF bonds. With total cost of land and improvements at $15,000 to $18,000 per lot, and revenues sufficient to repay debts in the $20,000 to $25,000 range, it was clear that this could be a fully self-funding program. The costs associated with setting up the TIF district, the infrastructure improvements, and the interest paid on the debt are all eligible expenses under Illinois' TIF legislation.

If at first the demand for housing appeared weak, the village could effectively reimburse current property owners for the purchase value of their vacant lots, make necessary improvements, and then literally give away an improved lot if a family decided to build a new home in the TIF district.

The TIF approach was patterned after a similar project in Ohio, Illinois, where the village agreed to create a TIF district to install new infrastructure if a local housing development group would wait to recover its costs from tax increments generated by the construction of new homes. Without the TIF district, there wouldn't have been any means to fund improvement of the land and sell lots at a marketable price. Without the development group (i.e., the contractors and builders) assuming some front-end risk, there would not have been a project either. The result in Ohio was 13 new homes, a 20 percent increase in school enrollments, increased school funding, and a total financial impact of more than $9 million in a town of just 450 people. This "Ohio Plan" was an example of a genuine partnership between public and private entities and one that Table Grove believed would work in their community too. The Table Grove Development Group expected to complete the legal requirements for setting up the TIF district and begin breaking ground for their first new home in the fall of 1998.

CONCLUSION

In Table Grove, community development has meant residents must assume responsibility for their community's future. At the same time, local leaders realized that goals have only been achieved through the prudent use of outside knowledge and resources, and by establishing effective partnerships among all of the public sector and private sector entities who have a stake in the community's future. The four key ingredients to Table Grove's success were:

1. Reliance upon the experience and intuition of the residents of the community to set a direction everyone can understand and a vision of the future the residents can share.

2. Willingness on the part of local residents to assume some risk, take a chance, and invest in the creation and activation of their community's plan of action.

3. Patience to establish the kind of learning environment necessary to keep everyone informed and engaged in the development process.

4. Commitment to the long term. Table Grove did not suddenly become what it was in 1993—it took years for the community to develop into what it was at that time. Likewise, local leaders understood it may be years before they have their grocery store, but their vision begins with creating a place where more people will one day call Table Grove their home.

DISCUSSION QUESTIONS FROM THE EDITORS

1. Where does the TIF money come from? The homeowners of the new houses built through TIF financing benefit from cheaper homes. Which institutions "pay" the costs of the TIF financing?

2. If the residents of Table Grove's objective was to have their own grocery store, would it make more sense to subsidize that grocery store (say, by purchasing the building and offering it rent-free) than by subsidizing medical care and housing? What are the advantages and disadvantages of Table Grove's approach?

3. In this case, a hospital located some distance away from the community took an interest in helping improve the town's health care service. What do you think the hospital's motivation might have been?

NOTES

1. This case is based on actual events and is presented with permission from the Table Grove Development Group. For more information about the Table Grove project, contact the Illinois Institute for Rural Affairs, Western Illinois University, 1 University Circle, Macomb, Illinois, 61455 or call (309) 298-2237.

2. United States Bureau of the Census on CD ROM. Accessible on the Internet at http://www.census.gov/.

3. TIF allows the community to use any new tax revenues in the TIF district to finance development projects in the district. The life of TIF districts is limited; they typically exist for ten to 20 years before they must be abolished.

CHAPTER 26

Private Cooperation for the Public Good

Maureen Kilkenny

INTRODUCTION

This is a story about how citizens in rural towns organized cooperatives, corporations, and networks with distant collaborators to fill roles that traditional private firms and government agencies wouldn't fill in their locations. It is about how private cooperation can overcome the market failures that arise from scale (dis-) economies and externalities. It is also about the implications of central place theory and the product cycle for business recruiting.

Rural citizens and businesses can and do successfully organize themselves without relying on government services, subsidies, or programs. Citizens can do some things unilaterally; other things require collaboration across communities, but not necessarily *neighboring* communities. Collaboration between neighbors is an asset on projects subject to scale economies and benefits, which *decline with distance*. But collaboration between neighbors is a liability on projects subject to scale economies whose benefits *decline with proximity*. In that case, given there are returns to scale, it is better to collaborate with far away entities. This case study is about the formation, activity, and outcomes at all three levels: *cooperative* activities of citizens across many towns (NIPCO); *unilateral* activities of private citizens in one town (Manning); and *collaborative* activity of citizens in three nonproximate towns (WITECC).

THE SETTING

Iowa may be best known to students of community development as the place where Brian Berry (1967) developed and tested "Central Place Theory." One of the problems facing rural Iowa towns today is the consolidation trend Berry documented. Since the turn of the twentieth century, farm productivity improvements have released rural people from the land, and transport costs have declined significantly. These changes have led to a redundancy in market centers. In Iowa, as elsewhere, the number and populations of many smaller towns continue to decline, and the larger towns get larger. The people of this case study understand that rural consolidation is a natural process. Furthermore, they understand that firm location is generally a two-stage process. First, a firm identifies an area that meets its criteria. Second, the firm chooses its site within that region. Only one town can succeed in attracting the firm, the other towns in the region "fail." They also know there will always be *some* small towns. They believe that those small towns which will thrive are those whose citizens are attentive and involved.

Western Iowa counties are relatively specialized in small-scale manufacturing. Rural towns compete internationally for footloose firms. Residents as well as industries prefer locations with good utility and communications infrastructures. But both types of infrastructure require large-scale investments, which can be hard to justify and even harder to finance in low-population, low-density places. When the market failed to provide the electricity and telecommunications infrastructure they needed to attract residents and businesses, the people in these communities formed cooperatives and nonprofits to provide it for themselves. Citizens of some of the member communities have been collaborating in a variety of ways for more than 60 years to support sustainable economic development in their small towns.

HOW THE COLLABORATORS MET

In the 1930s, rural electric cooperatives (RECs) were formed. This case study concerns communities in the rural electric cooperative called the Western Iowa Municipal Electric Cooperative Association (WIMECA), which unites the six communities of Anthon, Aurelia, Hawarden, Hinton, Manning, Mapleton, and Onawa; across six counties (not contiguous).   In 1949, the Northwest Iowa Power Cooperative (NIPCO) was formed from a coalition of nine RECs in the region, including WIMECA.[1] WIMECA and the other eight member RECs each have a representative on NIPCO's board of directors. The WIMECA and NIPCO models of regional partnership guided the development of partnerships for other regional development activities. In 1997, three small towns (all members of WIMECA and NIPCO) formed Western Iowa Technology Entrepreneurship and Capital Corporation (WITECC).

PRIVATE COOPERATION TO PROVIDE EXCLUDABLE PUBLIC GOODS

Recall that Manning is a member of the rural electric cooperative, WIMECA, which is a part of the regional power cooperative, NIPCO. In 1996, NIPCO invested more than $8 million to install a system used to manage the power network and which could accommodate internet access. Pioneer Holdings (a joint venture of NIPCO, MCI, and Long Lines, Ltd.) founded Pioneer Internet in 1996, which installed 400 miles of fiber-optic cable. This *synchronous optical network* (SON) provides internet access and a variety of telecommunications services linked to the international network to 65 western Iowa communities. While such infrastructure has some of the characteristics of a *public good*, it is also *excludable*. Thus, private provision is possible and can be efficient, especially if organized as a cooperative, since the risk of monopoly pricing and quantity distortions are minimized.

NIPCO also employs an economic development director whose mission is to foster new business start-ups and existing business expansions. Her web page is continuously updated with photos and specifications of available industrial sites and buildings in communities throughout the NIPCO region.[2] Notice how the operation of NIPCO overcomes many potential market failures. First is the efficient provision of electric power. Second is how they internalize some of the positive external economies from rural development. The more businesses and households there are consuming NIPCO services, the lower are the net costs to *all* NIPCO members. Third, NIPCO effectively captures the benefits of jointness in production because the network needed to manage the power grid and also provides an electronic communications infrastructure. All of these are examples of efficient *private* provision of *local public* goods. Recall that the difference between a pure public good and a *local* public good is that the benefits of the latter decline with distance or are limited to a specific region (Boadway and Wildasin 1984).

UNILATERAL DEVELOPMENT ACTIVITY: PROFIT AND NONPROFIT

Citizen groups in some of the NIPCO member towns have also been unilaterally active in their pursuit of economic development. This case study focuses on the town of Manning, Iowa (pop. 1,400). In the 1950s, the shopkeepers, businessmen, farmers, bankers, and householders of Manning started the *for-profit* Manning Development Corporation (MDC). The MDC's objectives were to support local industrial development and to diversify their economy. They raised funds locally by forming a corporation and issuing stock/selling shares. The capital was used to buy land and construct a building for a business park.

Over the decades, MDC/Manning attracted a series of manufacturing firms to the business park. Most of the businesses mass-produced electrical equipment. Compared to the stability over time of the land in farms in the region, they found the turnover rates in nonfarm businesses to be frighteningly dynamic. No firm stayed in Manning more than ten years. Some of the firms simply closed, and some relocated. The last manufacturer came in 1985; it relocated to Mexico in 1995 in search of lower wages.

Thus, the town of Manning learned firsthand about the *product cycle* (Vernon 1966; Norton 1986). This theory explains that products are most likely innovated, developed, and commercialized in a city site, due to the diversity of that environment. As the market grows and production of a product expands, the firm relocates to an urban fringe site. As the process matures and the need for scientific and technical labor declines, it opens plants in rural areas to economize on rents and wages. In the last stage, when it is no longer able to command a premium price domestically (because it has been supplanted by subsequent innovation), it relocates to other countries to serve the foreign market as well as to economize on labor costs. Like households hosting a progressive dinner, each community type, from the city to the village, hosts businesses during some stage in their life cycle. Businesses come and go from each type of community. No town or city can treat business recruiting as a "one-shot deal." They must be continuously vigilant.

The departure of the last assembly plant from Manning's business park spurred a debate about whether or not to invest in spec buildings (built to the specifications of the firm they were trying to recruit). According to the president of the Manning Community Betterment Foundation (MCBF), who is also a vice president at the locally-owned bank, they decided against it, to avoid being "put in a financial bind" if the company leaves before Manning recoups their investment. Rather than advertising Manning on the basis of the low-cost *space* and low alternative wage opportunities there, they decided to advertise and capitalize upon their relative abundance of talented, quality people and their vital community/quality of life. They decided to seek out firms willing to pay higher wages for higher quality.

The citizens of Manning realized that while their financial capital was limited, they were well endowed with human capital. To better leverage that human capital towards serving the public good, they also restructured their for-profit Manning Development Corporation into the *non-profit* MCBF. The switch to nonprofit status made the Manning group eligible for government grants and other nonprofit foundation support. Furthermore, as a nonprofit, they are able to plow back into Manning 100 percent of the capital gains from the sales of the property from the MDC. The nonprofit foundation is exempt from all taxes, including on capital gains. As soon as the MDC was dissolved, more than two-thirds of the MDC stockholders simply converted their old MDC investments into donations to the new MCBF.

According to Warren Puck, a local businessman active in the MCBF, a fundamental reason to switch to nonprofit status was that the MDC stockholders never saw a *monetary* return on their equity anyway. The reasons the townspeople people invested in their local economy were for the general betterment (ergo their new name), rather than direct personal gain. Warren Puck says, "This is my home. This is where I want to live. I'd like to encourage my children to stay here and provide an opportunity for them . . . . It's just part of a bigger picture." Founding member Joan Phillips says, "People here decided that the benefits of cooperating for the public good outweigh the sum of the costs to individuals." Those benefits are well understood to be indirect and/or real, not monetary. According to Ron Collins, Manning's newspaper publisher, "More or less, nonprofits created unity, because nobody was going to get more than anybody else, [which was] mainly nothing [in dollar terms]. And we don't have an empty store on Main Street. Not one."[3]

RURAL BUSINESS RECRUITING: A "CLUB GOOD"

Some activities that are subject to increasing returns to scale may also be partially rivalrous. For example, since a firm chooses only one of many small towns in the region they target, business recruitment is competitive. The more towns there are in one region competing for one firm, the lower the probability any one town has of attracting the firm. On the other hand, recruiting is subject to both static and dynamic economies of scale. The static scale economies are that the costs of gathering information and conducting promotion campaigns decline with volume. The dynamic scale economy is of the "learning-by-doing" variety. As noted above, business recruiting is not something a town can do once, then rest on its laurels.

The Manning activists are well aware of the difficulties of sustaining unilateral economic development activities. A small town like Manning can't afford to have lots of people volunteering time and energy. How long can the current "spark plugs" keep it up? If they slack off, they may miss an opportunity. But how can they sustain such a level of activity? A popular recommendation is that they should collaborate with neighboring towns. But the Manning citizens disagree with that strategy. They strictly prefer to collaborate with far-away towns. Indeed, the citizens of Manning have a sophisticated intuitive understanding of the challenges they face. They do not gloss over the rivalry of business recruiting (and public facility siting). They know that they are competing with their neighbors for the site to be chosen by a business interested in their general area. Formally, the expected value of the payoff declines the more neighboring towns there are in the coalition. This type of congestion classifies business recruiting activity as a *club good* (Boadway and Wildasin 1984; Buchanan 1965). The critical aspect of a club is the membership criteria. In this case, since the gains of collaborating on business recruiting are higher the farther apart are the collaborating towns, the criterion is to be sufficiently far apart.

Representatives of the emerging Manning Community Betterment Foundation (MCBF) went to a Sioux City economic development conference attended by representatives of similar community development groups, in September 1997. The MCBF people looked for "active people from the towns with the same issues" (Joan Phillips). They found their mates from the towns of Mapleton and Hawarden. The three towns are of similar size (populations from 1,200 to 2,400). They are in the same place in the *urban hierarchy* (Berry), but they are not neighboring communities, they are not close enough to be in competition with each other. They do not affiliate with nearby towns, especially towns above them in the hierarchy. As MCBF President Howard Roe says, "We might not go for the Fort Dodges [pop. 25,894] and the bigger towns like that. Anyway, they have their own professional community development offices. We do things for ourselves."

Manning, Mapleton, and Hawarden "all felt that their futures were dependent on affordable access to broadband telecommunications networks," says one of the activists. The three small communities recognized the potential payoff of their long-distance collaboration. They formed Western Iowa Technology Entrepreneurship and Capital Corporation (WITECC) within two months. WITECC incorporated in 1998 as a nonprofit, 501c(3) organization. The three communities work together to achieve some critical mass in their efforts to attract new businesses to their communities.

The outcome for Manning has been the realization of their business recruiting goal. They recently attracted a high-tech firm that capitalizes both on their internet connectivity and their skilled workforce. In 1998, WITECC and MCBF attracted the company ECI to Manning. ECI provides third-party technical support for two large CD-ROM manufacturers: Mitsumi and Smart and Friendly.[4] ECI has a development office in San Jose, California (Silicon Valley), which "makes all our contacts," according to Jerry Strawhacker, the director of Technical Support Services at ECI headquarters in Des Moines. The branch in Manning is their *only* technical support office.

Strawhacker explained that ECI generally targeted rural Iowa for its technical support office because of the quality rural labor force, and the tight labor market in Des Moines. They felt that city employees also have so many alternatives that it is hard to maintain a loyal workforce. But ECI didn't identify any particular rural town. Strawhacker says, "Manning came to us." That was possible because of the high visibility of the WITECC activists. It turned out that the president of ECI in Des Moines had been a personal friend of a WITECC member since the days when they both sat on a statewide economic development council. Once again, the citizens of the remote small town of Manning demonstrate the efficacy of distant connections (see also Granovetter 1973).

DISCUSSION QUESTIONS FROM THE EDITORS

1. The author notes the power company's involvement in economic development and says why power companies do this sort of activity. Would power companies be as interested in economic development if they did not have a local monopoly?

2. Manning attracted a company that provides technical support for CD-ROM manufacturers. Is the company likely to stay in Manning more than ten years? Why?

3. Manning partnered with two similar-sized towns that are not in its immediate area to attract business. How would one keep the alliance going if the other two towns are less successful in attracting business?

NOTES

1. Northwest Iowa Power Cooperative (NIPCO) http://www.nipco.com.
2. Northwest Iowa Power Cooperative (NIPCO) http://www.nipco.com
3. Transcripts from interviews of Warren Puck and Ron Collins in "Make Change NotMoney: A Look at the World of Nonprofit Business," September 3, 1998; American Radioworks archived broadcast: http://www.mpr.org

4. The location histories of these businesses nicely demonstrate the *product cycle*. See their corporate histories on their web pages: Enterprise Corporation International, http://www.eciusa.com; Mitsumi Electronics Corporation http://www.mitsumi.com.

CHAPTER 27

Welfare to Microenterprise: A Community-Based Approach to Sustainable Enterprise

Anthony E. Smith

INTRODUCTION

The redesign of the public welfare system with the Welfare Reform Act of 1996 and the dramatic change in the ground rules have ushered in an era of uncertainty for individuals on public assistance as well as state welfare agencies. In many communities, particularly rural areas such as the Appalachian region, job opportunities may be relatively scarce or low-paying. The challenge for job creation thus falls increasingly on creating entrepreneurial opportunities. Recent studies at the national, regional, and state levels confirm the challenges of job creation for individual transitioning from welfare to self-employment, particularly in rural communities (Boshara et al. 1997; Ryan McGinn 1997; Taylor 1997). This case study describes a community-based approach to building social, economic, and community assets to enable individuals to transition from welfare to self-employment. The study is organized into three sections: (1) developing a community-based approach to sustainable enterprise, (2) building a statewide partnership for changing state welfare policies, and (3) establishing an asset-building approach for enabling welfare[1] individuals to transition to self-employment.

BACKGROUND: OPPORTUNITY FOR CREATING A PARADIGM SHIFT

The catalyst and coordinator for this project was the Lightstone Community Development Corporation (LCDC), formed in 1994 as an affiliate of the Lightstone Foundation Inc. (LFI), a nonprofit corporation headquartered in Pendleton County, in the eastern panhandle of West Virginia. LCDC operates a

Sustainable Enterprise Microloan Fund which began in 1994 to provide technical assistance and small loans to individuals to start or expand small businesses which demonstrate stewardship of natural and/or community resources. The U.S. Treasury Department in 1998 certified LCDC as a Community Finance Development Institution (CDFI) for its record in enabling low-income individuals transition to self-employment in an economically depressed ten-county service area.

In 1998, LCDC was selected in a competitive grant program administered by the Appalachian Regional Commission (ARC) to demonstrate a national model for transitioning individuals from welfare to self-employment. LCDC developed a collaborative approach with state agencies and community-based microloan funds to change state welfare policy to enable welfare recipients to start a business without losing their welfare benefits during the first two years.

A key component of LCDC's collaborative strategy for the ARC project was to ask the West Virginia Small Business Development Center (WVSBDC) to be an active partner. The WVSBDC is part of the West Virginia Development Office, the state-level Commerce Department. The WVSBDC has direct access to policymakers such as the governor's office, legislators, and agency heads. The WVSBDC coordinates a network of 12 Small Business Development Center's that serves every county in the state. The centers provide free consulting for persons starting a business or already in business, and have worked with welfare recipients in the past.

The WVSBDC had initiated and received legislative support for a statewide microloan program, funded at $400,000 per year since 1994. The WVSBDC provides seed funds for regionally operated microloan programs, and retains oversight of the program. Lightstone had twice received seed funds through this program.

DEVELOP A COMMUNITY-BASED APPROACH TO SUSTAINABLE ENTERPRISE

LCDC's first lending activities were in support of a network of five county farmers' markets in the WV eastern panhandle. In 1994 and 1995, the Lightstone Foundation, together with the West Virginia University Extension Service, helped develop farmers' markets in three of the counties (Pendleton, Grant, and Hardy), and also provided technical and financial support to two existing farmers' markets in Mineral and Hampshire Counties. In seeking to strengthen links between family farmers and their communities, Lightstone Foundation and the farmers encountered a challenge in how these markets could benefit low-income households. Farmers wanted to participate in the West Virginia Women, Infants and Children (WIC) Farmers' Market Coupon Program because it would enable low-income households to receive $20 coupons which they could use to purchase fresh, locally grown produce directly from the farmers. Farmers could not afford to participate in the program, however, due to the long delays in getting coupons redeemed by the state treasury.

Discussion I

How can a community-based microloan program build assets in the community to overcome the limitations of a state subsidy program for low-income households?

In 1994, LCDC enabled farmers at these markets to accept WIC coupons by providing zero interest bridge loans to the farmers, ranging from $20 to $200 at a time, by redeeming the coupons directly to the farmers and then invoicing the state agency. LCDC's initiative thus enabled the farmers to serve low-income customers, and as it turned out, their WIC business accounted for more than 50 percent of their sales at the farmers' markets. For the low-income households, it represented an increase in family assets, as they were unable to participate in the Farmers' Market WIC Program without participating farmers. In 1995, the state agency, taking its cue from the success of LCDC's program, changed the ground rules for redeeming WIC coupons so that farmers could redeem them at local banks. The Farmers' Market WIC Program continued in effect at these farmers' markets the following years. This represented the first instance to which LCDC helped usher changes in state policies by demonstrating a community-based approach to building assets for family farmers and low-income persons.

In 1996, LCDC received a grant from the West Virginia Small Business Development Center (WVSBDC) for its revolving loan fund to support small business development. LCDC advertised the availability of its microloan program throughout its service area. Soon thereafter, LCDC began to receive referrals from several sources for loan applicants.

Discussion II

How can a community-based microloan program complement the lending activities of local banks by making loans to low-income individuals with a history of credit problems without going out of business?

Among the first loan applicants referred to LCDC were (1) a disabled Vietnam veteran wanting to start a portable band saw business, (2) a victim of domestic violence wanting to start a business consulting to small government in developing violence prevention programs, and (3) a person laid off after 22 years of working in a sewing company that went out of business, wanting to start a family landscaping business with his unemployed son.

In each case, the local Small Business Development Center (SBDC) worked with the entrepreneur to develop a business plan, a loan package, and marketing plan, and made the referrals to LCDC for loan consideration. LCDC worked closely with the SBDC and the clients in fine-tuning the business plan, and structuring the loans as lines of credit to reduce debt service to a minimum during start-up, as well as to build a history of repayment before making additional loan commitments. Both SBDC and LCDC continued to work with the entrepreneurs after the loans were approved to provide free consultations on record keeping and other business issues.

All applicants had credit history problems and had been turned down for loans from their local banks. LCDC staff met with these individuals and learned that the reasons for their credit problems were all related to instances of unemployment and/or family emergencies, such as health or transportation, which in some cases led to more than 30 checking account overdraws in a year. In every instance, they had met their financial obligations once the emergency had passed, and all were current with their accounts.

LCDC's loan review committee reviewed their applications, and recommended loan approval, ranging from $5,000 to $8,000 each. Each loan represented a strong example of stewardship of natural and/or community resources, and all represented ways of increasing wealth in the community by creating value-added capabilities and recycling of capital in the community. Each loan also generated purchases in their respective communities, so the loan funds were multiplied several times over in creating community wealth.

LCDC's board approved the loans, and in each instance approved them as lines of credit, contingent on a history of loan repayment. LCDC's board also developed a comprehensive set of legal and financial documents for execution by the loan applicants. The documents made it abundantly clear that these were loans and not grants, and that LCDC meant business. As each business grew and demonstrated its ability to repay its loan commitments, it was able to draw down on its line of credit. As of 1998, LCDC has experienced one default but no losses on its portfolio of nine loans, and all but one of the businesses are highly successful. From the one business that failed, LCDC was able to recover the full principal value of the loan from insurance proceeds for equipment stolen from the business, which later turned out to have been a case of fraud, and the entrepreneur in question is now serving time in jail. According to the WVSBDC, most other microloan programs in the state experience many loan defaults.

LCDC's success with its loans may be due in part to the high degree of due diligence in reviewing loan applications prior to making a loan, in part to the close working relationship with the entrepreneur after the loan is made, and in part to a strong set of legal documents that protect LCDC. In all instances, LCDC obtains an UCC-1 expedited judgment note on any and all collateral for its loans, which enabled LCDC to recover the insurance proceeds on equipment stolen from the one company that failed.

Discussion III

What is meant by "sustainable enterprise?"

LCDC's board of directors developed clear yet broad lending criteria for sustainable enterprise. The loan criteria include prudent lending guidelines, such as a sound business plan, credible character of the loan applicant, sufficient collateral for the loan (including the equipment purchased with the loan), and good credit (with exceptions for family circumstances, as noted above). In addition, LCDC's board felt that to merit a loan, a business loan applicant must demonstrate at least one of the three criteria below, and not detract from any of them:

- *Stewardship of natural resources*: enhances the natural environment and/or supports value-added processing of natural resources to minimize waste. The portable band saw business minimizes waste of wood in cutting (far less waste than a circular saw), while also creating more value added on site (band sawed boards fetch three to five times the price of a log, and keep the value in the community).
- *Stewardship of human resources*: enhances the quality of life, learning and/or career development opportunities for individuals, especially for disadvantaged populations. The domestic violence prevention consulting business enhances the opportunities for victims, or potential victims, of domestic violence.
- *Stewardship of community resources*: creates more wealth in the community by purchasing services or products in the community, thereby recycling capital so that every loan dollar leads to additional local expenditures. The landscaping business is committed to purchasing its equipment locally, thus creating more wealth in the community. Waste products from the business, such as leaves and grass clippings, are composted and reused.

Based on LCDC's current loan portfolio, for every $10,000 of LCDC loan funds invested in new or existing sustainable microenterprises, more than $10,000 in matching investment is leveraged from other public and private sectors, more than $30,000 in new product and service sales will be generated, and on average one to two jobs will be created. This translates to more than an $800 increase to the local revenue base for every $200 invested.

BUILDING A STATEWIDE PARTNERSHIP FOR CHANGING STATE WELFARE POLICIES

In late 1997, the Appalachian Regional Commission (ARC) issued a Request for Proposals (RFP) for welfare to work demonstration projects in the 11-state Appalachian region. LCDC chose to develop a collaborative approach to changing state policies and demonstrating practices at the local level to enable welfare recipients to transition to self-employment. LCDC was one of four projects, and the only microenterprise project, awarded a grant in March 1998.

Discussion IV

How can a community-based organization develop a collaborative approach to changing statewide policies?

LCDC served as the contract administrator for the ARC project, and subcontracted with the West Virginia Small Business Development Center (WVSBDC) to help implement policies and practices on a statewide basis. LCDC's subcontract with WVSBDC enabled the state agency to hire a full-time coordinator for the project for one year, and established guidelines for partnership on a number of levels through a Memorandum of Understanding (MOU) between LCDC and WVSBDC. The subcontract to WVSBDC reversed the traditional roles of these two organizations, as WVSBDC had twice previously funded LCDC with grants for LCDC's revolving loan fund.

LCDC also subcontracted with three other state microloan funds to help develop policy suggestions and for documenting any changes in their lending practices for welfare recipients that might grow out of the project. Subsequently, one of the microloan funds dropped out of the program, as it was unable to staff its operations. In the absence of a statewide microloan association, this project also enables the three microloan funds to share information about each other's operations. Prior to this time, the microloan funds had been brought together annually for a one-day training by the WVSBDC, but no regular communications were taking place.

Through its partnership with the other microloan funds, LCDC's project area comprised a total of 29 economically depressed West Virginia counties. This area included not only LCDC's ten-county service area, but another 19 West Virginia counties within the service areas of the three other microloan funds.

In addition to the three microloan programs, LCDC's other project partners include the West Virginia Department of Health and Human Resources (DHHR) and three social service agencies that voluntarily cooperated in this effort. The project better enabled these agencies to meet their federal and organizational goals to create employment for welfare individuals.

Discussion V

How can a strategic alliance among numerous community-based organizations and state agencies translate commitments into changed policies and practices?

This project thus enabled LCDC and its project partners to achieve a significant shift in their working relationships to support a community-driven policymaking environment. LCDC worked at several levels to achieve support for change in state policy, through three types of partnerships:

- *Social service agencies*: LCDC conferred with social service agencies to develop a broader definition of welfare eligibility to include the "working poor," that is, individuals qualifying for LIHEAP (Low Income Home Energy Assistance Program), WIC, Medicaid, individuals recently on welfare, or unemployed individuals who were at or below 80 percent of the national poverty level during the previous year. In addition, LCDC and its social service agency partners agreed to develop an approach to enhancing the social net for emerging microentrepreneurs.

- *Microloan funds*: LCDC consulted with the three other microloan funds on barriers for individuals on welfare to start their own business, including state welfare regulations which limit personal assets to $2,000. It was agreed that this was an impossibly low limit for starting a small business and a great disincentive for anyone currently on welfare. It was also agreed that at least a two-year grace period was required in which to develop a viable business.

- *State agencies*: LCDC coordinated with the WVSBDC to develop a plan for publicizing the project and for organizing a statewide conference for key stakeholders. Governor Cecil Underwood of West Virginia held a press conference about the project in early May 1998, which was broadcast in part the following day on statewide public radio. A number of state policymakers attended the press conference, including DHHR representatives, which was helpful in gaining their further support of the project. Then in June 1998, LCDC and WVSBDC convened a statewide conference that included participation of DHHR, the state job training agency, other state policymakers, the three other microloan funds, and other social service agencies. In preparation for the conference, LCDC worked jointly with the WVSBDC in developing a set of specific questions for DHHR and other policymakers regarding ways to overcome barriers to self-employment for low-income individuals. These questions included considerations of raising asset limits, providing at least two years of operating experience, and other considerations to support welfare individuals wishing to consider a self-employment option.

LCDC's executive director facilitated an interactive discussion at the conference, and DHHR and employment training representatives committed to exploring policy options. Conference attendees also committed to cosponsoring regional workshops to design policies and practices at the local level. LCDC agreed to coordinate these efforts with all parties concerned. In July and August 1998, LCDC cosponsored these interactive design workshops with the microloan funds, DHHR field offices, SBDC field offices, and other local stakeholders. The outcomes of these state and regional meetings were twofold:

- An amended state plan, filed by DHHR in August 1998 with its federal agency, to continue welfare benefits for individuals transitioning to self-employment in the 29-county project area, as a two-year demonstration project, by: establishing a business asset level of $10,000 for individuals; providing a two-year grace period for small businesses; stipulating that 40 welfare individuals per year for two years could qualify for business loans under this project; and identifying LCDC and its microloan partners as agencies to qualify welfare individuals for self-employment.

- Commitments at the local levels by key stakeholders to support a locally-designed, comprehensive approach to enabling welfare individuals to pursue self-employment.

ESTABLISHING AN ASSET-BUILDING APPROACH TO ALLEVIATING POVERTY

The methodology for addressing the issues of poverty grew not only out of LCDC's operating experience in making loans to low-income individuals, but also published research at the national level. Growing numbers of the "working poor" have no assets to buffer them from normal, everyday emergencies, including health, transportation, and daycare. Individuals in poverty do not have the resources to address these crises. Even if they are earning above minimum-wage income, the lack of assets can throw them into chaos when their lives are confronted by emergencies. LCDC thus adopted an asset-building approach to enabling individuals transition from welfare to self-employment.

Discussion VI

How would you design social, economic, and community asset-building strategies for alleviating poverty, particularly in rural communities?

In addition to the economic asset-building approach to alleviating poverty, LCDC had to address the social and community barriers to small business development which are peculiar to a rural, mountain region. The decline in family farming and high school dropout rates combine to create a region in which family-based small enterprises represent a desirable but difficult goal for families to achieve. Obstacles include literacy, transportation in a rural mountain region, access to credit, and distance to concentrated urban markets. Many small enterprises are family-owned businesses that require a relatively small amount of start-up capital but have difficulty obtaining access to credit. Even in cases where credit is available, the remaining obstacles combine to make it very difficult for prospective borrowers to develop a sound business concept, translate it into a viable business plan, and carry out all the required steps for starting a business.

Finally, LCDC incorporated findings from two national studies in its program design:

- a 1996 national survey which indicates that a state's economic viability is closely linked to its environmental health,[2] and
- a 1994 report suggesting that a regional approach to developing sustainable enterprises is generally considered the most cost-effective approach.[3]

LCDC thus incorporated three levels of asset-building into its program design—social, economic, and community assets—as follows:

1. *Develop Social Capital Plan*: Each participant is referred to one or more of several regional social service providers. Each applicant is encouraged to participate in training and counseling with a case manager to develop a plan for building social capital assets to address child care, health, housing, family budgeting, rehabilitation services, and other services as needed to enable the individual to achieve his/her economic and career goals. Transportation and daycare needs are met through subsidies, and SBDC business counselors have in some cases traveled to meet with participants. Tangible goals for the 1998–1999 program include:

   a. Build social capital of 20 welfare individuals.
   b. Build policy support for self-employment strategies for individuals transitioning off welfare.

2. *Develop Economic Capital Plan*: Each participant is referred to the regional Small Business Development Center for business training and to develop a business plan. LCDC's project coordinator works with each participant in developing a business concept that addresses issues of stewardship of natural and human resources, to ensure eligibility for LCDC's loan program. Upon completion of a business plan (which includes all of the above), the participant can apply for a microenterprise loan from LCDC for up to $10,000. Tangible goals for the 1998–1999 program include:

   a. Provide a projected 12 loans (six by LCDC, and six by three other participating West Virginia microloan fund agencies) totaling a projected $60,000 (based on an average projected loan of $5,000).
   b. Transition 20 welfare individuals into employment.
   c. Provide technical assistance and policy support to three other West Virginia microloan funds in providing loans to low-income individuals transitioning off welfare.

3. *Develop Community Capital Plan*: The LCDC project coordinator works with each participant in developing, documenting, and monitoring

implementation of a community capital plan as part of their business concept. This could include, for example, plans for purchasing locally, reducing waste or reusing resources in the enterprise, and/or tangibly enhancing the quality of life in the community. The stewardship principles are reinforced by offering participants the opportunity to have loan application fees waived and more favorable loan terms if they enter into a signed agreement to perform community service. Tangible goals for the 1998-99 program include:

a.   Discover microenterprise market development opportunities by cosponsoring two regional market development workshops.
b.   Generate and document increased levels of community wealth through sustainable enterprises.

MID-YEAR PROGRESS REPORT

As of December 1998, more than halfway into the one-year ARC project, some significant groundwork has been laid in policy changes and in developing regional social infrastructures for building social, economic, and community capital. In addition, a significant grant from the Office of Community Services (OCS) will enable LCDC to extend and develop this project further. To date some 20 welfare recipients have received some business training, with several of them emerging as strong candidates for microloans. In December, two welfare individuals were approved for business loans by LCDC, and several more are in the pipeline for loan approval in early 1999.

LCDC has encountered challenges in its partnerships with the three other microloan funds. One folded operations, the second has chosen not to cooperate with anyone, and the third has yet to develop a cooperative relationship with its local SBDC. Other challenges emerge as well, especially now that welfare rolls have dropped approximately 70 percent in West Virginia over the past year. In addition, there remain the other challenges of cementing relationships among very different organizational cultures, from community-based organizations, to welfare agencies, to small business development centers at the local and state levels.

Some midstream adjustments LCDC has instituted include:

- focusing its microloan partnership with one other microloan program that seems to have the capacity and the willingness to cooperate;
- redesigning the welfare referral process, so that all referrals from welfare agencies go through LCDC or the other microloan fund before they are referred to the local SBDC;
- establishing direct links with the welfare agency field persons who counsel welfare recipients; and
- organizing market development workshops, such as on providing child care and home-based weaving, to generate quality prospects for loan applicants.

CONCLUSION

While the results of LCDC's "welfare to microenterprise" project will continue to unfold over the next couple of years, certain change management strategies have already proven effective. These include methods for sustainable enterprise development and partnership strategies for changing state policies. As with the Farmers' Market WIC program, the "welfare to microenterprise" project positions LCDC as a community-based agent for changing state policies, by demonstrating what works at the community level. It also enables LCDC to enter into a variety of strategic partnerships at the local and state levels to develop a collaborative model for social change.

It appears that a community-based approach with strong partnerships at the state level can be a very effective means for rural communities in providing comprehensive approaches to enabling individuals to transition to self-employment. It remains to be learned whether the community-based infrastructure for building social, economic, and community assets for alleviating poverty will overcome the many challenges ahead in moving from "demonstration project" to permanent changes.

NOTES

1. The term "welfare" will be used throughout the text for simplicity and consistency, even though the Welfare Reform Act of 1996 refers to individuals on welfare as TANF (Temporary Assistance for Needy Families) eligible.

2. A recently published national survey conducted by the Institute for Southern Studies reveals that states with the healthiest economies (jobs, annual pay, business start-ups, etc.) also have the healthiest environments (toxic emissions, spending on natural resource conservation, etc.). The survey places West Virginia near the bottom nationally for economic and environmental health. See Hall 1994.

3. There is an emerging global consensus that a grass-roots, regionally-focused approach to sustainable development can be the most effective approach to achieving tangible results at the local level. See Mann 1994.

CHAPTER 28

Developing Services in Sparsely Populated Municipalities in Nordic Countries

Knut Ingar Westeren

INTRODUCTION

This chapter analyzes the service sectors in 36 municipalities, (ten each in Norway, Sweden, and Finland, four in Denmark and two in Iceland). The three characteristics used to select the municipalities are a peripheral location, a higher than average production in the agricultural sector, and a decline in population in the 1990s. In the European tradition, a peripheral location is often defined as a region having fewer than six inhabitants per square kilometer. Some of the municipalities included in the project have a higher population density, but they are situated on islands. Thus we can say that the municipalities discussed in this chapter represent a portion of Europe's real periphery.

This chapter first analyzes service sector trends in peripheral municipalities in the Nordic countries in the 1990s and evaluates whether the service sectors have been an engine of growth for the rural economy. Information is also provided about activities in which the municipalities had success in developing services, and strategies used to avoid reductions in services.

Two kinds of data collection were carried out. First, all service activities (private and public) in the municipalities and the changes in the number of activities during the period 1991–1996 were registered by sector. The study also asked all municipalities to describe the "success stories" that they had experienced in the service sector. All together, the municipalities reported 140 success stories. It is on the basis of these data that we discuss how different forms of cooperation between municipalities and other entities affect service availability in the region.

MAP 8
Developing Services in Sparsely Populated Municipalities

THE OUTPUT FROM THE SERVICE SECTOR AND DIFFERENT FORMS OF COOPERATION

The data were collected through visits to the municipalities. Information was collected primarily from municipal administrators. The criteria for defining "success stories" in the data collection process were the effects of success on the local community (see table 28.1).

Table 28.1
Effect of Cooperative Effort on the Community
The municipality obtained a new service activity that would otherwise not be available
The project gave rise to increased production/increased profits
The project reduced the unit cost for the production of the service
The project led to a higher than average quality for the service
The project contributed to an increase in the local participation of the population
The success of the project was dependent on a close connection to the agricultural sector or to organizations in the agricultural sector

We sought about six success stories in each municipality. By the end of the project period, we ended up with 140 stories, or a little less than four stories from each municipality.

The success stories were also classified according to:

- the sector in which the result of the production or outcome from the project appeared, and
- the form of cooperation on which the project depended.

The form of cooperation that the project depended on was classified in the following way (see table 28.2):

Table 28.2
Classification of Success Stories According to Form of Cooperation
Public-private cooperation (PU-PR)
Public-voluntary organization (PU-VO)
Public-public (PU-PU)
Private-private (PR-PR)

To understand the classification in table 28.2, it is necessary to comment on terminology and explain what we mean by public-private partnership, third sector, and voluntary organizations. Osborne and Gaebler (1992) discuss a number of alternative service delivery options. They found that the use of public-private partnerships exploded in the 1980s because these partnerships initiated service production that was cheap and well adapted to local communities' needs. According to Osborne and Gaebler (1992), a public-private partnership had to involve the public sector and other agents in the local community, which could be everything from (for-profit) firms to nonprofit organizations (third sector). The Committee for Economic Development (1986) gives an additional interpretation of the public-private partnership concept by including (and stressing the importance of) committees or task forces with public and private representation to recommend an economic strategy.

The concepts of third sector, voluntary organization, and nongovernmental organization (NGO) mean somewhat different things to different writers. In this chapter, the term voluntary organization is used for all nonprofit organizations (third sector) (Kuhnle and Selle 1992). This term includes a great diversity of organizations that play different roles in the local community.

The municipality in the Nordic periphery is the key player in the provision of public services. It plays this role as a service provider itself, a partner in developing services with the private sector, and in cooperation with, and financial support of, voluntary organizations. The first two categories in table 28.2 cover what Osborne and Gaebler (1992) call public-private partnership. We have chosen to split this into two categories because from the municipality's point of view it makes a difference whether the service is produced by a private firm in cooperation with the municipality or as a cooperative project between the municipality and a voluntary organization.

The development of voluntary organizations is important to the municipalities' ability to provide services, especially in peripheral communities. The voluntary organizations in the Nordic countries have a hierarchical and democratic structure with a local organization, a regional level and a national level. Another characteristic of these organizations in the Nordic countries is broad participation from many groups in the local communities. The following have historically been the most important voluntary organizations:

- Farmers' organizations
- Labor organizations
- Temperance organizations
- Different religious movements
- Language organizations
- Sports organizations
- Different social and humanitarian organizations

This list is representative for all Nordic countries, with the exception of language organizations which are found mainly in Norway.

From 1960 to 1980, the importance of leisure in society grew, which had an impact on the structure of voluntary organizations. The original and ideologically based interest organizations (the first four in the preceding list) have experienced a decline in membership numbers. At the same time, new voluntary organizations, such as the modern feminist movements and environmental organizations, are growing.

One important trend is that organizations are gradually becoming more professional. This trend can be recognized from two perspectives. First, organizations are increasingly hiring full-time employees who attempt to develop the organization to become as efficient and professional as possible. Second, services and activities are becoming more professional. We see this clearly in the sports organizations, but also in humanitarian and social organizations. The Red Cross provides a good example, as its use of technology and level of competence has increased considerably in recent years.

The voluntary organizations in the Nordic countries cooperate closely and are to a high degree integrated in the public sector, especially the local level; many local organizations receive financial support from their municipality. In recent years, the support that organizations receive has shifted from general support to project support. This is particularly occurring in the health and social sectors, whose services are an important part of the public safety net in the Nordic countries. The outcomes of voluntary organizations' activities are, therefore, evaluated in more or less the same way as activities within the public sector. In the culture and sport sectors, there has been more room for trial and error, and voluntary organizations have had more influence in deciding how the public support will be used.

Membership in the general social voluntary organizations declined through the 1990s. Nevertheless, leading politicians, such as former Prime Minister Torbjørn Jagland of Norway, have expressed the opinion that in the years to come voluntary organizations will have a more important role to play, often in cooperation with the public sector. This viewpoint can be considered a response to criticism of the growth of the public sectors and the increasing costs of public welfare programs.

Another change in the structure of voluntary organizations is the growth of more specialized organizations which emphasize their members' interest. Nearly every serious medical illness is now represented by an organization working for the interests of those suffering from such a disease. We see similar developments in the fields of culture, sports, and religious organizations.

Many organizations have begun to cooperate with the business sector and are pursuing sponsors. Compared to other countries, voluntary organizations in the Nordic countries are presented with a much larger set of rules and regulations limiting and regulating sponsorship and advertising. In recent years, however, Nordic countries have been experiencing a trend in the direction of the evaluation of many voluntary organizations by market forces.

SUCCESS STORIES AND DIFFERENT FORMS OF COOPERATION

Table 28.3 classifies success stories according to sector of production and form of cooperation. Sixty-two of the 140 success stories (about 45 percent) result from cooperation between the public sector and voluntary organizations. Another 27 success stories are based on cooperation between the public and private sector. Forty-four success stories originate from within the public and seven stories from within the private sector, respectively.

The results in table 28.3 show that voluntary organizations dominate in the provision of social and cultural services. As expected, private organizations are considerably more important in commercial and business activities, though voluntary organizations are also relatively strongly represented in tourism. This may be a result of the potential for considerable external effects in this sector.

Table 28.4 presents the 140 success stories by sector and effect. Effects are classified according to the categories presented in table 28.1. The results show that the most important effect of the success stories was that a municipality obtained a service that otherwise would not have been there (category 1). Another important effect is a reduction in the unit cost of a service (category 3). In about 15 percent of reported cases, cooperation resulted in increased production and profits (category 2), and in another 15 percent, the result was a higher quality of a service (category 4).

Table 28.3
Success Stories Grouped According to Sector of Production and Form of Cooperation

Sector	Form of Cooperation				Total	
	PU-PR	PU-VO	PU-PU	PR-PR		%
Primary sectors	3	1	0	3	7	5
Mfg. Industries	3	1	2	1	7	5
Retail trade	2	0	0	1	3	2
Tourism	10	8	1	1	20	14
Transport	3	2	1	0	6	4
Business services	4	0	1	0	5	4
Public administration	0	3	1	0	4	3
Education	0	4	11	0	15	11
Health services	0	7	9	0	16	11
Welfare institutions	1	16	9	0	26	19
Other social and community services	0	2	0	0	2	1
Cultural services, recreation, and sports	0	14	3	1	18	13
Cooperating sectors*	1	4	6	0	11	8
Sum	27	62	44	7	140	100
Percent	19	44	31	5	100	

Note: * Success stories are the result of the joint effort of two or more sectors.

CONCLUSION

The interest of this study lies not only in the successes that we found, but also in the success stories we had expected to find but did not. In particular, we found few success stories based on cooperative initiatives involving the manufacturing and service sectors. This is surprising for two reasons. First, municipalities spend considerable money to stimulate the establishment of new business activities in manufacturing. Second, a closer integration of voluntary organizations into the market did not produce results that were looked upon as a joint success. It looks as if the business sector is exploiting voluntary organizations for advertising and sales promotion, but there is not much cooperation for mutual benefits.

Table 28.4							
Success Stories Grouped by Sector and Effect							
	Effect						
Sector	**New Service**	**Increased Profit**	**Lower Cost**	**Higher Quality**	**Increased Participation**	**Agricultural Project**	**Total**
Primary sectors	0	0	0	0	1	6	7
Mfg. industries	4	3	0	0	0	0	7
Retail trade	1	2	0	0	0	0	3
Tourism	8	8	2	2	0	0	20
Transport	3	1	2	0	0	0	6
Business services	2	1	2	0	0	0	5
Public administration	0	0	1	0	3	0	4
Education	6	0	4	5	0	0	15
Health services	3	0	6	7	0	0	16
Welfare institutions	5	2	14	4	1	0	26
Other social and community services	0	0	0	0	2	0	2
Cultural services, recreation, and sports	6	3	4	1	4	0	18
Cooperating sectors*	3	1	4	2	1	0	11
Sum	41	21	39	21	12	6	140
Percent	29	15	28	15	9	4	100

Note: *Success stories are the result of the joint effort of two or more sectors

We also found only a few success stories in the agricultural sector as the result of cooperation between voluntary organizations and the public sector or private businesses, respectively. In some municipalities, we came across the keyword "change to more ecological production." When we looked more closely into the matter, we found some farms producing in ways more sensitive to their ecological systems. These farms often ran into problems when they attempted to start on their own at the local level. One of their problems was related to marketing their product.

Since the service sector was the main focus of the project, most of the success stories are in that sector. We found very few successes in the retail sector. The trade sector includes retailing and wholesale. Data from the project indicate that the retail sector kept its position in the municipality centers, but declined in the periphery. We had hoped to find stories of successful strategies for avoiding the reduction of retail services in the peripheral municipalities, but there were very few such stories.

Business services also show very few success stories. We could see that to a great extent municipalities have adapted to the first phase of changes brought by new information technology and the computer revolution. To a large extent, both private and public services were using computers; we found extensive use of computers in the administrative and executive parts of public services. We found very few examples of new small businesses that aimed at serving the local use of computers and information technology, and we found no voluntary organizations that had as their aim stimulating the formation of such businesses.

In the tourist sector, we found many success stories which can be grouped into two categories:

- the formation of organizations and associations providing advice and consulting services (like marketing) to existing tourist activities in the municipality, and
- project development, such as the development of new facilities.

The opera festival in Kolari, Finland, is a good example of cooperation between voluntary organizations and businesses in the tourism sector. Three factors seemed to contribute to the success of this project: (1) the existence of highly competent and professional voluntary organizations in the cultural sector, (2) the presence of a tourism infrastructure (hotels, restaurants, and camping/cottage facilities) capable of supporting the event, and (3) financial support from the municipality. Two other successful efforts concerned the development of more professionally delivered winter tourism services—in Trysil municipality in Norway, and Kittila municipality in Finland. In both instances, the professional capabilities of the voluntary organizations were critical to the positive outcome.

In the public sector, we found many success stories. The following example is from the education sector. In Grong municipality, Norway, pupils from grades 1 through 4 are now offered an athletic training program instead of a traditional physical education program. This is the result of a cooperative project involving the municipality and a local sports organization. The success of this project is based on creativity, a high degree of participation from all types of sports organizations in the municipality, the high level of professional competence of the sports organization, and financial support from the municipality.

While we found several success stories in education, very few were in higher education. We perceive this as a problem because many of the municipalities experience net out-migration of people with education beyond high school. Orsa municipality in Sweden provides an example of a possible counterstrategy. There the municipality supports courses at the university level. These courses are offered in cooperation with voluntary organizations, and they aim at filling the knowledge gap that is found locally. It is one of only a few success stories in this area.

Many projects were in the health and social sector. Voluntary organizations have been running health and social institutions for many years. Some of these organizations (e.g., the Red Cross) have been closely integrated in the municipal management of health and social services and received a budget in more or less the same way as municipal agencies. Escalating costs in recent years have led many of these organizations to hand over the institutions and the responsibility for running them to the municipality.

Efforts by voluntary organizations geared toward providing services to people with mental problems in Overhalla municipality, Norway, and Isojoki municipality, Finland, are two examples of successful projects by voluntary organizations in the health sector. In these two cases, the voluntary organizations, in cooperation with the municipality, provide services beyond those offered by the municipal agency. The public health system in the Nordic countries is responsible for the treatment of all diseases, including mental illness. A problem arises when a patient returns to the local community after the treatment in the hospital is completed. In Overhalla and Isojoki, local voluntary organizations provide a program that supports the return and reintegration of the patient into the local community.

Voluntary organizations are also very active in the provision of social services, particularly services to the elderly. The projects found in our study demonstrate great creativity. The services provided often complement those offered by the municipality. We also noticed the development of more services targeted to the needs and interests of particular groups. For example, in the past, the Red Cross provided general services to all elderly people in a district. Now we found more targeted offerings, such as a weekend for elderly people with rheumatic problems.

Two other sectors where there are many success stories are culture and sports. There is a trend toward more bureaucracy in sports organizations. This is considered a problem for small sports organizations in peripheral municipalities because it reduces their influence over their activities. For example, some of the bookkeeping requirements to receive national grants tax capabilities of small voluntary organizations. Other requirements reduce the ability to manage resources within an informal system that relies on borrowed equipment or informal equipment lending agreements. Several of the success stories identified in our study are of sports organizations that were able to develop their own facilities and were, therefore, not subject to as many government controls. They used large amounts of volunteer work from their members and support from the municipality. They were successful because they managed to carry out projects without much involvement of the county and national governments.

DISCUSSION QUESTIONS FROM THE EDITORS

1. Put yourself in the place of a municipal official. What are the advantages to cooperating with the private sector? With the voluntary sector? What are the disadvantages of these forms of cooperation?

2.   How is cooperation likely to be different in small towns versus large cities?

3.   The author notes that small organizations have difficulty meeting the bookkeeping requirements of national grants.   Could an intermediary provide bookkeeping capacity, similar to the systems discussed in the chapter by Anthony Smith in terms of making it possible for farmers to get payment?   Discuss the pros and cons of using an intermediary to achieve organizational economies of scale.

CHAPTER 29

Introduction: Successful Rural Businesses

Scott Loveridge

What makes a rural business successful? Are there peculiar characteristics of the rural economy that give it competitive advantages as compared to businesses based in urban areas? Or do rural businesses thrive in spite of their relative distance to markets? Many businesses, particularly the sole proprietorships frequently found in rural areas, appear to have come to their current locations more through accident than design. Yet it is clear that in today's economy, inefficient businesses cannot survive for long. Therefore, one must conclude that some characteristics of rural areas make these businesses viable on the world market. Business survival depends crucially on the following elements:

Information. The business must be able to correctly identify markets for its product, the status of competition, appropriate technology, and manage its assets. Rural areas create special challenges for businesses in information access. With the changes in information technology, barriers to good information in rural areas are dropping rapidly, but many transactions still depend on face-to-face interactions.

Capital. Businesses need cash to purchase new capacity, maintain inventory, and pay employees during times when sales are low. Economists refer to this as capital. Business start-ups and growing businesses have particular issues related to capital. They do not have established lines of credit. Urban areas tend to have more specialized financial personnel, either working for banks or venture capitalists, who are able to assess a new or growing business's ability to pay debt or provide a healthy return to investors. In rural areas, the low volume of this type of financial need translates into fewer institutions able to assess new opportunities. Sources of credit or equity in rural areas are more oriented towards traditional projects, such as home mortgages or agricultural loans. Rural financial institutions may not have the capacity to assess projects such as a new computer assembly firm.

Labor. Rural areas have a natural advantage in terms of the cost of labor. However, with the global economy, rural businesses in highly developed countries now compete with firms located in poorer countries that pay workers far less per hour and provide no benefits, or job security. Rural firms must also cope with shortages of specialized workers. Firms have the option of training their own workers or recruiting from outside the region. Worker training takes time—often years. Recruiting from outside the region requires paying an attractive salary, raising the firm's costs.

Natural Resources. Rural firms typically have an advantage in terms of their access to certain natural resources. Land is cheaper in rural areas than it is in urban areas. Firms may also locate near significant mineral resources used as inputs in their production process. On the other hand, urban firms have access to other natural resources. Urban areas frequently grow up around natural transportation hubs, such as a port or passageway.

Business Services. Rural firms must also cope with poor access to business services, such as accounting, equipment maintenance, and professional training opportunities. A typical solution is to develop this capacity within the firm, which is a cost disadvantage compared to outsourcing, especially for smaller firms.

Customers. Finally and most importantly, firms need customers. The disadvantages—in terms of access to customers—of being located in a sparsely settled area should be obvious. Perhaps less obvious are certain advantages of a rural location. Firms producing items designed for a rural lifestyle may have a certain advantage over urban firms, in that rural firms probably understand their customers better.

The above discussion provides an overview of some of the challenges and opportunities for rural businesses. As you read the case studies that follow, ask yourself how the featured businesses have coped with the challenges and taken advantage of the opportunities of a rural business setting. The contribution by Illeris demonstrates how an entrepreneurial, engaged community can successfully make the transition from a labor-intensive industrial base that depends on the domestic market to a skill-intensive, internationally competitive economy. The chapter by Wojan explores how the special aspects of rural labor markets make it possible, under good management, to thrive in today's economy. The contribution by Chugh documents the struggles and triumphs of a woman who has built a business from scratch. Finally, the chapter by Woods and Smith shows how the local community and a successful rural business interact with each other.

Map 9
Successful Rural Businesses

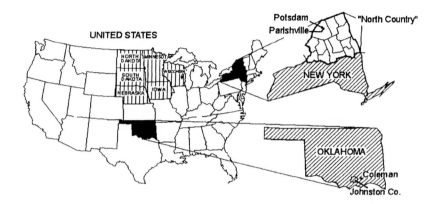

Adapting to Foreign Competition: The Textile and Clothing Industry in the Herning-Ikast Area of Jutland, Denmark

Sven Illeris

INTRODUCTION

This case study deals with the textile and clothing industry in western Jutland, a peripheral and largely rural part of Denmark. It is shown that this industrial district is characterized by deep historical roots, a local entrepreneurial culture, and strong networking traditions, and that its firms have been able to meet changing challenges with flexible responses. We discuss policies that governments can pursue to create optimal conditions for the future development of this kind of industrial district.

HISTORICAL BACKGROUND

The Herning-Ikast textile and clothing industry has its origin in the eighteenth century, when the poor farmers of this sandy, heath-covered region started knitting stockings from the wool of their sheep (Hansen 1983). In the nineteenth and twentieth centuries, some local people created manufacturing firms that put out much of the production (especially of undergarments) to farmers who had knitting machines on their farms. Thus, a tradition of local entrepreneurship and close networks between local partners emerged. In the district, which previously had no large towns, Herning-Ikast grew up at the new railway stations. They have now reached a population in the contiguous built-up areas of 30,000 and 15,000, respectively. The industry increased in the 1930s and 1940s, based on the protected Danish market, where everything that was produced could be sold.

Map 10
ADAPTING TO FOREIGN COMPETITION

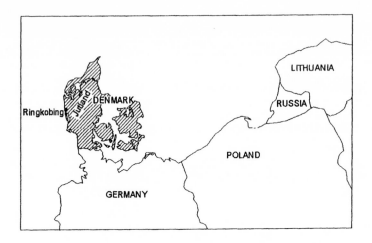

When trade was liberalized after World War II, the textile and clothing industry declined in most of Western Europe, due to competition from low-wage countries. Many experts predicted that the Herning-Ikast industry had no chance of surviving. The firms survived, however, as a result of Taylorist rationalization and specialization (e.g., in sewing operations). Because of their flexibility, which was based on network cooperation and awareness of rapidly changing fashions, the firms were able very quickly to launch and expand the production of new styles. They created a production network of specialized firms, even started exporting to other North European countries.

CHARACTERISTICS OF THE HERNING-IKAST TEXTILE AND CLOTHING INDUSTRY

What are the distinguishing characteristics of the Herning-Ikast district? First of all, it is a district of modest size. Within the county of Ringkøbing, the textile and clothing sector has employed about 12,000 persons during most of the post–World War II period, largely within a distance of 15 miles from Herning. To this figure, employment in derived activities should be added, such as dyeing, trucking, vocational schools, industrial organizations, etc. (another, much newer, local specialization is in computer services). The textile and clothing firms are small, typically employing about 50 persons and never more than 300. Most of the personnel are low-skilled women (seamstresses, etc.), as elsewhere in the textile and clothing sector.

The district as a whole contains firms with very different specializations. There are firms making knitwear, clothes for women and children, sportswear, up-market and discount products, and carpet producers. Production networks became widespread. For each order, cooperation was organized between local firms specialized in the components necessary for just that product. Firms compete, but at the same time they share information and cooperate with their competitors on the basis of mutual trust and shared social and cultural norms. The business networks are also personal networks. Everybody knows almost everybody else—in many cases, they have gone to school together or have family ties. And very important: all firms know each others specialities and strengths.

Local networking and the export and import of raw materials created a particular trade pattern. There are many local relationships and many international relationships, but there are few trade relations with the rest of Denmark. Copenhagen, the otherwise totally dominant national capital, only plays a very modest role for the Herning-Ikast industry.

A striking feature in the district is the entrepreneurial spirit. The firms are normally owned by the men who founded them, or by their descendents. These men are local residents and their firms are "home grown." Statistical data show that the frequency of new firm creation is high, but not the highest in Denmark. It is the extremely high survival rate of the new firms that is unusual. What is the explanation of the geographical differences in entrepreneurial activity? Danish researchers, especially Højrup (1983), point towards cultural traditions. Peripheral Jutland is dominated by the "life-mode of self-employment." This means that the people value being independent proprietors of enterprises.

One should bear in mind that this value is much more widespread than the number of self-employed persons. The local community honors those who have created firms. Many employees share this attitude. They hope someday to start on their own business and until then they respect, and are loyal to, their employer, rather than viewing him as an adversary. On the other hand, when an employee quits to create his own firm, the former employer tends to support him, for instance through subcontracts, if he does not become a direct competitor. This spin-off mechanism lies behind much of the above-mentioned networking.

As regards industrial relations in the Herning-Ikast district, we find a kind of balance. On the one hand, the management style is undoubtedly patriarchic—the employer wants to control everything. This fact, combined with the Taylorist repetitive, unskilled work, has given the district a bad reputation in union circles in Copenhagen. On the other hand, employers also care for their employees—who, incidentally, may be their neighbors or family members. Reciprocally, the typical employee is loyal to the employer. By all accounts, the general level of motivation is higher than in Copenhagen.

The wage level, especially for women, was previously low. In recent decades, it has approached the Copenhagen level. The large majority of workers are unionized. But the local unions tend to consider the interest of the firms more than do their national headquarters and show more flexibility regarding work rules. Strikes are extremely rare.

In spite of increasing wage levels, gradually it has become difficult to recruit young women to this type of work. In the 1980s, therefore, firms began to experiment with self-directed working groups and less monotonous work, partly to increase flexibility in production and partly to be able to offer more interesting jobs to young women.

CHANGING CONDITIONS AND BUSINESS STRATEGIES

As already mentioned, when international trade was liberalized after World War II, the first way in which the Herning-Ikast textile and clothing industry met competition was by cost-cutting and Taylorization.   In the face of stiffer competition from low-wage countries, this strategy gradually became untenable. The firms then turned toward higher quality products, product innovation, and new markets where higher prices could be obtained. A survey in 1990 showed an extremely high level of product and market innovations (Illeris 1992). Specialization into narrow product niches increased, too. Once more, the industry thrived.

The next shock was caused by the fall of the Berlin Wall in 1989. The industry soon was exposed to competition from neighboring east-central European countries in transition from planned to market economies. The European Union (EU) negotiated agreements with these countries which resulted in low customs tariffs for EU reimport of clothes, produced from raw materials exported from the EU (since 1998, there are no tariffs at all). At the same time, the Uruguay Round of GATT (General Agreement on Trade and Tariffs) negotiations abolished many restrictions on global textile and clothing trade.

Wages constitute an important part of the production costs. Polish hourly wages are only about 10 percent of Danish wages, and Lithuanian wages are lower still. Poland, in particular, also has an old tradition and much technical know-how in textiles, though quality standards were low during the communist regime. Even if productivity is lower in the transition countries, and transport costs must be added, sewing work can be outsourced to Polish firms at about one-third of what the same work would cost in Denmark. One problem with such a strategy is the lack of experience of Polish managers running a business in a market economy. Since management salaries are also much lower than in Denmark, however, Danish firms are anxious to train Polish managers and transfer know-how to them.

Monetary transport costs play only a minor role for textiles and clothes. Time costs, however, are of crucial importance for market segments where fashions change rapidly, e.g., clothes for teenage girls. Firms in this sector of the textile industry can only design clothes and plan production quantities on the basis of guesses of what can be sold. If it turns out that more or less is demanded, or that changes in the design are necessary, it is a question of survival for the firm to be able to change orders within few days. For a Danish firm, this flexibility exists if the sewing work is performed in Poland, where the goods are on a truck for only one or two days, and where the Danish manager can easily go and arrange changes. For this reason, Far Eastern partners are irrelevant for fashion-dependent products.

From 1990 on, prices of textiles and clothes began to decline in Western Europe. It became obvious that in Denmark, the industry would be wiped out if it did not restructure radically. The solution chosen was to outsource the labor-intensive sewing operations to transition countries. The cloth may still be cut and dyed in Denmark, but is then shipped to Poland for sewing (while remaining the property of the Danish firm). Finally, the clothes are shipped back to Denmark for marketing. The result has been a dramatic change in the Herning-Ikast industry.

Figure 30.1
The Value of Danish Sewing in Poland and of Danish Cloth Exports to Poland, 1987–1996

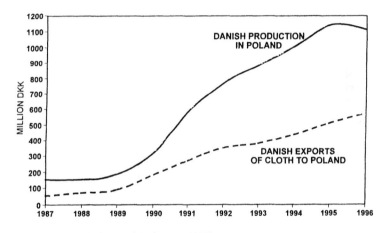

Source: Nielsen and Pedersen (1998)

Figure 30.1 shows the rapid increase of Danish cloth exports to Poland and of Danish sewing orders in Poland. Most of the Danish firms involved in this system are located in the Herning-Ikast district.

The restructuring process has so far not only saved a good deal of the textile and clothes industry, but has left the survivors with increased turnover and profits. The industry has at the same time continued its quality strategy and has been able to expand its markets. While in 1987, only 30 percent of the exports went outside the Scandinavian countries, in 1996, 60 percent of exports were shipped outside of Scandinavia.

Figure 30.2
Employment in the Textile, Clothing and Leather Industry in Denmark and the County of Ringkøbing, 1987–1997

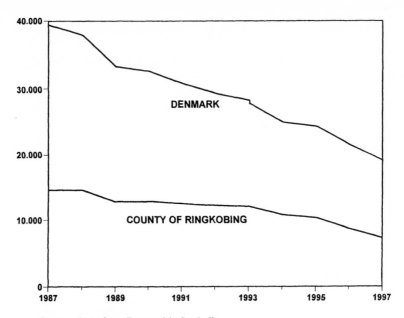

Source: Data from Denmark's Statistik.

The other side of the coin is, however, that the sector has shed labor in Denmark, as shown by figure 30.2. After 1993, employment declined in the county of Ringkøbing, too (outsourcing is estimated to have created a similar number of jobs in the transition countries as those made redundant in Denmark). The reduction has almost exclusively hit the unskilled workers, mainly the seamstresses who have all but disappeared in Denmark, except for a few working on test models and other special tasks. On the other hand, employment of white-collar persons working in design, management, and marketing has fallen much less, and recently even increased a little.

In other words, the typical Herning-Ikast textile and clothing firm has been transformed from a manufacturing firm to a firm whose economic values are created in knowledge-intensive service functions:

- finding out where the demand from various market segments is heading;
- designing clothes accordingly;
- buying appropriate materials;
- arranging for the physical production and the connected logistics;
- securing the quality of the products;

- selling and distributing products; and
- above all, managing this whole system in a sufficiently flexible way, so as to meet the turbulent changes in fashions and tastes.

The manufacturing sector thus merges with the wholesaling sector, which also increasingly designs and manages the manufacturing of clothes, on the basis of their intimate market knowledge. There are clear tendencies of integration with the retailing of clothes, too, by way of franchised shops.

Whether vertically integrated or disintegrated, a new pattern of specialization is emerging, one that is not based on types of clothes—such as sportswear—but on market segments, for instance clothes for middle-class teenage girls. Most Danish clothing firms aim at the broad medium market—"reasonable quality at a reasonable price"—but there are also up-market and low-price firms.

These developments have been under way for some time, and the outsourcing of manufacturing operations to foreign countries has radically changed the character of the firms. Since the operations are technically and geographically more and more complicated and involve many specialists, they require an increased business volume. A concentration into fewer, bigger firms is taking place, though the firms are still in the small-medium range. It is hardly possible anymore for an entrepreneur to start a firm by buying a secondhand knitting machine and putting it up in the garage. Barriers to entry have increased. Traditionally, the sector scorned theoretical knowledge, and around 1970, Herning refrained from begging the Danish government for a university— something all other towns did at that time. But now, the textile sector employs an increasing number of college-educated persons and is starting to co-finance research institutions.

Fortunately, most laid-off seamstresses were able to find other work. For some time already, the county of Ringkøbing has had the lowest unemployment rate of any Danish county. In the early 1990s, unemployment increased during the recession, but no more than elsewhere. Since 1994, unemployment has followed the general Danish downward trend to such a degree that in 1998, the rate of unemployment was about 5 percent (depending on the definition of unemployment) in the Herning-Ikast area. The seamstresses have found new jobs, mainly in other manufacturing industries (e.g., furniture) and in public social and health services (which previously were lagging behind in this part of the country). No increase in out-migration has been observed. Vacant buildings can easily be used for other production purposes or warehousing.

The outsourcing of sewing work to Poland has weakened the production networks in the Herning-Ikast industrial district. It is likely that other operations, such as knitting, cutting and dyeing will follow, and that not much will be left of the local production networks. This does not necessarily mean, however, that the industrial district will dissolve. For one thing, information networks may continue to be important. And for another, vocational schools that have close ties to the industry and permanently adapt their programs to the needs of the firms (now expanding into high-level education) will continue to offer the most skilled labor it is possible to recruit, which often constitutes a decisive location factor.

POLICY PERSPECTIVES

The Herning-Ikast textile and clothing district has developed and survived almost without any influence from government policies, except macroeconomic policies which have favored private firms in general. It is obvious that the entrepreneurial spirit and the networking tradition have historical roots; such qualities cannot be created overnight, especially in Europe where local cultural traditions are powerful. This does not mean, however, that local and national governments cannot encourage desirable developments in this direction. But results can only be expected in the long run, and only if local cultural traditions are respected. Governments in high-wage countries can help counteract the effects of competition from low-wage countries through support for education and training of the labor force and for research and innovation.

DISCUSSION QUESTIONS FROM THE EDITORS

1. Which would you rather have in your community, a homegrown textile firm with 50 employees, or a 50-employee textile firm that moved to the region from somewhere else? Why?

2. The case study region has exported its low-skill, low-wage jobs to Poland and increased its high-skill, high-wage jobs. What would you predict would happen to the location of jobs as Poland's economy improves?

3. What can local policymakers do to foster transition from low-skill, low-paying jobs to higher level jobs within the same industry? Is it always necessary to "export" the low-skill jobs?

CHAPTER 31

Fragile Virtue: Rural Labor Market Response to a New Competitive Environment

Timothy R. Wojan

INTRODUCTION

The shift from cost to non-cost factors of competition is commonly thought to have disadvantaged rural production in the 1980s and 1990s. Differentiated consumer tastes, in combination with demand for higher quality products have rewarded production systems that are both flexible and adaptable. It is argued that labor market characteristics of rural areas, reliant on routine production of standardized products, are ill-suited to fill these requirements. In contrast, urban areas have accommodated this change in the competitive environment by deploying pools of skilled labor that can perform a large variety of nonstandardized tasks and move rapidly from declining to emerging industries or firms. The change can be characterized as a replacement of the "robust regime" of mass production by a "resilient regime" of flexible accumulation.

Production systems described as "fragile" have provided an alternative response to the new competitive environment (Kochan et al. 1993). They are characterized by a high degree of interdependency between labor and management within firms, and amongst firms in supplier-contractor or co-production relations. The critical distinction from the "resilient regime" described above is that skills are developed internally rather than relying on external markets. This chapter investigates the experience of rural firms in the Upper Midwest that have derived competitive advantages from the application of high-commitment industrial relations/human resource (IR/HR) strategies that characterize "fragile" production systems.

RURAL RESPONSE TO THE NEW COMPETITIVE ENVIRONMENT

The examples that follow were drawn from four case studies in the Upper Midwest.[1] All of the counties examined are relatively small, with total urban populations of less than 10,000 and three of the four are not adjacent to a metropolitan area. The one adjacent county is also the smallest of the counties, with no urban population (settlements of at least 2,500 people) as of the 1990 census. Examples from the four case studies demonstrate two factors which serve to mitigate this decline in the economic value of rural workers: (1) the existence of a sector which is dependent on workers who acquire a substantial amount of skill on the job; and (2) the transformation of flexible low-skill manufacturers[2] into semi-skilled suppliers of just-in-time lead manufacturers. Firms in the first category, which will be termed "small-batch producers," are found in each of the case study counties, providing a rich story of alternative responses to the economic dislocation of the 1980s. The second category provides examples of the labor transformation required of firms that once used routine processes and produced for inventory to become competent just-in-time suppliers.

Employment Relations in Rural Small-Batch Firms

The necessity of flexibility in providing a wide range of products is dictated by the small or ephemeral character of the end-market, and the resulting inability to achieve economies of scale through the use of purpose-built machinery and a more highly disarticulated division of labor. The market approaches used by the various firms in the case study counties to achieve flexibility match the strategies of small-batch producers (Scranton 1991). The strategy employed by these firms allows the internalization of training benefits that has been central to increasing production capability.

Internal promotion, with workers acquiring firm specific skills over an extended time period (Koike 1988, 273), characterizes the skill formation process of a majority of production workers in the small-batch firms studied. New hires are generally not skilled in various manufacturing techniques. It is through intensive on-the-job training, workers' own mechanical aptitude and, for some, entry into an apprenticeship, that cumulative training generates skilled workers over time. While firms are generally eager to hire workers who received training from a post-secondary vocational education program, none of the firms are dependent on the output of such graduates for their hiring needs. While firms are prepared to provide training themselves, mathematical, problem-solving and innate mechanical abilities of a worker are seen as essential to the long-term development of skills.

The long tenure of skilled workers is commonly cited as an advantage of doing business in a rural community. The rate at which skilled workers leave, or are recruited by other firms, is low. This allows employers to capture (internalize) the benefits from training investment. It is the relative isolation of rural producers—often identified as a development impediment—that has advanced their ability to internalize the long-run return to labor training.

The Dual Commitment Relationship

A labor practice that is most evident among Forestville manufacturers is an implicit covenant between employer and worker to ensure the long-term viability of the employment opportunity through time. This dual commitment relationship should not be seen as a guarantee of employment through all economic contingencies. Rather, the firm commits to provide meaningful work, to market its products aggressively to ensure such work, and to increase employee skills. In turn, the employee commits to work for the same employer for the long term and to develop his/her skills. Although this dual commitment relationship is not part of a formal labor contract, firm owners and observers of the Forestville economy understand and support this commitment.

Employers are interested in creating a secure work environment and increasing morale, so that they will keep the investment in skill acquisition internal to the firm. By retaining workers as they increase their skills and experience, employers gain a highly skilled workforce that enables them to produce nonstandardized goods of high quality. Employees benefit because stable employment at reasonable wages allows them to stay in their communities.

The fact that both employer and employee have strong ties to the community reduces the risks assumed by both parties by increasing their mutual dependence. Cyclical risks, such as the recession in many manufacturing industries extending through the mid–1980s, are mitigated through the custom and small-batch market strategy followed by the firms. However, this approach cannot eliminate redundancies in all situations. Firms, therefore, distinguish between core and contingent workers. Contingent workers in Forestville are not temporary workers to cover short-term demand fluctuations. The contingent workforce is comprised of regular, full-time employees with benefits. The provisional basis of their employment is made explicit, and they have an opportunity to eventually change their status. Should employee attrition or long-term growth in the customer base warrant creation of a permanent position, candidates are drawn from this contingent pool.

The assessment of the welfare effects of the dual commitment relationship would require more detailed data and information regarding the risk aversion of workers and employers. One might guess that workers pay for the benefits of the dual commitment relationship with lower wages than those paid by other firms. This does not appear to be the case, however, as suggested by the wage comparisons in table 31.1.

The relationship observed in Forestville is unique to the extent that employers feel an obligation to provide secure work for employees, even if the economy is doing poorly. However, the economic benefits of retaining skilled

Table 31.1
1987 Average Hourly Wage Rate Production Workers, Upper Mississippi Valley Region

County Type	Average Wage Rate /Hour
All Rural Counties with Production Worker Employment < 4,000	$7.92
Rural Machinery Industry Counties, Prod. Worker Employment < 4,000*	$9.88
Riverton	$7.20
Poplar Grove	$9.25
Prospect Falls	$8.37
Forestville	$9.62

Note: * Machinery industry employment or establishment numbers disclosed in 1987 Census of Manufacturers.
Source: Census of Manufacturers

employees are recognized by small-batch firms in all of the communities. Since laying off skilled employees exposes firms to the risk of permanently losing some of them, firms attempt to avoid or postpone releasing redundant workers. The small-batch firms share the belief that skill acquisition is a cumulative process that provides a strong incentive for a durable employment relationship. The prevalence of the small-batch producers in these rural counties—places where one might expect to find a low-skill labor force—suggests interdependence between the market, production technology, and the labor process. A belief in the existence of a trainable, permanent workforce can be combined with general purpose machinery to produce highly differentiated products. In contrast, a belief in the existence of a low-skill labor force—or knowledge on how this segment of the labor market can be secured—can be combined with purpose-built machinery to manufacture standardized products.

It is the relative isolation of rural areas that has made the pursuit of either strategy feasible. The rural small-batch firms demonstrate how this condition of limited alternatives may also be used to align the long-term interests of employers and employees in the areas of cumulative skill acquisition and firm competitiveness. The fact that this condition has existed for some time has allowed these rural producers to make incremental changes in IR/HR practice, moving closer to the "high-commitment" archetype. However, this does not mean that the transition has always been simple. The next example suggests that innovations in employment practice have at times threatened the existence of these rural firms. The fact that survival depended in part on the limited alternatives of workers and also on the past goodwill of management may provide some clues as to why these innovations have enjoyed only limited diffusion in the U.S. economy.

Group Incentives to Innovate versus Individual Incentives to Produce

Despite the long-term nature of employment relationships, it would be incorrect to characterize these relationships as static. Changes in the method of remuneration are one example of innovations in employment relations implemented by a number of firms. These innovations sought to tie remuneration to performance rather than fixed-wage schedules. Given the strong work ethic of the rural labor force which employers lauded, the transition to more flexible wages, which would presumably benefit groups of hard workers, should have been an incentive-compatible change to the wage schedule. However, in those instances where the prior wage protocol had worked to establish its own set of incentives, changes in worker remuneration were tumultuous. In the example that follows, this change came closest to threatening the solvency of the firm as any crisis in its 50-year history.

The firm produces high quality aluminum castings for a diverse set of industries. The economic crisis of the 1980s had weeded out nearly a third of all foundries in the United States, reducing their number from 3,500 at the start of the crisis to about 2,500 by the end of the decade. The competition among remaining firms was tough in terms of both quality and price. The firm in this case study realized that the only way to remain competitive was to increase its capability to innovate. The one major obstacle to any plant- or group-level innovation was the piecework wage schedule that rewarded individual innovation. Because the awards accrued to individuals, they were not eager to share their innovations with other employees who were perceived as competitors. Management felt that meaningful innovation in production would require group innovation and the sharing of all relevant information among workers. When the firm introduced the gain-sharing scheme in contract negotiations in 1987, the compensation plan was seen as the prerequisite to the implementation of innovations in worker participation and work redesign; the interest in increasing wage flexibility was subordinate.

The firm was not expecting the disruption in work generated by the replacement of one set of incentives with another. By eliminating the personal incentives built into the piecework system, workers shirked their duties, resulting in work slowdowns. It is not clear whether the work slowdown was the result of worker distrust of the new collective wage formula or of uncertainty about a group's ability to win premiums in the new system. The new system eventually resulted in significant productivity improvements by 1992. Although workers eventually demonstrated their capability to cooperate in teams to mutual benefit, the transition from the old to the new reward system was not smooth.

Initiating work redesign under the old system was nearly impossible, as changes to the production system might alter the value of a worker's accumulated tacit knowledge of the production process. Incremental changes to the production process pose a limited threat to this knowledge and may even augment it. However, the introduction of radical change can negate a significant portion of this implicit knowledge, in effect reducing the value of specific skills accumulated over time. As long as the piecework system existed, any change other than incremental change would be seen as a threat to each worker's collection of tacit knowledge.

The example suggests that the crises facing manufacturing firms in the 1980s went beyond external changes in foreign competition or in the market, but extended to the relationship between labor and management. Wage issues and substantive changes in work design or employee involvement posed threats to workers and tested their relationship with management. The necessity of these changes did not guarantee the success of the new policy. This example illustrates that even competent firms faced the possibility of insolvency resulting from failed innovation.

Yet the firm survived and successfully introduced the innovation in worker remuneration. Are there particular characteristics of the rural environment that allowed the firm added flexibility to deal with the crisis? Again, the condition of limited alternatives suggests itself as the salient difference between rural and urban areas. Management was cognizant that long-term benefits of a strategy change might impose substantial short-term costs. The fact that management had regularly expressed its long-term commitment to employees, combined with limited demand for specialized labor in the local market, might have persuaded workers that refusing to accept the short-term costs associated with change could result in the loss of long-term benefits. This is not to suggest that urban firms are not able to implement these innovations. Rather, it provides added insight into why deep labor markets might impede adoption of high commitment IR/HR labor strategies.

Employment Relations in Just-in-Time Supplier Firms

The discussion now turns to the examination of the transformation of firms from producers of intermediate goods for inventory who rely on routine production practices, to flexible producers capable of satisfying the just-in-time supply requirements of end-producers.

Long production runs and the slack in the manufacturing process resulting from the production for inventory made the mass production strategy economically and technically feasible. The length of the production runs made investment in single-purpose machines and dies cost-effective, while at the same time minimizing the requirements of worker discretion. Production for inventory provided a manufacturing system which was "robust" to worker absenteeism, poor workmanship, or mechanical failure, as inventory in reserve could always be drawn down in the event of a disruption (Kochan et al. 1993).

In contrast to numerically flexible production, just-in-time production requires a core workforce that can perform a variety of tasks to produce the goods required by the customer for that day or week. It is the variance in workload across several products that would make hiring and laying off single-task workers intractable. Even if demand were stable, there would be advantages to having a long-term core workforce. The premium placed on quality makes the operation of quality control on the production line central to the objectives of the firm. Indeed, any defective parts are likely to impede assembly of the product in the lead firm's plant. Employers are dependent on the tenacity of the labor agreement and require more trust in the quality control performed by individual employees (Kochan et al. 1993).

The ability of rural subcontractors to meet the quality and delivery requirements of lead firms is based on the employees' acquired skills and their attention to detail. Workers with farm backgrounds made up a significant but decreasing share of the manufacturing labor force. Employers lauded the very high mechanical aptitude and strong work ethic of these employees. The length of tenure with a particular firm is also very important to the development of manufacturing processes dependent on sustained efforts at skill formation of workers over a relatively long time period. The loyalty of the workforce was identified as the greatest advantage of a rural relative to an urban location.

The example demonstrates that employment characterized by routine, standardized work does not necessarily define the highest level of industrial functioning of the local labor force. The transformation described in this case study also suggests that some rural workers may be left behind. General training of workers in problem-solving skills off the shop floor produced the same measurable variation in performance as would be expected in a classroom setting. Management expressed the concern that some workers were unable to, or chose not to, excel in these skills. However, it was clear that these skills were becoming an integral part of work reorganization. Dismissal of employees unable to develop these skills was seen as inevitable. The example strongly suggests the importance of maintaining the quality of public education; rural areas with better education systems may have a significant advantage in transforming traditional rural IR/HR systems.

The labor flexibility enjoyed by these firms is not the result of merely trading flexibility in changing the size of the labor force for functional flexibility. There are times when the number of job orders is insufficient to employ a full regiment of core employees. Under the current system, a layoff presents the chance that well-trained employees may not return when the firm is able to rehire. For the employee, the perception of job insecurity works to undermine the long-term relation between firm and worker. This tends to reduce worker involvement in quality control and productivity improvements that are central to effective just-in-time management. To protect against these undesirable results, the firm maintains a core group of employees who are hired on a long-term basis. The size of this workforce approximates the number of personnel needed to operate the plant during an economic downturn. To cover labor demands above this level, the firm relies on temporary employees. This temporary workforce can be as large as 40 percent of all production labor.

There are indications that managerial prerogative with respect to the maintenance of a large temporary workforce may be severely restricted by quality control certification such as ISO 9000.[3] Since all new employees are required to pass through the same training procedure, the training investment in temporary employees is very high given their short tenure. In the one firm that is certified but has significant demand for low- or semi-skilled workers, about 5 percent of the production workforce is temporary. Making quality control operative in each job is an implicit goal of ISO 9000 standards that will be increasingly difficult to satisfy with a large share of temporary workers.

CONCLUSION

The quality control dilemma facing rural just-in-time suppliers is one justification for the superiority of urban locations. If fluctuation in demand cannot be smoothed using unskilled temporary employees, then the existence of external markets for workers in urban areas may provide a more feasible solution. A similar argument can be made regarding small-batch firms with respect to their need for highly skilled employees. Emerging industries characterized by substantial volatility and production uncertainty may make the internal development of workers' skills infeasible. Firms in these industries may have no choice but to rely on external markets for skilled workers. And yet, the strategy of relying substantially on external labor markets is contrary to high performance, high commitment IR/HR practice. There is wide agreement that work has become less idiosyncratic, transforming the former necessity of internal markets to deal with problems of asset specificity into a management option, as illustrated in the case studies presented here. In the "fragile model" of industrial development, it is the "professionalization" of work within a specific firm context that argues for the internalization of skill formation and promotion. In contrast, the "resilient model" regards the "professionalization" of work as transcending firm boundaries. Urban locations will likely be necessary to follow this latter strategy.

DISCUSSION QUESTIONS FROM THE EDITORS

1. Why does the author use the term "fragile virtue" in his title?

2. Will the loyalty systems the author describes here be able to withstand the pressures of the global economy, especially competition from low-wage countries?

3. What might happen to an employer whose labor force is 40 percent contingent during an economic boom?

NOTES

An earlier version of this chapter is available as TVA Rural Studies Staff Paper 98-5, at http://www.rural.org/publications/. A version of this paper was presented at the 43rd North American Meetings of the Regional Science Association International in Arlington, Virginia, November 14–17, 1996. The author thanks Cynthia Rogers, Glen Pulver, and Jonathan Zeitlin for constructive comments. The usual caveat applies. The views expressed herein are the author's and do not necessarily represent the views of the U.S. Department of Agriculture or the Economic Research Service.

1. The names of the counties have been changed in this discussion. Readers wishing to investigate the cases more thoroughly are invited to contact the author for the genuine county names. The counties are located in southern Minnesota, Missouri, and Iowa and northern Wisconsin.

2. They were flexible in the sense that they were able to switch from large to small production runs with relative ease.

3. International Organization for Standardization ISO 9000 Series defines international quality control standards that "establish procedures by which firms can be certified as competent to justify, and in that sense warranted to make claims regarding their ability to perform as promised" (Sabel 1996b).

CHAPTER 32

Tale of a Successful Small Business in a Rural Community

Ram L. Chugh

INTRODUCTION

The formula for Sandy Maine's highly successful soapmaking business is hardly one that you would find in any economics textbook or formal M.B.A. program: Start with no formal training or real business background. Work with less than a $15 investment and without any formal business plan to start. Be willing to share everything you learn with any of your potential competitors, and locate in a place where both the raw materials for your product and anyone interested in buying what you produce, for the most part, are at least a half a world away.

Such an approach would seem more a recipe for misery than success, but the Parishville, New York, soapmaker has enjoyed exponential growth in sales every year for nearly 20 years, thanks to a positive attitude, a willingness to "play hunches," and a commitment to sharing her knowledge with her peers— and the fruit of her labors with a wide variety of hometown and worldwide charitable organizations.

Through the wise use of emerging technologies like the Internet and a stubborn insistence to simplify her operations as much as possible, Maine has been able to merge her New Age values with some old-fashioned hard work to not only develop a niche in her market, but to actually exert influence over the entire specialty soap industry. Maine's resolute spirit and vision of what could be has helped her to see beyond the geographical, technical, and organizational limitations of the north country region to develop a well-established and ever-growing enterprise.

The SunFeather Natural Soap Company is located in the small rural community of Parishville (population 1,900) in northern New York. This company was included among the 24 successful businesses profiled in our 1986 study (Chugh and Gandhi 1986), which examined the significance of small businesses in northern New York's economy. We decided to do a follow-up study on SunFeather Soap to find out how well it was doing in the current market.

SOCIOECONOMIC PROFILE OF NORTHERN NEW YORK

To develop a proper appreciation of the success of SunFeather Soap, it is important to understand the socioeconomic environment of this vast rural region. The 1986 study covered the 14 counties of St. Lawrence, Franklin, Clinton, Jefferson, Lewis, Herkimer, Hamilton, Essex, Oswego, Oneida, Saratoga, Fulton, Warren, and Washington in northern New York, commonly known as the north country region. The total area covered is 17,202 square miles, bounded by the St. Lawrence River in the north, Lake Ontario in the west, Lake Champlain in the east and Mohawk River Valley in the south. The Adirondack Mountains and the adjoining forest reserve lie in the center and separate the region into two parts. The northern New York region borders the Canadian provinces of Ontario and Quebec. It is the most rural region in the state, sparsely populated, and geographically quite isolated.

In 1990, the population density of the region was about 55 people per square mile, versus the state average of 381. Its total population of about 1.24 million in 1995 was 6.8 percent of the state's total, but its land area covers more than 38 percent of the state. Most communities are small in size with populations ranging from a low of 400 to a high of about 25,000 inhabitants. The average community size in the region is about 2,500 people. The region generally suffers from higher incidence of unemployment and lower per capita income than the rest of the state. The 1994 per capita income in the north country region was $17,828, as opposed to the state per capita income of $25,720.

Because of the low level of economic growth and lack of economic opportunities, the region experiences many problems typical of rural areas. These include higher rates of poverty and unemployment; inadequate infrastructure; inadequate transportation networks; limited access to health care and social services; out-migration of young people; and a low tax base. The political fragmentation, resulting in many small local governments, results in higher costs of public services because of diseconomies of scale. The region also suffers from a harsh winter climate.

On the positive side, the region has vast natural resources in agriculture, mining, forests, lakes and waterfalls, ski facilities and winter sports, clean air and water, and excellent tourism opportunities. Similarly, its proximity to the rich Canadian market just across the border is considered an important asset. The region, therefore, does have potential for economic growth. It is primarily because of such assessments of the economy of the region that some community leaders refer to it as the "underdeveloped empire of the Empire State." Promoting rural development and creating jobs are the major priorities of the region.

SUNFEATHER NATURAL SOAP COMPANY, INC.

Few entrepreneurs capture the spirit of independence and individualism better than Sandy Maine, who turned what friends and family originally called a "silly idea" into a million-dollar enterprise. Maine started her business in 1980, when she was 23 years old. We interviewed Sandy in her office to get a good feel about her work environment. She talked to us candidly about her start, her growth, and what the future holds for her burgeoning business.

Getting Started

Q: How did you first get started in business? Were you an entrepreneur looking for a product to market or were you a soapmaker looking to get into business?

A: I guess you could say that I'm an entrepreneur because I first got started at age seven with this business. I had a couple of different things that I did, like a lemonade stand and a modeling clay business on the air force base that I lived. Then I decided to get serious and go to college and make something of myself [laughs]. That lasted until I got out of college and worked one year in the workforce at which time I decided to start another business. The soap business came to mind. And that grew out of my love for the wilderness, herbs, and gardening. I was searching for something to inspire me and I wanted to inspire other people through my work.

Q: You mentioned that you grew up on air force bases. Your father was in the service. Did your mother work or were there any other family members that served as role models for your future business career?

A: My mother worked at odd jobs, but my grandmother was a business person. She had a doughnut shop and she had three or four other businesses during her life—which was odd in that era for a woman. There was no big family business. But the spirit was there.

Q: Had you been making soap as a hobby before you decided to go into business?

A: No, but I was really interested in it. My grandmother made soap and I had her tell me all about it. I was really intrigued by it and we went around and visited all of her friends . . . and they told me all about how they used to make soap. I also saw it as a way I could integrate my interest in herbs, flowers, and the woods, because you can put those things into soaps.

Planning to Start the Business

Q: Was there anything, besides the fact that you were here at the time, that made you want to start this business in the north country as opposed to someplace else?

A: A lot of it had to do with living in Winthrop at the time, working in the Adirondacks and meeting my husband, Louie, who has roots here. It just seemed like a rich, wholesome place. I came up here in 1976 and got involved in the culture while in college and really didn't want to leave once college was over.

Q: When you first got started, what kind of business preparations had you made? Did you take some M.B.A. courses or anything like that?

A: It's a good thing I didn't, because I probably would never have done this; I probably wouldn't have believed it was possible. It was just better that I went on my instincts. I learned as I went along. Probably if I had gotten the M.B.A. and had started the business, I probably would have been a lot further ahead than I am now [laughing].

Sources of Funding for the Initial Investment

Q: Did you have the benefit of a large amount of capital to start out?
A: I was on unemployment and I had $15 and my first order for raw materials cost about $15, and I was working out of my kitchen. They say a lot of people start businesses when they are unemployed because they have a lot of time. What I made, I put back into buying more materials. I did that for about five years. The business kept growing and generating cash and I kept turning it back into the business and living a simple lifestyle.

The Early Days

Q: Did you find any advantages to building your business in the north country?
A: I never thought about it strategically, like, "Oh, if my business was only closer to Vermont or near central New York." I just was here and I was doing it here. But the advantages, now as I look back, were that there are some very hard-working people here; the cost of living is low, so you don't have to pay $10 an hour to have a good worker. I could pay minimum wage and pay more as the business grew. The business really succeeded because of dedicated workers who were reliable, honest, and hard-working, not always well-educated, but they were here, and that works for a production line type business.
Q: Did you find that there was a lot of help to get your business off the ground?
A: We were always looking for help because I felt inadequate. As the business got bigger, I began to think that I should have a business plan or be doing my bookkeeping in a different way. We went to the Technical Assistance Center in Plattsburgh, New York, and that worked out pretty well. It got me thinking about what I should be doing and what I should be thinking about. That was helpful because then I would go to the library and get books and read and do research on my own and find my way . . . I'm still looking at books and getting ideas through researching on the Internet, and finding my way.
Q: Do you feel like you were breaking new ground as a woman entrepreneur in the 1970s?
A: It wasn't a factor for me. I always did just what I felt like doing. I didn't have any gender awareness as far as that goes. Also, because I was in this "feminine craft," it wasn't like I was going out in a hard hat or anything like that. Nobody noticed that I was "breaking tradition."

Marketing

Q: Early on, where did you start to market your product?
A: I realized very quickly that the local market just wasn't going to do it for me. So I started venturing out to other areas. There, I could sell ten times or, 20 times more, by going to a more populated area. Then doors started to open up and I started doing trade shows, like the Rochester Gift Show and the New York International Gift Show. Then I started adding sales staff so I didn't have to go to all of the shows.
Q: How have you expanded your product line over the years?

A: In the beginning, we had about 12 different kinds of soap and now we have more than 150 different kinds (500 different products).

Q: How is your product marketed right now; how could I find your products?

A: Well, you can look at the Internet, go to Japan and buy it . . . . We've sold into 14 different countries at different times; most recently we've been working with a distributor in France, and we've sold to Saudi Arabia, Kuwait. It's in every state, lots of different "mom and pop" gift stores, The Nature Company, lots of health food stores, we also have catalogues. We're here, there, and everywhere.

Q: Was the decorative packaging something you came up with or did you go to an outside firm with that kind of expertise?

A: At first I'd sit down at the drafting table and draw all of the pictures and do all the lettering. My first catalogue was all done by hand with a calligraphy pen. Over time, you find there are people who can do a much nicer job than I could. I still have the ideas for the product and how I want them to look, but I could envision the product and work with a graphic designer and get a much more professional outcome.

Q: Besides the soap and soapmaking kits, what do you produce here?

A: The "washy squashy" children's modeling soap . . . soapmaking supplies, raw materials, soapmaking books, home party plans to capitalize on this whole wave of people wanting to make soap at home or start their own soapmaking business.

Supporting Business Growth

Q: Has it been harder growing your business in the rural north country region than in a more populated place?

A: That's been a big question for me the last few years. There seems to be a limitation on talent here. The people who work for me have had a limited set of experiences. I've tried to expand their world view different ways, like by sending them to California for computer training, taking others to the Soapmaker's Guild gathering, but still I often wonder what would this business look like if our managers were more worldly and had more experience to offer the business.

Q: Do you see this as a big void in the north country?

A: Well, the grass always looks greener on the other side. What if I had highly functioning managers who just knew how to accomplish the maximum? Would I be able to pay them? It's a tough question.

Q: What special strategies have you developed to overcome this void and the remoteness of the region?

A: Well, being a mail order company, shipping in and out really hasn't been a problem. I don't think I could ever have reached the level of sales by just marketing locally. Louie and I have spent some time in Ithaca during the school year and I've been doing some experimenting down there and the response has just been phenomenal. By tending to a specific store, the sales have been ten times what they would have been if they just had been ordering from us. Being there and creating the interest, it just seems like the climate is hospitable. And here it's always been a struggle.

Q: How has technology played in marketing or producing your product?

A: It seems that where we've kept the technology simple, that's where there have been the least problems. I was always in favor of upgrading our technology because I felt that to be the way a healthy business organized itself. Starting back in 1986 when I got my first computer. I said hey if we're going to grow, we've got to have some computer savvy here. And we jumped in head first. Then we jumped in about three years ago and got a whole network. And now I'm like aaagh! [laughs] Without Louie here, I could not handle some of the problems that come up and I don't feel like I know my customers very well anymore.

Q: Has the Internet played a big part in your sales?

A: Internet sales have been minimal. We get about six requests a day for information. Most of them are interested in soapmaking, soapmaking supplies. My first book had a dramatic effect on our retail sales. My publisher has sold over 60,000 copies and all of those people have written us and a good portion of them have become customers. During the premier year of my book (1996), our retail sales just skyrocketed. That offered a great deal of free publicity for my business, the craft, and me.

Q: How has your volume of business risen over the years?

A: It's been a nice gentle up. In the first seven years, we had some dramatic doubling of sales. The first year, we did $90; the second year, we did $900; the third year, we did $9,000; the fourth year, we did $90,000. Now we're way past $900,000. But it's been 15–20 percent growth every year and I don't know what we're looking at this year. It will probably be about a million and a quarter.

Q: Early on, did you have to secure financing to help your business grow, and were there any problems associated with that?

A: I remember at some point I got my first big loan from my dad; I borrowed $7,000. That seemed like a huge amount of money to me at the time. I don't even remember what I used it for, but I must have put it to good use. Then a couple of years ago, we borrowed $100,000 to upgrade our computer system and to bring a new product, "washy-squashy," to the marketplace. We also hired a person who had more professional skills. It didn't feel scary to be borrowing that much money, and actually the "washy-squashy" ended up becoming 30 percent of our sales, so it was an on-target kind of spend.

Q: Looking back over the period that you've been in business, are there any regrets over things you did or should have done?

A: Sometimes I regret the amount of involvement it has taken. But I've also had a tremendous amount of freedom, so you can't complain too much about how hard you have to work, when you don't have to work when you don't want to. Certainly, I don't work more than 30 hours a week now and that's comfortable, but at one time it was seven days a week, 12–15 hours every day. But I loved it.

Q: What did your family think when you first got started?

A: Well, it did not go over that well, but they didn't bother me too much about it. I did take a lot of teasing. Even my friends made fun of me. A lot of people thought I was silly.

Q: What made you think that you weren't doing something silly, that you could make a go of it?

A: I just knew it was what I wanted to do. I just knew it was going to work. I just knew it.

Competition

Q: Is there a concern that writing books on soapmaking and selling soapmaking kits will deflate your actual sale of specialty soaps?

A: I really believed in sharing, the spirit of sharing. My thought process was how many Americans use soap. Everyone does. How many Americans use specialty soaps? Only about 5 percent. So there's 95 percent of this market that's not being tapped. I can't service this whole market. If other people were making soap, it would just snowball, which it is. I already have more than my share of the soap market. I just felt like, how could I go wrong? Most of the women here didn't agree with my philosophy. They were much more protective, and when people who wanted to be soapmakers would come to visit . . . they were considered infiltrators or spies. But my philosophy is a lot different. I think generosity comes back, and it certainly has come back for me.

Q: Have you felt the pressure of competition as more people get into the business?

A: We heard from some of our sales people in the field that other soap suppliers are selling to this store and that now. I know I've lost some accounts, but I've gained more than I have lost. There have been more accounts opening up and our growth has been steady. I don't think we would have had all the interest and the growth if all these books weren't being written. Also, I'm selling a lot of supplies to the new soapmakers, so I'm diversifying my business there and somehow it's all working out. I think the generosity is a positive thing.

Q: Is the soap or the packaging different for products you export to foreign markets?

A: The soap is the same. Canada wanted us to put French labeling on our packaging, but the cost was too high. We just can't seem to sell into Canada, and we've tried really hard . . . the exchange rate works against us. By the time it gets on the shelf, it's so expensive that the Canadians won't buy it. And now we've got soapmakers in Canada, so I feel that they should be able to supply Canada.

Q: Are you guided by anything when determining the pricing of your products?

A: Well, I found that most of the companies that are starting out now (are underpricing their product). I tell people, you're going to need to charge as much or more than I do—even if you're working out of your home—in order to grow.

Outlook for the Future

Q: What about the future?

A: Well, today I was going to call somebody about selling the business [laughs]; it's been a frustrating day. It's like a soap opera here sometimes. Trying to figure out where you draw the line between work, and friendship, and commitment; that's when it gets hard sometimes.

Q: Is there a specific way that you would like to see your business grow? Do you have certain benchmarks you are looking to reach?

A: What we're trying to do is simplify it as much as possible, make it as profitable as possible, and make it as easy to run as possible.

Q: Do you keep certain products in your line even if they don't make a big profit?

A: If I feel that a product is inspirational in a certain way to the world then I don't really care if I'm making a lot of money on it. I definitely keep products on that aren't really money earners because they make the line look interesting and they serve another function.

Q: Are there other niches within the industry that you're looking to expand in?

A: I'm really interested in hemp, because hemp is going to become major in the next 20 years. It's something we could produce domestically that could help revive the family farm. It's something that can be produced in the north country, and it makes an excellent oil for soapmaking. My biggest new direction is in the home parties. I would almost be happy to sell my business and just focus on that at some point. I think there's tremendous potential for that, but it would take a tremendous amount of administrative planning and work to develop that.

Q: Do you get a lot of your raw materials locally?

A: No. I get a lot of oils from India, France. A lot of my essential oils come from all over the world. My main ingredients, olive oil and coconut oil, come from the Philippines and Europe.

Q: Is there something that ties this business to the north country region?

A: I think you could pick this business up and put it just about anywhere that has overnight mail. But if I had to pay $10 an hour for people to wrap soap, that would be a factor.

Q: Still there's a feeling that you are connected to the region. In what ways do you give back to the community, and do you think that's important?

A: It's part of our mission and our philosophy. We give around 10 percent of our gross income to different organizations. We tie the money to certain product lines, including a women's empowerment project in Nepal. We give to about 14 different organizations. It might be $50, it might be $200, but it all adds up. So we do have that feeling of wanting to give back.

Q: Do you have any advice for people who might want to start a business in the north country?

A: I think it's an excellent place to set your business down. It seems like if there was some way to bring their own management team in (from the outside), that would be the optimum kind of thing. Maybe those people are around; maybe they're not. You really have to be versatile to do this kind of thing, you have to be able to jump over the logs and climb into the trees to get a bearing on your direction.

CONCLUDING OBSERVATIONS

Sandy Maine provides a fascinating case study of a successful entrepreneur in a small rural community. Looking back to our conversations with her in 1986, one cannot help but be impressed with her persistence and perennial sense of optimism. Undoubtedly, she has grown a great deal. She is now a very confident and self-assured businesswoman and has become proficient in dealing with the changes in her business. She now thinks strategically and is proactive in her approach. Consequently, she is able to plan ahead and deal effectively with the growing competition and the changes in consumers' tastes.

In our 1986 interview, Sandy Maine appeared quite enthusiastic and determined to succeed in her new venture, but she was clearly entering uncharted waters, plunging into an undefined and undeveloped industry without any real idea of where it would take her. She did not fully know the market, what niche her soap products would find there, or where they would eventually lead.

The fragrance soap industry was little more than a homespun hobby in 1986. There were no professional associations or established network of experts on which Maine could rely. She also could not turn to banks or economic development consultants for advice or support, because they knew even less about this fledgling industry than she did. She was moving forward in the dark, without the benefit of adequate seed money to start her enterprise or a clear roadmap to success. Each step forward was taken on faith, without any assurance of where it would lead. But with every passing year since 1986, Maine gained the experience and confidence that emboldened her to pursue new avenues, try out new products, and embrace the adventure that is business. She honed and expanded upon her instinctive marketing skills, using avenues as diverse as trade shows and the Internet to increase her share of the market. With experience, she developed a keen sense of the potential success of her products and became adept at creating merchandise that filled particular needs in her industry. She never shied away from new ideas or technology, which has helped her to expand her operation throughout the United States and around the world.

Most refreshing is the effect that business success has had on Maine's personal and family life. Rooted in values learned from childhood, Maine's business venture has remained a family operation despite its exponential growth. The support of her husband and family continue to play an integral role in her decision-making process and tremendous business success since its inception in 1986. Despite the many demands on her time, Maine has never compromised her family life.

Similarly, she had not allowed her phenomenal success to change her attitude and treatment of employees, customers, and even rivals with the same down-to-earth casualness that makes everyone around her feel at ease. Her long road to prosperity appears to have given this self-made entrepreneur a greater understanding and appreciation for life beyond her business. Another notable development since 1986, has been Maine's conscious effort to build social responsibility into her enterprise, turning the profits made from specific products into revenue streams for a number of personal causes, from the empowerment of women in Nepal to the care and protection of abandoned pets at the local animal shelter.

In 1986, Maine entered the fragrance soap business with about a half dozen products. Today, her company produces more than 500 soap and soap-related products, and she is recognized as both an innovator and role model in the industry. Maine let her determination, zeal, and positive outlook guide her to success despite all of the barriers before her. In the process, she has shown a tremendous ability to be flexible and adaptable and has exhibited a willingness to work with others—including her competition.

DISCUSSION QUESTIONS FROM THE EDITORS

1. Does Sandy Maine run a business or does she have an avocation? Has this attitude helped or hurt her? Why?

2. Commenting on doing business in the region, Maine notes the lack of management ability in the local area. What could local policymakers do to alleviate this problem?

3. What do you think will happen to SunFeather Soaps when Sandy Maine sells the business or retires? Will it remain locally owned? Will it remain in the region? Will it continue to donate to local charities?

NOTE

I wish to express my deep appreciation to Sandy Maine for agreeing to be interviewed for this study. She was generous with her time, and even took time to review the earlier drafts of this chapter. She can be reached at the SunFeather Natural Soap Company, Inc., 1551 Highway 72, Potsdam, New York 13676. Her Internet address is: www. electroniccottage.com/sunfeathersoaps. I also wish to express my sincere thanks to James Murphy of the Merwin Rural Services Institute at SUNY Potsdam for his assistance in conducting and transcribing this interview. This paper is dedicated to my wife, Seema, and daughter, Pooja.

CHAPTER 33

The Impact of an Entrepreneurial Business in Rural Oklahoma

Mike D. Woods and Tom Seth Smith

INTRODUCTION

Sundowner Trailers, Inc., located in Coleman, in rural southeast Oklahoma, was founded in 1976 to produce and sell quality livestock trailers. The firm is family owned, and employed more than 700 in 1998. Topics discussed in this case study include the firm's growth history and interaction with local economy, innovation in products and services, use of SBA (Small Business Administration) assistance, and contributions to community projects.

GROWTH HISTORY AND INTERACTION WITH LOCAL ECONOMY

Sundowner Trailers, Inc. was founded in 1976 by the Shipman family of Coleman, Oklahoma. The company produced custom horse and livestock trailers. Three brothers, Larry, John, and Gary, began the company and were joined by another brother, Jerry, in 1980. They operated out of a hay barn in Coleman on the property of their father, Wayne Shipman.

In the early years, the brothers often found themselves working well into the night to meet production deadlines and fill orders, hence, the name "Sundowner." The brothers handled every stage of production, from welding construction, to painting, to trim and finishing. The early commitment to quality has been a driving force of the company.

When Sundowner Trailers, Inc. was founded, the three brothers were its sole employees. Employment grew slowly at first and reached 165 by 1992. By 1994, there were already 410 employees, and three years later, in 1997, employment was 600. Sundowner Trailers, Inc. enjoyed steady growth in sales, selling approximately $10 million worth of products and services in 1991, and by 1997 sales had grown to almost $70 million. The facilities in rural Coleman also expanded to keep up with demand; they now cover more than 30 acres. A unique marketing and production strategy has so far resulted in steady growth with no wide fluctuations in employment. The combination of "built to order" trailers with inventory production for the most popular models, creates a need for a stable labor force.

Coleman, Oklahoma is in southeastern Oklahoma, on the eastern edge of Johnston County. It is an unincorporated community; thus, census data for Coleman are not available. The estimated population of Johnston County in 1996 was 10,460. Unemployment rates were 5.9 percent in 1996, and 7.3 percent in 1997.

USE OF SBA ASSISTANCE

Firms with great potential for growth often do not have access to adequate capital. Programs offered by entities such as the Small Business Administration (SBA) are intended to provide assistance. In the early years, Sundowner Trailers, Inc. applied for and received an SBA 504 loan. This type of loan provides financing for fixed assets, and allowed Sundowner to continue its rapid growth. Rural Enterprises of Oklahoma, Inc. (REI) was the certified development company that, in cooperation with a local bank, processed the SBA loan.

In later years, the firm was able to secure financing from other sources. In fact, a second SBA loan was approved but never utilized. The original loan, however, allowed continued expansion at a critical point in the firm's development. Margaret Blankenship, REI's marketing manager, recalls assisting the firm with business plan development on a home computer when there were only 55 employees. The owners were willing and able to find the technical expertise to aid their firm in securing needed financing.

Discussion I

Sundowner Trailers, Inc. has enjoyed remarkable growth in recent years. What entrepreneurial characteristics or traits would you expect a company like this to exhibit?

INNOVATION IN PRODUCT/SERVICE STRATEGY

Entrepreneurs have many characteristics that are distinctive, according to the scholars who study them. Peter Drucker (1985) notes that entrepreneurs often take an idea for a product, assume risks, and commit to a vision for the business. Sundowner has certainly brought many innovations to the horse trailer industry, which is not thought of as "high tech." Drucker notes that entrepreneurial activity and innovation is not limited to "high tech" businesses. Successful entrepreneurs in any industry search for an opportunity and have a willingness to innovate and accept change.

The founders of Sundowner Trailers, Inc. understood the process of trailer production and put it to use when they started production in their father's hay barn. They were willing to commit to a high standard, and felt their efforts would be successful. Margaret Blankenship recognized their "vision" when assisting with the preparation of an early business plan. Sundowner Trailers, Inc. decided early on to focus on quality and produce for the "higher end" of the market, emphasizing value, not price. In a 1997 nomination statement for an SBA award, Rural Enterprises of Oklahoma, Inc. notes several innovations and standards, including: commitment to brand name accessories, quality input use, living quarters to accompany the horse trailer, guarantees on workmanship, development of a dealer network, and creation of a research and development group.

Sundowner trailers are built as standard models or to fill customer orders from various options. The company's trailers usually include brand name tires, reflectors, and exterior running and license plate lights, sealed and enclosed wires, safety chains, and breakaway switches. Popular options to standard designs include paint schemes, logos, lettering, and graphics, winches and generators, cabinets, access and side doors and windows, and aluminum wheels.

In the beginning, Sundowner built only steel trailers. These trailers are built of the finest quality galvanized materials available, and are finished much like automobiles, with careful attention given to construction and finish—even to the extent of using Akzo-Sikkens paint, the same paint used on Mercedes and Lexus automobiles. In 1988, production was expanded to include aluminum trailers in response to customers' needs. As in their steel trailers, only the finest materials and latest technology available go into the production of aluminum trailers.

In 1994, Sundowner introduced a living quarters option to their trailers in response to customer demand. Besides having a stall to transport livestock, these trailers include a bedroom area, small kitchen with a stove and refrigerator, and a bathroom with a shower. The living quarters are certified for use in all states requiring certification. The living quarters are manufactured and installed in Elkhart, Indiana, by Sundowner Interiors, Inc., which was formed in 1994 to exclusively build and install the living quarters options on the company's trailers. Sundowner Trailers, Inc. owns a 26 percent minority interest in Sundowner Interiors, Inc.

In 1996, Sundowner began offering "slide out" living quarters as an option on its trailers. The side wall section of the trailer expands to give more living space when using the trailer. This concept has already had a significant positive impact on the recreational vehicle market. It has been tested in the horse trailer industry and has received wide acceptance. Sundowner will build several different sizes to meet individual needs.

Trailer accessories, such as stacked saddle racks and bridle hooks, have become popular add-on items. To meet market demand for these accessories, the company established a parts and trailer accessories department, which is also responsible for filling customer orders for replacement parts. The parts and accessories department occupies a warehouse facility at the company's plant complex. These facilities provide warehousing of fabricated and purchased parts to give customers prompt and efficient service. All parts orders are received via facsimile from dealerships and are shipped promptly.

Sundowner Trailers, Inc. guarantees the workmanship and materials of the main trailer structure and all other parts manufactured by Sundowner that attach to the main trailer under a limited warranty for a period of five years on aluminum trailers and one year on steel trailers. The paint on the steel trailers is guaranteed for two years. The warranty does not include normal wear items, such as brakes, bearings, and tires. The company's warranty obligations are limited to repairs and replacement of parts. Sundowner has recently enhanced the warranty by allowing unused periods to be transferred to succeeding purchasers of Sundowner trailers.

Sundowner Trailers, Inc.'s vigorous and aggressive marketing program made them leaders in their role as a major manufacturer of steel and aluminum trailers. The company's marketing plan includes a dealer network of approximately 75 dealerships on the 48 contiguous states, and in Canada. Sundowner has sales managers assigned to sales territories covering every part of this vast area.

Sundowner University was established in 1997 to assist with the dealer network. Sundowner employees, Personnel Manager W. C. Daniel, and some outside sales professionals are brought in to assist with training of dealers in sales, finance, product knowledge, customer service, accounting, and ordering. This commitment to education has been very important for the company's success.

Sundowner Trailers, Inc. recently established a research and development group that has already had a positive impact on translating customer demands and employee suggestions into new products. The group consists of seven full-time employees who work closely with both the marketing and production departments. A new research and development facility was constructed during 1995 to conduct experiments and construct new trailer prototypes. At Sundowner, quality begins on the drawing board. Computer aided engineering and CAD/CAM computer software programs are used to assist with new product design and structure, thereby substantially reducing trial and error in the development process.

CONTRIBUTIONS TO COMMUNITY PROJECTS

While the contribution of Sundowner Trailers, Inc. in terms of jobs is very significant for the local economy, other contributions to the region are also impressive and contribute to the quality of life in the area. Several local high schools and national technical schools benefit from donations of welders, building materials, and other supplies, and training programs in the local schools benefit from assistance provided by Sundowner Trailers, Inc.

Discussion II

Sundowner Trailers, Inc. operates in a rural region. What issues would you expect the firm deals with which may be unique to a rural area?

A significant challenge for Sundowner Trailers, Inc. is finding sufficient labor. Typically, employees travel up to 50 or 60 miles to their job in Coleman. The personnel director notes that the company searches for the proper attitude and work ethic. The company provides the training, but the housing supply has been a problem, as it has in other rural areas. Even if employees wish to move closer to their job in Coleman, often there is no available housing.

Employees recruited by Sundowner Trailers, Inc. are typically from a rural area, and many grew up on a farm, often with prior experience working with machinery, an advantage for the company. Sundowner also built ties with local schools, and feels that it offers a viable employment option for residents of the area.

Sundowner Trailers, Inc. offers 20 scholarships, paying $1,000/year, for students attending any university or technical school. All children or grandchildren of any employee can apply for one of these scholarships. The personnel director believes that this investment in the region's youth will pay off in the long run with an improved labor force. There is also the attitude that it is the "right thing to do." The personnel director is a former local school administrator. This facilitates forging and maintaining close ties with local schools.

Sundowner sponsors the annual Coleman Basketball Tournament and supports little league teams in the region. Donations of cash and materials have been provided to local fire departments and community foundations. In recognition of its commitment to its community and region, in 1996,

Sundowner Trailers, Inc. received the Quality Jobs Award from the state of Oklahoma for contributions to the local economy.

CONCLUSION

The brothers who founded Sundowner Trailers, Inc. have made an impact on rural Oklahoma. Knowledgeable observers note the founders had a "vision" and the entrepreneurial drive to be successful. The firm has grown rapidly, but was careful not to overreach. Some options or ideas were rejected. This is a family business that has enjoyed sound management. More than 600 jobs have been created by the company; they have significantly increased the job options of rural Oklahomans.

References

Adams, B. N. 1969. "The Small Trade Center: Processes and Perceptions of Growth of Decline." In R. M. French, editor, *The Community: A Comparative Perspective.* Itasca, IL: F. E. Peacock.

Albrecht, D. E. 1998. "The Industrial Transformation of Farm Communities: Implications for Family Structure and Socioeconomic Conditions." *Rural Sociology* 63:51–64.

Albrecht, D. E. 1993. "The Renewal of Population Loss in the Nonmetropolitan Great Plains." *Rural Sociology* 58:233–46.

———. 1986. "Agriculture Dependence and the Population Turnaround: Evidence from the Great Plains." *Journal of the Community Development Society* 17:1–15.

———. and S. L. Albrecht, 1997. "Changing Employment Patterns in Nonmetropolitan America: Implications for Family Structure." *Southern Rural Sociology.*

Albrecht, D. E., and S. H. Murdock, 1990. "The Sociology of U.S. Agriculture: An Ecological Perspective." Ames, Iowa State University Press.

Allen, J. C. 1995. "An Examination of the Social Disruption Hypothesis as Meat Processing Moves to Town." Paper presented at the annual meeting of the Rural Sociological Society, Washington, D.C., August 17–20.

Barkema, A. D., M. Drabenstott, and J. Stanley. 1990. "Processing Food in Farm States: An Economic Development Strategy for the 1990s." *Economic Review* (Federal Reserve Bank of Kansas City) 75(4):5–3.

Barkley, D. L., and M. S. Henry. 1996. "Economic and Fiscal Impact of Savannah Lakes Village, South Carolina." University of Arkansas Cooperative Extension Service Report, Little Rock: University of Arkansas.

Barré, P. 1998. *Districts industriels.* Mimeo. Louvain-la-Neuve, Belgium: Institut des Sciences du Travail.

Bartik, T. J. 1991. "Who Benefits from State and Local Economic Development Policies?" Kalamazoo, MI: W. E. Upjohn Institute for Employment Research.

Beale, C. L. 1993. "Salient Features of the Demography of American Agriculture." In D. L. Brown, D. Field, and J. J. Zuiches, editors, *The Demography of Rural Life*, 108–27. Publication #64, University Park, PA: Northeast Regional Center of Rural Development.

Beale, C. L. 1978. "People on the Land." In T. R. Ford, editor, *Rural U.S.A.: Persistence and Change*; 37–54. Ames; Iowa State University Press.

Becker, G. S. 1981. "A Treatise on the Family." Cambridge, MA: Harvard University Press.

Bender, L. D., B. L. Green, T. H. Hardy, J. A. Kuehn, M. K. Nelson, L. B. Perkinson, and P. J. Ross. 1985. "The Diverse Social and Economic Structure of Nonmetropolitan America." Washington, DC: U.S. Department of Agriculture, Economic Research Service.

Bender, N. K. 1999. "Enhancing Tourism Development Through Partnerships." In H. G. Vogelsong, editor, *"Proceedings of the 1998 Northeastern Recreation Research Symposium."* Radnor, PA: U.S. Department of Agriculture, Forest Service, Northeastern Forest Experiment Station.

———. 1995. *Agricultural Tourism: Opportunities for Farmers and Rural Communities.* Fact Sheet. Putnam, CT: Northeast Connecticut Visitors' District.

Benko, G., M. Dunford, M. Heurley, and J. Heurley. 1997. "Les districts industriels:vingt ans de recherche." *Espaces et sociétés*, 88/89. Paris Editions L'Harmattan.

Berry, B. 1967. *Geography of Market Centers and Retail Distribution.* Englewood Cliffs, NJ: Prentice-Hall, Inc.

Besser, T. L. 1998. "Employment in Small Towns—Microbusinesses, Part-Time Work, and Lack of Benefits Characterize Iowa Firms." *Rural Development Perspectives* 3(2): 31–39.

Birch, D. L. 1987. *Job Creation in America.* New York: The Free Press.

———. 1979. "The Job Generation Process." Research report prepared for the Economic Development Administration, U.S. Department of Commerce. Cambridge: Massachusetts Institute of Technology Program on Neighborhood and Regional Change.

Blackford, M. G. 1991. *A History of Small Business in America.* New York: Twayne Publishers.

Blakely, E. J. and T. K. Bradshaw. 1985. "Rural America: The Community Development Frontier." In H. K. Schwarzweller and F. Fear, editors, Research in Rural Development, 2:3–29. Greenwich, CT: JAI Press.

Boadway, R., and D. Wildasin. 1984. *Public Sector Economics.* Boston: Little, Brown, and Co.

Boshara, R., R. Friedman, and B. Anderson 1997. "Realizing the Promise of Microenterprise Development in Welfare Reform." Washington DC: Corporation for Enterprise Development.

Bridger, J. C. 1992. "Local Elites and Growth Promotion." In *Research in Community Sociology*, 95–113. Greenwich, CT: JAI Press.

———. 1989. *The Growth Machine: A Qualitative Assessment. Master's Thesis in Rural Sociology.* University Park: The Pennsylvania State University.

Bridger, J. C., and A. Harp. 1990. "Ideology and Growth Promotion." *Journal of Rural Studies* 6:269–277.

Bridger, J. C., and A. E. Luloff. 1999. "Toward an Interactional Approach to Sustainable Community Development." Journal of Rural Studies.

Broadway, M. J. 1994. "Hogtowns and Rural Development." *Rural Development Perspectives* 9(2):40–46.

Brown, R. B. 1993. "Rural Community Satisfaction and Attachment in Mass Consumer Society." *Rural Sociology* 58(3):387–403.

Buchanan, J. M. 1965. "An Economic Theory of Clubs." *Economica* 33:1–14.

Bülow, K. 1996. *Pilot Programme of Industrial Services for the Furniture Industry: Report and Recommendations*. Galway, Ireland: Connemara West Centre.

Busse, T. 1994. "The Case of the Branch-North Branch Consolidation Study." *Minnesota Cities* 79(7): 8–11.

Campbell, E. 1998. "Irrigated Acres Grow in North Dakota." *AGWEEK* (July 20): 24–25.

Castle, E. C. 1991. "The Benefits of Space and the Cost of Distance." In K. E. Pigg, editor, *The Future of Rural America*, 41–55. Boulder, CO: Westview Press.

Castle, E. N. 1998. "A Conceptual Framework for the Study of Rural Places." *American Journal of Agricultural Economics* 80(3):621–631.

Castle, E. N., editor. 1995. *The Changing American Countryside: Rural People and Places*. Lawrence: University Press of Kansas.

Cetron, M. 1994. "An American Renaissance in the Year 2000." *The Futurist* 28(2, March–April): 27–38.

Christenson, J. A. 1989. "Themes in Community Development." In J. A. Christenson and J. W. Robinson, Jr., editors, *Community Development in Perspective*. Ames: Iowa State University Press.

Christenson, J.A., and H. Robinson. 1980. *Community Development in America*. Ames: Iowa State University Press.

Chugh, R. L., and P. P. Gandhi. 1986. *North Country Successes: Case Studies of Successful Entrepreneurs in the ANCA Region*. Albany, NY: The Nelson A. Rockefeller Institute of Government.

Cochrane, W. W. 1979. *The Development of American Agriculture: A Historical Analysis*. Minneapolis. University of Minnesota Press.

Committee for Economic Development. 1986. *Leadership in Dynamic State Economies*. Washington, DC.

Congress of the United States, Office of Technology Assessment. 1991. "The Challenge for Rural America." In *Rural American at the Crossroads: Networking for the Future*, 35–55. Washington, DC: U.S. Government Printing Office.

Cook, A. K. 1990. "Retirement Migration as a Community Development Option." *Journal of the Community Development Society* 21(1):83–101.

Coulson, L. A., and D. L. Darling 1996. "Coping Strategies of Successful Rural Communities." *Kansas State University Agricultural Experiment Station Report of Progress* No. 754, March.

Davis, N. 1994. "Nature-Based Tourism in Eastern Connecticut." Connecticut Challenge Grant Application. Putnam, CT: Northeast Connecticut Visitors' District.

de Schrevel, M. 1994. "Filière Agro-alimentaire." *Entreprendre Aujourd'hui*, Supplément 7.

Dillman, D. 1985. "The Social Impacts of Information Technologies in Rural America." *Rural Sociology* 50(1):1–26.

Drucker, P. F. 1985. *Innovation and Entrepreneurship: Practice and Principle New York*: Harper and Row.

Dupraz, P., and B. H. de Frahan. 1998. "Agriculture and Employment in E.U. Rural Areas; Case Study: Département Les Ardennes, France." Louvain-la-Neuve: Université Catholique de Louvain and Rennes: Institut National de la Recherche Agronomique.

Dupraz, P., B. H. de Frahan, and G. Faucheux. 1998. "Agriculture and Employment in E.U. Rural Areas; Case Study: the Province of Luxembourg, Belgium." Louvain-la-Neuve: Université Catholique de Louvain and Rennes: Institut National de la Recherche Agronomique.

du Toit, D. F. 1984. "Confessions of a Successful Entrepreneur." In D. E. Gumpert, editor, *Growing Concerns: Building and Managing the Smaller Business.* New York: John Wiley and Sons.

Economist. 1997. "Europe's Tiger Economy." May 17: 21–24.

Edwards, R. 1979. *Contested Terrain: The Transformation of the Workplace in the Twentieth Century.* New York: Basic Books.

Esposti, R., F. Godeschalk, T. Kuhmonen, J. Post, F. Sotte, and I. Terluin. 1999. *Employment Growth in Rural Regions of the EU: A Quantitative Analysis for the Period 1980–1995.* The Hague: LEI-DLO.

Office Statistique des Communautés Européennes. 1981–1997. *Regions—Statistical Yearbooks.* Luxembourg: *Office des Publications Officielles des Communautés Européennes.*

Office Statistique des Communautés Européennes. 1996. *Office Statistique des Communautés Européennes Yearbook '96, A Statistical View on Europe 1985–1995.* Luxembourg: Office des Publications Officielles des Communautés Européennes.

Office Statistique des Communautés Européennes. 1985. *Statistiques de Base de la Communauté. Luxembourg: Office des Publications Officielles des Communautés Européennes.*

Fishkin, J. 1995. *The Voice of the People: Public Opinion and Democracy.* New Haven, CT: Yale University Press.

Flora, C. B., J. L. Flora, G. P. Green, and F. E. Schmidt. 1991. "Rural Economic Development Through Local Self-Development Strategies." *Agriculture and Human Values* 8(3, Summer): 19–24.

Flora, C. B., J. L. Flora, J. Spears, and L. Swanson, with M. B. Lapping and M. Weinberg. 1992. *Rural Communities: Legacy and Change.* Boulder, CO: Westview Press.

Flora, J. L., J. J. Chriss, E. Gale, G. P. Green, F. E. Schmidt, and C. B. Flora. 1991. From *The Grassroots: Profiles of 103 Rural Self-Development Projects. Agriculture and Rural Economy Division Staff Reporter* No. 9123. Washington, D.C., Economic Research Service, USDA.

Flora, J. L., G. P. Green, C. B. Flora, F. E. Schmidt, and E. Gale. 1992. "Self-Development: A Viable Rural Development Option?" *Policy Studies Journal* 20(2):276–288.

Flora, J. L., J. Sharp, C. Flora, and B. Newlon. 1997. "Entrepreneurial Social Infrastructure and Locally-Initiated Economic Development." *Sociological Quarterly* 38(4):623–645.

Fraase, R. G., D. E. Walsh, and D. E. Anderson. 1974. An Analysis of the Economic Feasibility of Processing Pasta Products in North Dakota. Bulletin 496. Fargo: North Dakota Agricultural Experiment Station.

Fuguitt, G. V. 1971. "The Places Left Behind: Population Trends and Policy for Rural America." *Rural Sociology* (36)4: 449–470.

Fuguitt, G. V., D. L. Brown, and C. L. Beale. 1989. *The Population of Rural and Small Town America.* New York: Russell Sage.

Garrett, P., N. Ng'andu, and J. Ferron. 1994. "Is Rural Residency a Risk Factor for Childhood Poverty?" *Rural Sociology* 59:66–83.

Glasgow, N. L. 1990. "Attracting Retirees as a Community Development Option." *Journal of the Community Development Society* 21(1):83–101.

Golden Growers Cooperative. 1998. *Testing the Dream,* 1997 Annual Report. Fargo, ND.

Goreham, L. 1992. "The Growing Problem of Low Earnings in Rural Areas." In C. M. Duncan, editor, *Rural Poverty in America.* New York: Auburn House.

Granovetter, M. 1973. "The Strength of Weak Ties" *American Journal of Sociology* 78(6):1360–1380.

Gray, B. 1989. "Collaborating: Finding Common Ground for Multiparty Problems." San Francisco: Jossey-Bass.

Green, G., J. L. Flora, C. Flora, and F. E. Schmidt. 1990. "Local Self-Development Strategies: National Survey Results." *Journal of the Community Development Society* 21(2):56–73.

Grossbard-Shechtman, S. 1985. *Contemporary Marriage: Comparative Perspectives on a Changing Institution.* New York: Russell Sage Foundation.

Haas, W. H. III, and W. J. Serow. 1990. *The Influence of Retirement In-Migration on Local Economic Development.* Final Report to the Appalachian Regional Commission. ARC Contract 89-48 NC-10269-89-I-302-0237. Asheville: North Carolina Center for Creative Retirement, University of North Carolina, September 29.

Hall, B. 1994. "Gold and Green," *Southern Exposure.* Institute for Southern Studies.

Hansen, N. 1991. "Factories in Danish Fields: How High-Wage, Flexible Production Has Succeeded in Peripheral Jutland." International Regional Science Review 14(2):109–132.

Hansen, V. 1983. "The Danish Hosiery Industry; a Specific Rural Industry in Central Jutland." In B. K. Roberts and R. E. Glasscock, editors, *Villages, Fields and Frontiers: Studies in European Rural Settlement in the Medieval and Early Modern Periods,* 385–400. BAR International Series 185. Oxford: BAR.

Harp, L. 1984. "The Entrepreneur Sees Herself as Manager." In D. E. Gumpert, editor, *Growing Concerns: Building and Managing the Smaller Business.* New York: John Wiley and Sons.

Heffernan, W. D. 1982. "Structure of Agriculture and Quality of Life in Rural Communities." in D. A. Dillman and D. J. Hobbs (editors), *Rural Society in the U.S.: Issues for the 1980s.* Boulder, CO: Westview press.

Hodson, R. 1984. "Companies, Industries and the Measurement of Economic Segmentation." *American Sociological Review* 49:335–348.

Højrup, T. 1983. *Det glemte folk.* Hørsholm: Statens Byggeforskningsinstitut.

Honadle, B. W. 1998. "Projecting the Public Services and Finance Implications of Municipal Consolidation: Evidence from a Small-City Consolidation Study." *The Regionalist* 3(30, Fall).

————. 1996. "Participatory Research for Public Issues Education: A Strategic Approach to a Municipal Consolidation Study." *Journal of the Community Development Society* 27(1): 56–77.

————. 1995. "The Barriers to Citizen-Led Municipal Consolidations: An Analysis of Minnesota's Municipal Boundary Adjustment Law." *Hamline Journal of Public Law and Policy* 17(1): 63–82.

Hunst, M., and G. Howse. 1998. *Minnesota Agricultural Statistics, 1997.* St. Paul: Minnesota Department of Agriculture.

Hustedde, R. J. 1996. "An Evaluation of the National Issues Forum Methodology for Stimulating Deliberation in Rural Kentucky." *Journal of the Community Development Society* 27(2).

Hyman, D., and B. Clinehens. 1998. "Citizen Representation in Local Issues Forums: Common Ground or Uncommon Agreement?" In K. Pigg, D. Hyman, and B. McKenzie, editors, *Sustainability and Community: Critical Connections.*

Proceedings of the Thirtieth Annual Meeting of the Community Development Society, Kansas City, MO.

Hyman, D. and J. Steff. n.d. *Seeking Common Ground II: Growth an the Quality of Life in Nittany Valley*. Centre County, PA: Public Issues Forum Steering Committee, *monograph*.

Hyman, D., J. Steff, and J. MacIsaac, editors. 1996. *Seeking Common Ground: Growth and the Quality of Life in Nittany Valley*. State College, PA: Public Issues Forum Steering Committee.

Illeris, S. 1992. "The Herning-Ikast Textile Industry: An Industrial District in West Jutland." *Entrepreneurship and Regional Development* 4(2):73–84.

Industrial Development Agency. 1996. *Achieve European Competitive Advantage: Guide to Tax and Financial Incentives in Ireland*. Dublin, Ireland.

Institut National de la Statistique. 1996. *Statistiques Régionales 1995*. Bruxelles: Institut National de la Statistique.

Institut National de la Statistique. 1994. *Statistiques Régionales 1993*. Bruxelles: Office Statistique des Communautés Européennes.

Institut National de la Statistique. 1991. *Annuaires Statistiques de la Belgique 1991*. Bruxelles: Office Statistique des Communautés Européennes.

Institut National de la Statistique. 1981. *Annuaires Statistiques de la Belgique 1981*. Bruxelles: Office Statistique des Communautés Européennes.

Institut National de la Statistique et des Etudes *Economiques*. 1995. Tableaux de l'Economie Champenoise 1994/1995. Reims: Institut National de la Statistique. Et des Etudes Economiques. Direction regional Champagne-Ardennes.

Institut National de la Statistique et des Etudes Economiques. 1993. *Population, Emploi, Logement, Evolutions 1975, 1982, 1990*. Paris: Institut National de la Statistique. Et des Etudes Economiques.

Isserman, A. M. 1994. "State Economic Development Policy and Practice in the United States: A Survey Article." *International Regional Science Review* 16(1&2):49–100.

Jensen, L., and D. J. Eggebeen. 1994. "Nonmetropolitan Poor Children and Reliance on Public Assistance." *Rural Sociology*, 59:45–65.

Jensen L., and M. Tienda. 1989. "Nonmetropolitan Minority Families in the United States: Trends in Racial and Ethnic Economic Stratification, 1959–1986." *Rural Sociology*, 509–532.

Johansen, H. E. and G. V. Fuguitt. 1984. *The Changing Rural Village in America: Demographic and Economic Trends Since 1950*. Cambridge, MA: Ballinger Publishing Company.

Johnson, R. K. 1998. "ND Bison Co-op in the Black." *AGWEEK* (June 22): 8.

Kassab, C. 1992. *Income and Inequality: The Role of the Service Sector in the Changing Distribution of Income*. New York: Greenwood Press.

Kassab, C., and A. E. Luloff. 1993. "The New Buffalo Hunt: Chasing the Service Sector." *Journal of the Community Development Society* 24:175–195.

Kaufman, H. F., and K. P. Wilkinson. 1967. "Community Structure and Leadership: An Interactional Perspective in the Study of Community." State College: Mississippi State University, Social Science Research Center, Bulletin No. 13.

Kochan, T., J. Cutcher-Gershenfeld, and J. P. Macduffie. 1993. "Integrating Employee Participation, Work Redesign, and New Technology: Experience in the USA." In W. M. Lafferty and E. Rosenstein, editors, *The Challenge of New Technology and Macro-Political Change*. New York: Oxford University Press.

Koike, K. 1988. *Understanding Industrial Relations in Modern Japan*. New York: St. Martin's Press.

Krannich R. S., and A. E. Luloff. 1991. "Problems of Resource Dependency in U.S. Rural Communities." *Progress in Rural Policy and Planning* 1(1):5–18.

Kraybill, D. S. 1998. "The View from Economics: Discussion of Castle's Conceptual Framework." *American Journal of Agricultural Economics* 80(3):635–36.

Kretzman, J. P., and J. L. McKnight. 1993. *Building Communities from the Inside Out.* Chicago: ACTA Publications.

Kristensen, P. H. 1992. "Industrial Districts in West Jutland, Denmark." In F. Pyke and W. Sengenberger, editors, *Industrial Districts and Local Economic Regeneration,* 122–173. Geneva: Institute for Labour Studies.

Kuhnle, S., and P. Selle. 1992. *Government and Voluntary Organizations.* Avebury: Aldershot2.

Larson, O. F. 1981. "Agriculture and the Community." In A. H. Hawley and S. M. Mazie, editors, *Nonmetropolitan America in Transition,* 47–193. Chapel Hill: University of North Carolina Press.

Leistritz, F. L., and R. R. Hamm. 1994. *Rural Economic Development, 1975–1993: An Annotated Bibliography.* Westport, CT: Greenwood Press.

Lewis, T. R. and J. E. Harmon. 1986. *Connecticut: A Geography.* Boulder, CO, and London: Westview Press.

———. 1995. *Farms and Family Fun in Eastern Connecticut.* Brochure. Putnam, CT: Northeast Connecticut Visitors' District.

Litcher, D. T. 1989. "Race, Employment Hardship, and Inequality in the American Nonmetropolitan South." *American Sociological Review* 54:436–446.

Lobao, L. M., M. D. Schulman, and L. E. Swanson. 1993. "Still Going: Recent Debates on the Goldschmidt Hypothesis." *Rural Sociology* 58:277–288.

Logan, J. R., and H. L. Molotch. 1987. *Urban Fortunes: The Political Economy of Place.* Berkley: University of California Press.

Lovejoy, S. B. and R. S. Krannich. 1982. "Rural Industrial Development and Domestic Dependency Relations: Toward an Integrated Perspective." *Rural Sociology* 47(3):137–52.

Loveridge, S. 1996. "On the Continuing Popularity of Industrial Recruitment." *Economic Development Quarterly* 10(2):151–158.

Loveridge, S., and G. Morse. 1997. "Implementing Local Business Retention and Expansion Visitation Programs." University Park, PA: North East Regional Center for Rural Development (Report #72), The Pennsylvania State University.

Luloff, A. E. 1996. "The Doing of Rural Development Research." In H. E. Echelberger, editor, *Rural America: A Living Tapestry,* 25–30. General Technical Report NE-228. Radnor, PA: U.S. Department of Agriculture, Forest Service.

Luloff, A. E. and L. Swanson. 1995. "Community Agency and Disaffection: Enhancing Collective Resources." In L. J. Beaulieu and D. Mulkey, editors, *Investing In People: The Human Capital Needs of Rural America.* 351–72. Boulder, CO: Westview Press.

Luloff, A. E. and K. P. Wilkinson. 1979. "Participation in the National Flood Insurance Program: A Study of Community Activeness." *Rural Sociology* 44(1):137–52.

Luther, V., and C. B. Flora. 1998. *Clues to Rural Community Survival. Lincoln:* Heartland Center for Leadership Development.

Mann, E. 1994. "Economic System and Sustainable Communities," Readings Compiled for Defining Sustainable Communities. Tides Foundation.

Mansbridge, J. 1984. *Beyond Adversary Democracy.* New York: Basic Books, and Chicago: University of Chicago Press.

Mathews, D. 1994. *Politics for People: Finding a Responsible Public Voice.* Chicago: University of Illinois Press.

McAllister, W. K., and D. Zimet. 1994. *Collaborative Planning: Cases in Economic and Community Diversification.* FS-575. Washington, DC: USDA Forest Service.

McLaughlin, R. T. 1990. "Making Connections through R&E: An Educator's Case Study." In G. W. Morse, editor, *The Retention and Expansion of Existing Businesses: Theory and Practice in Business Visitation Programs.* Ames: Iowa State University Press.

Mehrhoff, W. A. 1995. "The Minnesota Design Team: A Process of Place-Making Stimulates a State's Communities." *Small Town* (September–October): 4–13.

Miller, J. P., and H. Bluestone. 1987. "Prospects for Service Sector Employment Growth in Nonmetro America." In *Rural Economic Development in the 1980s: Preparing for the Future.* Washington, DC: USDA, Economic Research Service, Staff Report #AGE870724.

Molotch, H. L. 1976. "The City as a Growth Machine: Toward a Political Economy of Place." *American Journal of Sociology* 82(2):309–332.

Morse, G. W., editor. 1990. *The Retention and Expansion of Existing Businesses: Theory and Practice in Business Visitation Programs.* Ames: Iowa State University Press.

Murdock, S. H., and F. L. Leistritz. 1988. *The Farm Financial Crisis: Socioeconomic Dimensions and Implications for Producers and Rural Areas.* Boulder, CO: Westview Press.

National Issues Forums Institute. 1996. *Organizing for Public Deliberation and Moderating a Forum/Study Circle.* Dayton, OH.

Nelson A. Rockefeller Institute of Government. 1997. 1997 New York State Statistical Yearbook. Albany, NY: The State University of New York.

Nielsen, G., and S. H. Pedersen. 1998. Dansk tekstil & tøj 1987–1997—en branche i bevægelse. Herning: Dansk Tekstil og Beklædning.

Nord, M., K. Krealing, D. Christensen, L. P. Claude, P. D. Fickes, C. R. Humphrey, A. E. Luloff, M. R. Schwartz, and S. M. Smith. 1994. "Economic Restructuring and Rural Community Transformation in Pennsylvania." *Agricultural Economics and Rural Sociology* Research Report 246. University Park: Pennsylvania State University.

Norton, R. D. 1986. "Industrial Policy and American Renewal," *Journal of Economic Literature* 24 (March):1–40.

Noyelle, T. J. 1986. "Economic Transformation." *The Annals, AAPSS* 488:9–17.

Oakerson, R. J. 1998. "Politics, Culture, and the Rural Academy: A Response to Castle." *American Journal of Agricultural Economics* 80(3):632–34.

Offe, C. 1985. *Disorganized Capitalism.* Cambridge, MA: The MIT Press.

Organization for Economic Cooperation and Development. 1994. *Creating Rural Indicators for Shaping Territorial Policy.* Paris: OECD.

Osborne, D., and T. Gaebler. 1992. *Reinventing Government.* Reading, PA: Addison-Wesley.

Pulver, G. C. 1995. "Economic Forces Shaping the Future of Rural America." In L. J. Beaulieu and D. Mulkey, editors, *Investing in People: The Human Capital Needs of Rural America,* 49–64. Boulder, CO: Westview Press.

Ramsay, M. 1996. *Community, Culture, and Economic Development: The Social Roots of Local Action.* Albany, NY: State University of New York Press.

Reeder, R. J., and N. L. Glasgow. 1990. "Nonmetro Retirement Counties' Strengths and Weaknesses." Rural Development Perspectives 6(2):12–17.

Reeder, R. J., M. J. Schneider, and B. L. Green. 1993. "Attracting Retirees as a Development Strategy." In D. L. Barkley, editor, *Economic Adaptation: Alternatives for Nonmetropolitan Areas,* 127–144. Boulder, CO: Westview Press.

Rogers, D. L. 1982. "Community Services." In D. A. Dillman and D. J. Hobbs, editors, *Rural Society in the U.S. Issues for the 1980s*, 146–155. Boulder, CO: Westview Press.

Ryan McGinn Samples Research, Inc. 1997. "Needs Assessment Survey." Unpublished small business survey conducted for the West Virginia Small Business Development Center.

Sabel, C. F. 1996a. *Ireland: Local Partnerships and Social Innovation. Paris: Organization for Economic Cooperation and Development.*

———. 1996b. "A Measure of Federalism: Assessing Manufacturing Technology Centers." Research Policy 25:281–307.

Salmon, S. 1998. "The View from Anthropology: Discussion of Castle's Conceptual Framework." *American Journal of Agricultural Economics* 80(3):637–39.

Schneider, M. J., and B. L. Green. 1989. *Retirement Counties: A Development Option for the Nineties.* Special Report 135, Arkansas Agricultural Experiment Station, Division of Agriculture, University of Arkansas, February.

Scranton, P. 1991. "Diversity in Diversity: Flexible Production and American Industrialization, 1880–1930." *Business History Review* 65:27-90.

———. n.d. "Advances and Dilemmas: American Consumer Goods Industrial Districts, 1880–1940." Mimeo, NJ: Rutgers University.

Sirianni, C., and L. Friedland. 1996. "Deliberative Democracy." An essay on the Internet for the Civic Practices Network: www.cpn.org/sections/tools/models/deliberative_democracy.html.

Small Business Division. 1996. *New York State Business Fact Book.* Albany, NY: New York State Department of Economic Development.

Smith, S. M. 1993. "Service Industries in the Rural Economy: The Role and Potential Contributions." In D. Barkley, editor, *Economic Adaptation: Alternatives for Nonmetropolitan Areas*, 105–127. Boulder, CO: Westview Press.

Smith, T. L. 1974. "Sociocultural Changes in 12 Midwestern Communities, 1930–1970." *Social Science* (49)4:195–207.

Soltow J. H. 1980. "Origins of Small Business and the Relationship Between Large and Small Firms: Metal Fabricating and Machinery Making in New England, 1890–1957." In S. W. Bruchey, editor, *Small Business in American Life.* New York: Columbia University Press.

Sommer, J. E., F. K. Hines, and M. Petrulis. 1993. "Agriculture Still Key to Economic Health of the Rural Great Plains." Rural Development Perspectives 8(2):28-36.

Stull, D. D., M. J. Broadway, and K. Erickson. 1992. "The Price of a Good Steak: Beef Packing and Its Consequences for Garden City, Kansas." In L. Lamphere, editor, *Structuring Diversity: Ethnographic Perspectives on the New Immigration:* 35-64. Chicago: University of Chicago Press.

Summers, G. 1986. "Rural Community Development." *Annual Review of Sociology* 12:341–71.

Summers, G. and K. Branch. 1984. "Economic Development and Community Social Change." *Annual Review of Sociology* 10:141–61.

Summers, G. F., and D. L. Brown. 1998. "A Sociological Perspective on Rural Studies." *American Journal of Agricultural Economics* 80(3):640–43.

Taylor, M. 1997. "Promoting Entrepreneurship in Central Appalachia." Mountain Association for Community Economic Development.

Torgerson, R. 1994. "Co-op Fever: Cooperative Renaissance Blooming on Northern Plains." Farmer Cooperatives (September):12–14.

Tuscaloosa News. 1993. October 10, 11, 18, 23; November 28. Tuscaloosa, AL.

———. 1994. February 9, 10, 15, 17, 18, 19, 20, 24, 28; April 8, 10, 18, 21; June 11; July 16; September 15, 16; October 10; November 7, 13; December 6, 7, 11, 21, 24. Tuscaloosa, AL.

———. 1995. January 22. Tuscaloosa, AL.

U.S. Small Business Administration. 1996. The State of Small Business: A Report to the President. Washington, DC: U.S. Government Printing Office.

Vaughn, D., and M. Blankenship. 1997. Nomination for Entrepreneurial Success Award, Small Business Administration.

Vernon, R. 1966. International Investment and International Trade in the Product Cycle. Quarterly Journal of Economics 80(2):190–207.

Von Meyer, H., I. J. Terluin, J. H. Post and B. Van Haeperen (eds.). 1999. *Rural Employment Dynamics in the EU; Key Findings for Policy Consideration Emerging from the RUREMPLO project*, The Hague, Agricultural Economics Research Institute (LEI), Report 4.99.08.é

Wilkinson, K. P. 1970. *"The Community as a Social Field."* Social Forces 48(3):311–2.

———. 1991. The Community in Rural America. New York, NY: Greenwood Press.

Wojan, T. R. 1996. *Structural and Macroeconomic Explanations of Rural/Urban Income Divergence.* Unpublished Ph.D. Dissertation, Madison: University of Wisconsin.

Zeuli, K. A. 1998. Unpublished Case Study of Dakota Growers Pasta Company. St. Paul: University of Minnesota.

Index

About the Contributors

DON E. ALBRECHT is professor of rural sociology at Texas A&M University, in College Station.

DAVID L. BARKLEY is professor of agricultural and applied economics at Clemson University, Clemson, South Carolina.

NORMAN K. BENDER is a senior extension educator, economic development at the Cooperative Extension System of the University of Connecticut in Norwich.

JEFFREY C. BRIDGER is assistant professor of sociology at the University of Kentucky in Lexington.

RALPH B. BROWN is professor of sociology at Brigham Young University in Provo, Utah.

RAM L. CHUGH is special assistant to the president for public affairs and SUNY distinguished service professor of economics at the State University of New York, College at Potsdam, Potsdam, New York.

LUMANE P. CLAUDE is extension associate, Cornell Cooperative Extension Service in New York City.

LINDA J. COX is a community economic development specialist, Department of Agricultural and Resource Economics, University of Hawaii in Honolulu.

DAVID L. DARLING is professor of agricultural economics at Kansas State University in Manhattan.

GREG DAVIS is extension agent at Ohio State University in Columbus.

NINI DAVIS is executive director, Northeast Connecticut Visitors' District.

PIERRE DUPRAZ is a researcher at the Institut National de la Recherche Agronomique at the Catholic University of Louvain, Belgium.

CORNELIA BUTLER FLORA is director of the North Central Regional Center for Rural Development, Iowa State University in Ames.

DOLORES FOLEY is assistant professor of public administration at the University of Hawaii in Honolulu.

BRUNO HENRY DE FRAHAN is professor at the Catholic University of Louvain, Belgium.

MARK S. HENRY, is professor of agricultural and applied economics at Clemson University, Clemson, South Carolina.

BETH WALTER HONADLE is director of the Center of Governmental Research and Public Service and professor of political science at Bowling Green State University in Bowling Green, Ohio. She chaired the consolidation study commission discussed in her case study.

CLARK D. HUDSPETH is a graduate student in the Department of Sociology, Anthropology, and Social Work, Mississippi State University.

DREW HYMAN is professor public policy and community systems at Pennsylvania State University in University Park.

SVEN ILLERIS is professor of geography at Roskilde University in Denmark.

MAUREEN KILKENNY is assistant professor of economics at the Iowa State University in Ames.

STEVEN KLINE is a research associate in the Illinois Institute for Rural Affairs, Western Illinois University in Macomb.

JOSEPH LAPILIO is a board member and community development coordinator of the Wai'anae Coast Coalition and Queen Lili'uokalani Children's Center in Wai'ane.

WILLIAM LAZARUS is associate professor and extension economist, Department of Applied Economics, University of Minnesota.

F. LARRY LEISTRITZ is professor of agricultural economics at North Dakota State University in Fargo.

SCOTT LOVERIDGE is professor in the Center for Community, Economic, and Workforce Development, WVU Extension Service and Director of the Regional Research Institute at West Virginia University in Morgantown.

A. E. LULOFF is professor of rural sociology at Pennsylvania State University in University Park.

VICKI LUTHER is an executive staff member of the Heartland Center for Leadership Development in Lincoln.

GEORGE W. MORSE is professor of agricultural economics at the University of Minnesota, Twin Cities Campus, St. Paul.

JANET S. ODOM is a graduate student in the Department of Sociology, Anthropology, and Social Work, Mississippi State University.

L. CHRISTOPHER PLEIN is assistant professor of public administration at West Virginia University in Morgantown.

STUART A. ROSENFELD is president of RTS, Inc. in Chapel Hill.

PETER V. SCHAEFFER is professor of agricultural and resource economics, and director of the Division of Resource Management at West Virginia University in Morgantown.

ANTHONY E. SMITH is the executive director of Lightstone Foundation, Inc., a regional nonprofit organization serving the Potomac Highlands region. Lightstone Foundation is located in Moyers, Pendelton County, in eastern West Virginia.

TOM SETH SMITH is executive director, Rural Enterprises of Oklahoma, Inc.

JEROLD R. THOMAS is district specialist for community development, Ohio State University Extension, Northwest District in Findaly.

RACHEL B. TOMPKINS is president, Rural School and Community Trust, Washington, D.C.

BÉATRICE VAN HAEPEREN is lecturer at the Catholic University of Louvain, Belgium.

KNUT INGAR WESTEREN is professor of economics at North Trondelag College in Steinkjer, Norway.

TIMOTHY R. WOJAN is a member of the staff of the Economic Research Service, United States Department of Agriculture in Washington, D.C.

MIKE D. WOODS is professor and extension economist with the Oklahoma Cooperative Extension Service, Oklahoma State University in Stillwater.

ANDREW A. ZEKERI is assistant professor of rural sociology at Tuskegee University, Tuskegee, Alabama.

DAVID ZIMET is extension economist at the University of Florida in Gainesville.